M
14.95

WITH

THE AUTHOR Tim B
Archaeology and Social Anth
in the UK and Cyprus. He is
has worked in the area of Byzantine Studies and publi
Balkans and East Mediterranean history. He is at present
at the University of Huddersfield, UK.

Professor Denis Judd is a graduate of Oxford, a Fellow of the Royal Historical
Society and Profess
published over 20
Prince Philip, Geo
stories for children
Empire: The British l
the BBC *History M*

Other Titles in the S

A Traveller's Histo
A Traveller's Histo
A Traveller's Histo
A Traveller's Histo
  Caribbean
A Traveller's Histo
A Traveller's Histo
A Traveller's Histo
A Traveller's Histo
A Traveller's Histo
A Traveller's Histo
  The Hundred Y
A Traveller's Histo
A Traveller's Histo
A Traveller's Histo
A Traveller's Histo

JUL 1 8 2005

A Traveller's History
of Cyprus

THE TRAVELLER'S HISTORY SERIES

'Ideal before-you-go reading' *The Daily Telegraph*

'An excellent series of brief histories' *New York Times*

'I want to compliment you ... on the brilliantly concise contents of your books' *Shirley Conran*

Reviews of Individual Titles

A Traveller's History of Japan
'It succeeds admirably in its goal of making the present country comprehensible through a narrative of its past, with asides on everything from bonsai to *zazen*, in a brisk, highly readable style ... you could easily read it on the flight over, if you skip the movie.' *The Washington Post*

A Traveller's History of London
'... dip into Richard Tames's literary, lyrical *A Traveller's History of London*'. *The Sunday Telegraph*

A Traveller's History of France
'Undoubtedly the best way to prepare for a trip to France is to bone up on some history. The *Traveller's History of France* by Robert Cole is concise and gives the essential facts in a very readable form.' *The Independent*

A Traveller's History of China
'The author manages to get 2 million years into 300 pages. An excellent addition to a series which is already invaluable, whether you're travelling or not.' *The Guardian*

A Traveller's History of India
'For anyone ... planning a trip to India, the latest in the excellent Traveller's History series ... provides a useful grounding for those whose curiosity exceeds the time available for research.' *The London Evening Standard*

A Traveller's History of Cyprus

TIM BOATSWAIN

Series Editor   DENIS JUDD
Line Drawings   *PETER GEISSLER*

Interlink Books
An imprint of Interlink Publishing Group, Inc.
New York • Northampton

First published in 2005 by
INTERLINK BOOKS
An imprint of Interlink Publishing Group, Inc.
46 Crosby Street, Northampton, Massachusetts 01060

www.interlinkbooks.com

Text copyright © Tim Boatswain 2005
Preface copyright © Denis Judd 2005
Line drawings by Peter Geissler
Maps by John Taylor

The front cover shows the mosaic floor of the Roman villa at Curium c. *Fifth century* AD.
Photo: C.M. Dixon

Library of Congress Cataloging-in-Publication Data
Boatswain, Tim.
 A traveller's history of Cyprus/by Tim Boatswain.
   p. cm.
 ISBN 1-56656-605-3 (pbk.)
 1. Cyprus–History.   I. Title.
 DS54.5.B63 2005
 956.93–dc22

                              2004028790

Printed and bound in Canada by Webcom

To order or request our complete catalog
please call us at **1-800-238-LINK** or write to:
Interlink Publishing
46 Crosby Street, Northampton MA 01060-1804
e-mail: info@interlinkbooks.com
www.interlinkbooks.com

Table of Contents

Preface

Cyprus stands in a unique geographical relationship to Europe, the Middle East and the Mediterranean and, since 1869, to the Suez short route to the east. It was its strategic importance to a post Second World War Britain engaged in the painful process of essential global military readjustment that precipitated one of the fiercest and most painful of colonial freedom struggles in the mid and late 1950s.

This anxiety over Cyprus's strategic role was not surprising, given that Disraeli had acquired the island for Britain in 1878 as a potentially invaluable military and naval base, as well as a token of the 'peace with honour' he had brought from the recent Berlin Conference. Ironically though, when Britain subsequently most needed Cyprus for the naval and military assaults on Egypt in 1882 and in 1956–7, it was both times found partly inadequate, and the Royal Navy used Malta with its deep water docking facilities instead.

Even today, Cyprus is invaluable to the West for a number of surveillance and strategic considerations that have been lent a new urgency as a result of the threatening surge of radical Islamic militancy. The island is also at the centre of the debate as to whether one day to admit Turkey to the European Union unless the problem of a divided Cyprus is solved first.

For those totally unaware of the island's past and current international status and dilemmas, Cyprus is an increasingly desirable and popular holiday destination – whether to the north, or more commonly, to the south. Here the tourist and visitor can bask in the sun, eat delicious food, drink fine local wine, party all night, and still get out and see the wonderful Roman mosaics at Paphos or the fine Byzantine interior of Asinou church.

As they contemplate these delights, they would be well advised to have Tim Boatswain's immensely readable and informative guide with them. The book is a treasure house of rich details, broad historical vistas and scholarly insights, written by someone who knows both the world of classical antiquity and modern Cyprus extremely well.

This book is also a miracle of compression, for even the briefest of glances at Cyprus' long and often tangled history reveals a kaleidoscope of civilizations, conquerors, rulers, religions, individuals, natural disasters, triumphs, failures and cultural achievements. But Tim Boatswain strides confidently through all of this, dispensing vivid narrative and shrew appraisal at every turn.

Merely to give a flavour of Cyprus' extraordinary early history is enticing enough. Of the personalities who were then part of Cypriot history, apart from Phoenician traders, Egyptian pharaohs and Roman emperors, Mark Antony gave the island to Cleopatra, St Paul preached there, the Venetian Doge visited it in 1123, Richard the Lion Heart sold it to the Templars in 1191 (then bought it back a year later) and the future Henry IV of England visited it in 1392.

The powers that have ruled the island include the Phoenicians, the Assyrians, the Persians, the Ancient Greeks, the Egyptians, the Byzantines, the Venetians, the Plantagenets, the French, the Ottoman Turks and the British. It is small wonder then that Cyprus has so varied and fascinating a past, and so rich and intriguing a present.

As the southern, major part of the island, the Republic of Cyprus, settles into its latest role as a member of the European Union, it is to be hoped that its future, and that of the northern section, will be both prosperous and peaceful. That the traveller will return culturally enriched and the recipient of peerless hospitality is beyond question.

Denis Judd
London

Foreword

The line which divides them ... is an unhappy and unequal division, but after the atrocities of recent years these two peoples, whatever their political agreement, will live apart. Already the two halves of the island are stamped with their personalities. The north has fallen into neglect, the south into over-exploitation.

Colin Thubron, *Journey into Cyprus*

When I first thought about writing this history of Cyprus I was very conscious that the island today is physically and culturally divided and a strong sense of injustice and hurt lingers in both the Greek and Turkish Cypriot communities. The 'Cyprus problem' is how to reunite the island and allow these two communities to live in peace with each other. The issues that resist a settlement are many and complex, but as Christopher Hitchen has pointed out, the most important question '... is the relationship between Greek and Turkish Cypriots, which poses a difficult conundrum: can two widely separated national groups find a peaceful co-existence involving two languages, two religions and two interpretations of history?'

The 'interpretation' of the history of the island is at the heart of the matter. Each community has an intense historical memory and looks back to past roots, claiming an affinity and shared cultural inheritance with their ethnic motherland. At the same time the two communities have perceived themselves as victims of history – a history which has inflicted on each of them a series of blows.

Greek Cypriots see themselves, as victims of the harsh rule of the Ottoman Empire and the long memory of the occupation and the desire for a united Greek world have burned bright in the hearts of many Greek Cypriots. The British rule of Cyprus merely prolonged their agony and, although eventually independence was achieved, there was no union with Greece. Even after independence many perceive their democratic rights, as the majority, were subverted by an externally imposed constitution and a recalcitrant Turkish Cypriot minority. The ultimate humiliation and victimisation took place when their country was divided by military force in 1974 and they lost 'everything'.

Many Turkish Cypriots equally believe themselves to be victims. For although their experience of being on the defensive is more recent it is also raw. Stripped of their imperial privileges by the British they found their civilisation less valued than the Greek heritage by their rulers. During the armed struggle for independence they were exploited by the British and set against the Greek Cypriots. After independence they were threatened and violently attacked by the majority community. Although partition brought them peace, their state is an international pariah under economic embargo and while the prosperity of the Greek Cypriot community grows they stagnate.

Recent efforts to solve the Cyprus problem have been intensified with Cyprus' membership of the European Union from 1 May 2004. Technically, membership includes the whole island, the Republic of Cyprus, which is a legally recognised entity. However, in reality, this only means the Greek Cypriots in the South unless a settlement can reunite the island. In a flurry of activity Kofi Annan, the Secretary-General of the United Nations, negotiated, cajoled and finally forced the issue of his own settlement plan by putting a referendum to both communities. Although the North voted in favour, essentially on the promise of the economic advantages of the EU, the South rejected the settlement. The majority of Greek Cypriots felt that Kofi Annan's deal did not go far enough in returning territory, restoring influence and ensuring security for their community. The question now is can there be any further movement, and what will clinch a settlement? The Greek Cypriots have held out for a better deal but what if there is no new deal?

Where bitterness exists today in each community it feeds upon the past and any view of the past that does not accord with a particular perception is bound to be suspect, especially if written by a member of a past imperialist nation, which still holds an interest in the island. Therefore, if I have offended I ask the forgiveness of my Greek and Turkish Cypriot friends, and the only defence I can offer is I have genuinely laboured to record Cyprus' wonderful but turbulent history without prejudice or favour.

CHAPTER ONE

Introduction

Geography

Cyprus is the third largest island, after Sicily and Sardinia, in the Mediterranean with an area of 3,572 sq. miles (9,251 sq. km). It is situated in the north-east corner of the Mediterranean (latitude 34°33′–35°34′ north and longitude 32°16′–34°37′), 38 miles (sixty km) from the southern coast of Turkey, fifty-six miles (ninety km) west of Syria and 211 miles (338 km) north of Egypt. The nearest parts of Greece are the islands of Rhodes and Karpathos, which are over 225 miles (360 km) to the north-east.

Its greatest length is 140 miles (233 km) and, at its widest point, is roughly sixty-one miles (ninety-eight km). Its coastline runs for some 486 miles (778 km) and the island's shape has been variously described as looking like the flayed hide of a deer or a guitar.

The island has two mountain ranges. Along most of the northern coast is the Kyrenia Mountains, or Pentadaktylos, literally meaning the 'five-fingered' and said to have been caused by the Byzantine hero Dighenis who imprinted the indentations of his left hand as he vaulted over the mountains. In the centre and south-west is the Troödos massif, a mountainous cluster, which reaches its peak in Mount Olympos (1,953 m above sea level). Between the two mountain ranges lies the fertile plain of Mesaoria.

Climate

Cyprus' climate is described as Mediterranean but is, in reality, more influenced by the Aegean than its position warrants. This is due to the

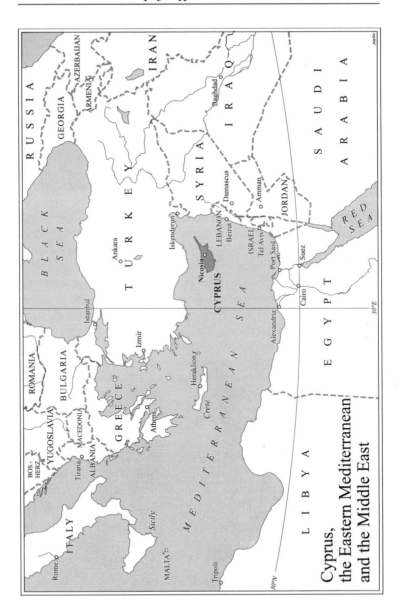

Cyprus,
the Eastern Mediterranean
and the Middle East

Etesian breezes that blow from the north-west during the summer. From June to September it is hot and dry and then from November to March it is mild and can be wet – the island has recently tended to suffer from a lack of rain, which has created water shortages. In between there are very short and changeable autumn and spring seasons.

The island enjoys a large amount of sunshine with an average of over eleven hours daily during the summer. The average annual rainfall is approximately 550 mm but over the last few decades, as indicated above, there has been a decrease in the annual rainfall. Snow rarely falls on the lowlands or on the Kyrenia range but often occurs in the winter on ground above 1,000 m on the Troödos.

The Name 'Cyprus'

Our earliest sources from the Middle East refer to the island under a variety of names. However, the origin of the name 'Cyprus' is unclear. It may be derived from a Greek word for copper as the island was known in the ancient world for the mining and export of this mineral. On the other hand it could be the name of the ore was derived from the name of the island. The Roman author Plissy the Elder states that the Romans got their best copper, *aes Cyprium* from the island. Another possible derivation is that the Greek *Kupros* is a translation of the Hebrew word for the henna plant, *Kopher*, which is found in abundance on the island.

Strategic Importance

Despite its limited geographical size and small population of around 800,000 people, Cyprus' geographical and political significance in the area has always been disproportionate. The reason for this has been the island's strategic position in the east Mediterranean.

Cyprus lies on an axis of movement, both north–south and east–west. It stands at the crossroads of three continents, Europe, Asia and Africa. It is, therefore, hardly surprising that throughout history the major powers in the region have taken an interest in controlling and settling the island. Its strategic position has always ensured that Cyprus has played a key role in history, but it has also resulted in the island becoming a victim of others' power politics.

CHAPTER TWO

Prehistoric Cyprus,
c. 7000–750 BC

Mesolithic (Middle Stone Age) Period (c. 8800 BC)

The history of Cyprus goes back more than 11,000 years to the 9th millennium BC. The first evidence of human occupation comes from a cave at Akrotiri Aetokremnos ('Eagles' Cliff'), on the south coast. Hearths and chipped stone implements were found in the context of animal bones, identified as pygmy hippopotami and pygmy elephants, along with remains of birds and fish. It is suggested these first humans on the island were hunter-gatherers who had crossed over either from the north, Anatolia or from the east, Syria.

Neolithic (New Stone Age) Period (c. 7000–4000 BC)

Around 7,000 BC Neolithic (New Stone Age) settlers, probably from Syria and Palestine, appeared. They settled near the coast or up river valleys. Their economy was a mixture of fishing, hunting and farming. Their settlement sites were near arable land and a good water supply. These first farmers fashioned their tools out of obsidian and flint and their vessels out of river stones. Some attempts appear to have been made to produce pottery but were apparently unsuccessful.

This culture has been named after Khirokitia, the largest and best-preserved site on the south coast half way between the cities of Limassol and Larnaca. The people lived in round buildings, the lower parts often constructed of stone. Evidence of a collapsed roof

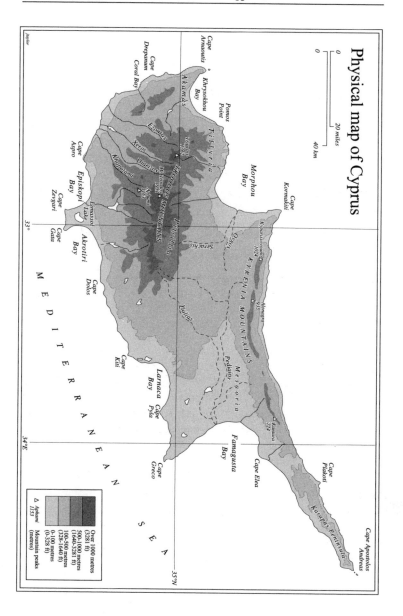

Physical map of Cyprus

from one building indicates that some houses may have had upper stories. However, the dwellings are generally shown in archaeological reconstructions with beehive roofs. The inhabitants buried their dead under the floors of their houses. Often the corpses were in a crouching position, like foetuses. Some skulls, which appear to have been deliberately deformed, were in a raised position and surrounded by offerings, possibly suggesting some type of ancestor cult. They were buried facing east, the source of light, and a few were found with boulders crushed on their chests, presumably to fix them firmly in their resting-place. The presence of obsidian, which is not naturally found on the island, in form of arrowheads and tools provides evidence of trade, most probably with Anatolia. Amulets of carnelian and mother-of-pearl, along with violin-shaped figures, were probably offerings to the deceased.

This Neolithic culture came to an end some time after 5,500 BC and was followed by a break in any settlement for nearly a millennium. The next groups of inhabitants appear to have had no connections with their predecessors, although they did sometimes occupy the same sites. This new culture, often referred to Sotira, after the site in the south, is dated between 4,500 and 4,000 BC. It features new architectural techniques: square-built houses below ground level, and different religious practices, with the dead being buried outside dwellings. An important innovation was the use of handmade pottery. The most distinctive style was known as 'combed-ware', because designs featured the use of a multiple-toothed instrument. The distribution of pottery and stone artefacts indicates there was contact and exchange between the various communities.

The end of this culture appears to have been fairly rapid, perhaps due to famine or earthquake. It is noticeable that in these early cultures there is not the same continuity in the archaeological record that can be observed on the adjacent mainland or the island of Crete. It is difficult to understand the causes of the disruption, but the dominant view is that in this stage in the history of Cyprus outsiders were not involved in the demise of these cultures.

Chalcolithic (Copper–stone Age) Period (c. 4000–2300 BC)

Despite a lack of clear continuity there do appear to have been some linkages between the Sotira and the next culture, for example, subterranean dwellings. However, these were to evolve into substantial circular stone buildings as found at Erimi, which is not far from Sotira and has given its name to the period. A new style of pottery, known as Red on White emerged, with a greater range of shapes and larger vessels, suggesting a wider set of uses, including storage.

Metalwork appears for the first time although it was not common. Tools and jewellery of the period are made of relatively pure copper. There is a debate whether metallurgy was an indigenous development, heralding the beginning of the exploitation of the island's copper resources, which were to play such a significant part in Cyprus' history, or were imported from Anatolia. There are small traces of

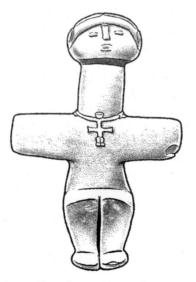

A stylised figurine in cruciform shape *c.* 3000 BC found at Yiala which the Erimi culture carved probably as an offering to the dead

tin in these early metal objects which might suggest an origin from outside Cyprus.

Representational art is a distinguishing feature of the Erimi culture, in particular human figurines, of a cruciform shape, made out of picrolite (a type of serpentine). Although the shapes are fairly abstract, where gender is indicated it is female. Lack of wear and frequent finds in graves suggests they were probably in many cases offerings to the dead.

Differentiation in terms of scale of houses and graves, along with the introduction of stamp seals point perhaps to different levels of wealth and status, suggesting a stratification of society into different classes.

Around 2500 BC some significant changes occur in the north of the island. Initially these changes took place in the river valleys of the north-west and then gradually penetrated other parts of the island. The site of Philia, near Morphou, has given its name to this next culture. Settlements changed with the introduction of the rock-cut chamber tomb, with a blocked approaching passage, known as a '*dromos*', and a new style of pottery known as Red Polished Ware.

However, the evidence, mainly based on cemeteries, is slight as to how these changes came about and, as is often the case with these early periods, archaeologists are left to speculate on the nature and causes for transition. It does seem that the metalwork and pottery are related to that found in southern Anatolia. This has led some to argue that settlers, perhaps fleeing from threat or catastrophe and bringing new artefacts, religious practices and burial customs, crossed over to the island. On the other hand there is evidence of some continuity which has supported those who suggest that these changes and developments are a purely Cypriot, indigenous, response to opportunities and influence brought about by trading the island's copper throughout the East Mediterranean. However, the first real evidence of the exploitation of the island's copper deposits comes in the middle, and of trading copper at the end of the next age.

Bronze Age Period (c. 2300–1050 BC)

The culture of the *Early Bronze Age* is best exemplified by the burial site at Vounous, to the east of Kyrenia. Here the tombs are amply provisioned with metalwork, including tools, weapons and pins for fastening robes, pottery and the bones of slaughtered animals. This all suggests a belief in an afterlife where 'you can take it with you'. The large number of representations of bulls and bulls' heads, found at various sites, implies the worship of a bull cult. This evidence could also indicate a connection with Anatolia, where representation of bulls is commonplace at the famous prehistoric Anatolian site of Çatal Hüyük.

The transition to the *Middle Bronze Age* (*c.* 1950 BC) does not appear to have been marked by any great upheavals. Settlements are found across the island, apart from in the more mountainous regions. These settlements exhibit regional variations in their material culture, but the growing number of bronze artefacts attests to the increasing importance of copper mining and trade. Features that emerge during this period are the construction of forts and evidence of mass burials. It is unclear what created the need to defend settlements, but it may indicate internal disturbances, as there is no evidence of major disruption from outside forces.

The *Late Bronze Age* (1650–1050 BC) was a period of great change. Patterns of settlement now changed significantly with the development of coastal trading sites, such as Enkomi, Kition, Hala Sultan Tekké and Maroni. The growing prosperity of these settlements testifies to the flourishing trade of the period. The material evidence now confirms contacts with the Near East, Egypt and Greece in the West.

Along with flourishing industry and commerce the first evidence of writing is found. Writing could be seen as essential for such a developing society, depending upon trade with neighbouring countries. The earliest writing, the so-called Cypro-Minoan, became current throughout the island – although written documents on baked clay tablets, similar to those from cultures in the Near East, have only been found at Enkomi. There appear to be about eighty signs, but so far no one has been able to decipher Cypro-Minoan script. What is tantalising is that it is believed that these tablets were not just inventories, like those from Minoan Crete or Mycenaean sites, but were texts of some sort. It has been suggested they might be poems, like those found in Sumerian and Akkadian.

The island now begins to take its first tentative place in world history. There are texts from the palace of the Egyptian Pharaoh Akhenaten (1379–1362 BC) at El-Amarna, mentioning a place named Alasiya. Some have identified these as correspondence between the pharaoh and the king of Cyprus, but not all scholars accept that Alasiya is Cyprus. It is recorded that the king of Alasiya sent copper ingots as tribute to Egypt for the security it provided in the region. In one letter the king of Alasiya explains he has been unable to send the amount of copper promised as most men in his country have been killed and he does not have a labour force to smelt it. It is thought this may relate to an invasion by peoples from Anatolia, but it is difficult to find corroborating evidence. There are also tablets from the Hittite Empire in central Anatolia which refer to Alasiya as being ruled by them, but again there is no other evidence for this claim.

At the end of the thirteenth century and the beginning of the twelfth the East Mediterranean was thrown into chaos by a wave of destruction. The Egyptian texts refer to bands of raiders, known as the 'Sea Peoples', 'laying waste all before them'. In about 1186 Rameses III records a victory over a group that invaded Egypt. Mycenaean sites on the mainland of Greece were reduced and abandoned and some of the coastal centres on Cyprus, like Enkomi and Kition were destroyed.

From this time on there was growing Aegean influence on the island. Some have seen this as a steady but gradual settlement from mainland Greece; others have suggested a wave of settlement, even arguing that the 'Sea Peoples' and Mycenaeans are the same. Whatever the truth the archaeological evidence reveals a mixture of local Cypriot features, alongside influences from the Near East, Egypt and the Aegean.

In the twelfth century these settlers from the Aegean are often associated with the Homeric Achaeans. They rebuilt some of the destroyed sites; for example at Enkomi a 'cyclopean' wall (like those found at Mycenaean sites) was constructed and the town was rebuilt on a grid plan. Public buildings were erected out of stone blocks, including a sanctuary with a sacrificial altar. This has been named the sanctuary of the 'Horned God' because of the quantity of horned animal skulls around the altar and a bronze statuette found in one of the inner rooms. The figure is of a young male, wearing a 'kilt' and what appears to be a horned cap. It has been identified as a cult statue of a god who was later

A male bronze figurine almost 2 ft tall found at the sanctuary of the 'Horned God' in Enkomi *c.* 1500–1200 BC

known as Apollo Kereates (Horned Apollo). He was worshipped in Arcadia (in the Peloponnese of Greece) as protector of cattle and could have been introduced into Cyprus by Achaean settlers.

At Kition the sanctuary area was next to a set of workshops where copper was smelted. It seems there was direct communication from the workshops into the adjacent sanctuaries. It would appear that the production of metal was under the direct protection of the gods. It reveals the importance of copper to society and the control the religious authorities could exercise over its use and export.

The eleventh century started with new contacts with the Aegean. Immigration from the Bronze Age Greek world was probably on a larger scale. New ceramic styles may have been introduced by those fleeing the so-called Dorian invasion in Greece. There were also strong influences from Crete from the Sub-Minoan period. Figurines of the goddess with upraised arms and associated in Crete with fertility have been found in several sanctuary sites. A new pottery style, the Proto-White Ware suggests Sub-Mycenaean influence. The Cypro-Minoan script disappears to be replaced by Cypro-Syllabic, which is connected to the Greek language.

The Hellenisation (Greek culture) of Cyprus that started in the twelfth century BC was now firmly established. This Greek influence was to have enormous importance on the historical and cultural development of the island. At the same time oriental influence from the Near East was sustained and integrated to create a unique Cypriot culture.

Iron Age (Geometric) Period (c. 1050–750 BC)

The introduction of iron into the island was not a sudden event but had been a gradual process, beginning in the previous era. The label often applied to the period between 1050 and 850 BC is 'Dark Age'. In reality, despite that title, the period sees the island's development advancing apace. The Achaean settlers that had come in greater numbers now established new urban sites, sometimes near earlier settlements. These new settlements were to become the capital cities of the ancient Greek kingdoms of Cyprus: Kourion, Paphos, Marion, Soloi, Lapithos and Salamis.

Later sources from the ancient Graeco-Roman world record a series of legends, which often link the foundation of these cities with Homeric heroes. Even if these stories concerning the founders are largely fictional the archaeological record confirms the considerable influence these Aegean immigrants had on the material culture of the island. There is metalwork that is distinctively Mycenaean in character. White Painted Ware pottery, with dark ornamentation on a white background, which is Aegean in origin, becomes dominant throughout the Cypriot Iron Age. Mycenaean chamber tombs, again quite different from local Cypriot tombs, are found at several sites.

At Salamis, which had replaced Enkomi as the leading settlement in the west of the island, a series of tombs has been excavated that reflect the heroic, aristocratic and regal society of Homer. Despite a large

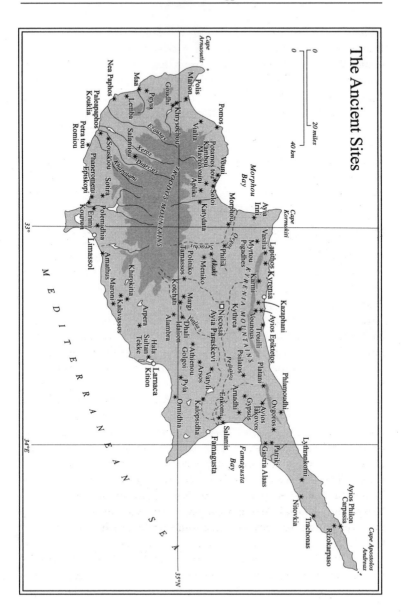

The Ancient Sites

0
0

20 miles

40 km

Cape Arnaoutis
Polis
Marion
Nea Paphos
Maa
Peyia
Goudhi
Lemba
Khrysochou
Erimos
Vialia
Salamiou
Pomos
Xeros
Youni
Diarizos
Khapotami
Potamos tou Soloi
Kambou
Mavrovouni
Apliki
Paleapaphos
Kouklia
Petra tou
Romiou
Sousklou
Phaneromeni
Episkopi
Erimi
Kourion
Sotira
Polemidhia
Limassol
Amathus
Maroni
Khirokitia
Kalavassos
Apera
Sultan
Tekke
Hala

TROODOS MOUNTAINS

Morphou Bay
Cape Kormakiti
Ayia Irini
Morphou
Karydata
Philia
Politiko
Tamassos
Meniko
Kotchati
Margi
Idalion
Golgoi
Alambra
Athienou
Arsos
Pyla
Omodhia

Lapithos Kyrenia
Vasilia
Myrtou Karmi
Pigadhes
Akaki
KYRENIA MOUNTAINS
Younous
Troulli
Kythrea
Ayia Paraskevi
Ovisos
Serachis
Peduaeus
Psilatos
Platani
Nicosia
Yialias
'Dhali'
Vavla
Larnaca
Kition

Kazaphani
Ayios Epiktetos
Phlamoudhi
Ovgoros
Ayios Iakovos
Gypsos
Arnadhi
Enkomi
Kalopsidha
Salamis
Famagusta
Famagusta Bay
Gastria Alaas
Pariki
Lythrankomi
Ayios Philon
Carpasia
Rizokarpaso
Trachonas
Nitovkia
Cape Apostolos Andreas

M E D I T E R R A N E A N   S E A

33°
34°E
35°N

number of grave goods that have an oriental origin, suggesting trade with the Near East, the mode of burial is remarkable in the way it replicates funerals from the *Iliad*. In the *dromos* at the entrance to the tomb chamber a chariot with two sacrificed horses still harnessed was buried, just as, in Homer's *Iliad*, Patroclus' team had been sacrificed by his friend Achilles. Sheep and cattle were also slaughtered and placed as offerings, along with wine and olive oil in pottery vessels, amphorae. The body was cremated on a pyre, the ashes collected, wrapped in cloth and placed in a bronze urn within the tomb. The tomb was then covered with a large mound of earth.

However, during this age the Mycenaean Greeks were not the only immigrants seeking to establish settlements in Cyprus. Some time in the ninth century the Phoenicians from what is now Lebanon began expanding westward, establishing colonies not just in Cyprus, but in Sicily, Sardinia, North Africa and Spain. Kition on the south coast of Cyprus was resettled by the Phoenicians and there is evidence that it was called 'New Town' (Qart Hadasht) as Carthage in North Africa and Cartagena in Spain were also named.

It has been suggested that the settlement at Kition was founded by Ethbaal (887–856 BC), the King of Tyre, the leading Phoenician city of the time. He had been the chief priest of Astarte, the Phoenician goddess of fertility and death, and had seized the throne in a palace coup. If he had been responsible for the colony this would explain the impressively grand temple dedicated to his patroness Astarte which was erected at Kition. Ethbaal was also the father of the notorious Jezebel, who married the king of the Israelites, Ahab, and, for her sins, came to a nasty end (Old Testament, 2 Kings, IX, 11–28).

CHAPTER THREE

Archaic to Classical Period,
750–323 BC

Advancing from those 'ages' labelled after the development of metal technology in the East Mediterranean, Cyprus now moves into a truly historical (with written records) period. Civilisation had advanced in the region with the growth of literacy, the use of currency and the establishment of complex states, which manifested various imperial ambitions. The early records of Egypt, Mesopotamia and the Hittites (from Anatolia in what is now Modern Turkey) seem to have expressed a political interest in Cyprus, and in the Archaic period the island is actually subject to a series of neighbouring overlords.

Assyria

The Assyrian Empire under its ruler Tiglath Pileser III and his famous successor Sargon II began a series of conquests which led to the subjugation of Palestine, Phoenicia, Syria and Cyprus by 709 BC. The records, which are often just inscriptions, are inevitably very fragmentary. At Kition King Sargon set up an inscribed stele, recording the submission of seven kings, whose names are a mixture of Greek, Phoenician and one possibly indigenous Cypriot. They had to pay gold, silver (surprisingly copper is not mentioned), timbers, and were 'to kiss the conqueror's feet in Babylon'. Later, during King Sennacherib's reign an inscription from Ninevah suggests Cyprus is no longer under direct Assyrian control as it records the flight of the King of Sidon to the island. Then around 670 BC a cylindrical seal of Esarhaddon refers to the ten kings of Cyprus. A couple of years later ten Cypriot kings join Assurbanipal on his ultimately unsuccessful expedition against Egypt.

15

How long it took for this political system based on local kings to develop in Cyprus is not apparent. Tradition has suggested that the earliest settlers had had political leaders and it is reasonable speculation to suggest that the trading settlements that emerged in the Late Bronze Age needed firm political structures. It is not possible to know whether the Greeks had become the ruling elite by this time. However, seven out of the ten Cypriot kings named on Esarhaddon's seal, mentioned above, have Greek names.

On the other hand Kition always seems to have been ruled by a Phoenician. By the first century BC there were eleven city kingdoms that were autonomous and struck their own coinage: Amathus, Idalion, Kition, Kourion, Kyrenia, Lapithos, Marion, Paphos, Salamis, Soloi and Tamassos. Increased Phoenician influence during this century appears to have resulted in Phoenicians ruling at Lapithos and even Salamis for a short period.

Egypt

After Assurbanipal's death the Assyrian Empire waned and in 612 BC Ninevah was sacked by the Medes and Babylonians. Although Egypt was itself defeated by the Babylonians at Carchemish in 605 BC the vacuum in the East Mediterranean left by the collapse of the Assyrians enabled the Pharaohs of XXVI Dynasty to build up their fleet which came to dominate the seas around Cyprus. The Pharaoh Amasis is given the epithet *Philhellene* (loving the Greeks) by the Greek historian Herodotus (*Histories*, ii, 178). He not only married a Greek from Cyrene but also seems to have relied on Greeks to provide soldiers for his army. Herodotus tells us around 569 BC he went on to subjugate and receive tribute from Cyprus.

Cyrus and the Persian Empire

Although Amasis was able to retain the throne in Egypt for forty-four years, and the archaeological evidence suggests the city kingdoms of Cyprus enjoyed considerable prosperity, it was not a time of stability in the Near East. A new power to the east was emerging. From the mountainous land of Persia a new dynasty, the Achaemenid family, spawned the all-conquering King of Kings, Cyrus (*c.* 559–530 BC). In a series of stunning conquests Cyrus expanded his empire. The first kingdom to fall was that of the Medes, their king, Astyages being captured around 553 BC. Next was Lydia with its capital Sardis, to the west of Anatolia falling in 546 BC. Herodotus (*Histories*, i, 86ff) gives a graphic and romantic account of the encounter between Cyrus and the Lydian King, Croesus (who was legendary for his wealth – hence the saying 'to be as rich as Croesus'). By 539 Babylon (near modern Baghdad) had fallen and the one remaining power not under Persian control in the Near East was Egypt.

Cyrus himself did not undertake a campaign against Egypt as, around 530 BC, he died fighting in the north-east of his empire. His son, Cambyses, however, who had, in fact, previously been entrusted with the conquest of Egypt by Cyrus, after he had settled succession disputes

A bichsorne ware jug from Arnadi showing a bull sniffing a lotus flower
*c.*750–650 BC

in Persia, prepared to attack. As his army passed though, Phoenicia submitted voluntarily and Cyprus, presumably in recognition of the inevitable, abandoned its allegiance to the Pharaohs. Cambyses' invasion, no doubt supported by the powerful Phoenician fleet, was completely successful and after a hard fought battle in 525 Egypt fell to Persian rule.

DARIUS

Cambyses did not last long on the Persian throne and the next significant ruler to emerge was Darius (522–486 BC). He divided the Persian Empire into provinces and *satrapies*, and Cyprus was in the fifth satrapy, which included the lands of the eastern Mediterranean coastline. The control of Cyprus by the Persians may have been relatively relaxed as the Cypriot kings were still minting their own coins without any representation of the Great King, as Darius now styled himself.

Within the Persian Empire there is evidence of a greater freedom of movement than previous times and the East Greek cities of Ionia (the east coast of modern Turkey) seem to have had increased contact with Cyprus. This connection is revealed in the growing influence of Ionian forms and styles on Cypriot art in the sixth century BC. And when the Ionian Greeks rebelled against their Persian masters in 499 BC, according to Herodotus (*Histories* v. 104), Onesilos, the king of Salamis, induced all the Cypriot city kingdoms, apart from Amathus, to join the revolt.

The Persians, under Artybius, landed a force on Cyprus to put the rebellion down and, although the Ionians sent a fleet to the aid of Cyprus which successfully defeated the Phoenician fleet, the Cypriots were crushed in a land battle. During the fight Onesilos is said to have killed the Persian commander only to discover that some of the Cypriot kings had deserted to the Persian side. In the subsequent rout he was slain and decapitated, his head displayed as a trophy by the people of Amathus. Whatever the truth of the detail, the story does illustrate a conflict between allegiance to the Greeks of the West and the Phoenicians (a proxy for the Persian Empire) of the East. This tension between West and East is a recurring aspect of Cypriot history and culture up to the present day.

Following their victory the Persians began to lay siege to those Cypriot cities that still resisted and the Ionian fleet sailed away. Excavations at Old Paphos have revealed the course of the siege there. A huge siege mound was built against the north gate of the city. It appears the Persians used sculpture and monuments from a nearby sanctuary as in-fill. This has unwittingly left a valuable record of Cypriot art and inscriptions that can be dated to or before this event (*terminus ante quem*). The inhabitants tried to undermine the mound with tunnels and fires but it was to no avail and Paphos eventually fell to the Persians. The last Cypriot city to fall was Soloi which held out for five months until finally its walls were undermined.

Although the eleven city-kingdoms were allowed to continue in existence, pro-Persian kings seem to have been installed. However, the evidence from coinage suggests the kings were still allowed to mint their own currency inscribed with their Cypriot or Phoenician script, depending upon the ethnic origin of the issuers.

XERXES

Darius had sworn revenge on the Athenians from mainland Greece, who had aided the Ionian Greeks in their revolt against Persia. The Athenians described the Ionians as their 'kith and kin', as the Attic (the area around Athens) dialect of Greek was similar to Ionian Greek and it was thought those who settled in Ionia had originally come from Attica. The Athenians had sent ships and soldiers and even joined in the sacking of the Persian satrapy's capital, Sardis. Darius' sea-borne expedition of 490 BC had ended in the unexpected and surprising Athenian victory at Marathon to the north-east of Athens. Ten years later Darius' son Xerxes organised a massive sea and land invasion of Greece, and Herodotus (*Histories*, vii, 89) records that the Cypriots contributed 150 warships (triremes) to the Persian fleet of 1,200. A further snippet of evidence reveals the paradox of tension and fusion between eastern and western culture on Cyprus. Herodotus records that the Cypriot leaders apparently wore turbans, eastern style, while the crews were in Greek dress. This tends to confirm the evidence that the Greek leaders in Cyprus had been replaced by Phoenicians or Persians after their revolt.

In 480 BC, at the battle of Salamis (an island off the Greek mainland coast and not to be confused with the city in Cyprus) Xerxes' navy was completely defeated by the Greek allies. Perhaps unsurprisingly the Cypriots, no doubt conscious of their Greek heritage, apparently did not fight well for their Persian masters. In the following year the Persian land forces which had stayed on in Greece were routed at the battle of Plataea.

The Greeks now determined to hit back at Persia, free their Greek cousins on the mainland of Asia Minor and secure the trade routes in the eastern Mediterranean. However, although the Greeks subscribed to the concept of Hellenism – the character and spirit of being Greek – there was a lack of unity amongst the city-states. Each city-state (*polis*) competed with its neighbour and different political ideals and structures made co-operation difficult. Although the threat of Persia had created a strong defensive alliance amongst the city-states, it was much more difficult for them to co-operate as an offensive force.

However, the Spartan general Pausanias, the victor at Plataea, with 50 triremes, did lead an expedition to Cyprus and quickly drove the Persians from most of the island. After this success he sailed to the Hellespont where he captured the city of Byzantium and opened up the straits into the Black Sea. But his tyrannical behaviour and possibly treasonous dealings with the Persians led to the Athenians taking over the leadership of the Greeks from the Spartans.

After further Athenian successes Xerxes (465 BC) was assassinated. This was followed by a revolt against the Persians in Egypt. The Egyptians called for help from the Athenians and Cyprus provided the base for an expedition. Things, however, went badly for the rebels and the Athenian expeditionary forces ended up being annihilated (454 BC). The failure of the Athenian expedition to Egypt had consequences for Cyprus: the Persians were now able to support their Phoenician allies on the island in wresting power from the Greeks.

KIMON

In 450 BC the Athenian commander, Kimon, was sent with a fleet of 200 ships to Cyprus. In a great victory the Athenians destroyed the Phoenician fleet off Salamis and sent sixty warships to aid the Egyptians who were still resisting the Persians. However, their siege of the main Persian base at Kition was unsuccessful. Kimon died that winter and the Greek forces suffered disease and famine. With the death of Kimon there was no appetite to continue the war against Persia and probably in early 448 BC a peace was negotiated by the statesman Kallias. Although the Ionian Greeks were granted some form of autonomy Cyprus was left under the rule of the Persians. The geographical distance of Cyprus from the mainland of Greece always leaves the island more likely to be subject to the powers of the Near East.

Phoenician influence increased at the expense of Greek throughout the island. The evidence suggests that Phoenician dynasties ruled at Lapithos, Marion as well as Kition. Kition had brought Idalion under its control, destroying the Greek temple to Athena. Later Kition purchased Tamassos from its king. Even the Greek Teucrid dynasty was ousted from Salamis and the throne was seized by a Phoenician. As a consequence the political systems operating in the city-kingdoms became more totalitarian, reflecting Phoenician culture rather than Greek.

EVAGORAS

In 411 BC the Teucrid prince, Evagoras who had fled Cyprus returned with his followers and was able to recover the throne of Salamis. He dominated Cypriot politics for the next forty years. A patron of all things Hellenic he was the first ruler to use Greek letters on his coins. The archaeological evidence at Salamis reveals large amounts of imports, pottery and metal work from mainland Greece. The style and design of these imports must have had a significant impact upon Cypriot artists. One such example is the bronze head of Apollo now in the British Museum, known as the Chatsworth Head because of its time at Chatsworth House, Derbyshire, home of the duke of Devonshire. It is an example of the Early Classical period from the mid-fifth century. It was originally found at Tamassos along with parts of the body, which unfortunately were immediately destroyed. The head is hollow cast and would have originally had inlaid glass eyes. The elaborate hair was cast separately and attached. Criticised for being rather heavy in style, it is, nevertheless, impressive in sheer smoothness and solidity.

In 410 Evagoras received an honorary citizenship from Athens as

The 'Chatsworth Head': a bronze Apollo possibly imported from mainland Greece from the classical period *c.* 460 BC

recognition for the help he afforded them in its conflict with Sparta and it its allies, known as the Peloponnesian War. When Athens was defeated in 404 BC many Athenians fled to join his court at Salamis. Later he secured aid for Athens from the Persian King Artaxerxes II. A revived Athenian alliance destroyed the Spartan fleet off Cnidus in 394 BC and the grateful citizens of Athens erected a statue of Evagoras beside the victorious admiral Conon in Athens. By about 391 BC with the support of Athens and the regimé of Achoris in Egypt he was able to rule over most of the cities of Cyprus. However, Athens and Sparta were exhausted by war and sought a peace which included Persia. In 386 BC the Peace of Antalkidas was concluded with the Great King. This treaty once more consigned Cyprus to Persian domination. Although Evagoras nobly resisted the subsequent Persian onslaught his forces were defeated both on land at Kition and at sea off the coast of Salamis. However, through clever negotiation he was able to retain his throne at Salamis, contingent on a payment of tribute to the Persian throne.

In 374 BC Evagoras was murdered. The great Athenian orator Isocrates honoured him with a panegyric, giving him as an example of the successful and humane autocrat. He was succeeded by his son Nicocles and then Evagoras II. Neither had his charisma or influence, but the resistance to Persian rule continued. According to the historian Diodoros of Sicily around 351 BC all the city-kingdoms joined Egypt and Phoenicia in a revolt against Persia. The Persians apparently were able to exploit dissension among the rebels and the revolt was suppressed and Salamis itself after a siege forced to surrender.

Philip of Macedonia

In 350 BC, while resistance in Cyprus to Persia was once more being snuffed out, on the mainland of Greece the king of Macedonia, Philip, was extending his kingdom into the western territory of Epirus. And in that same year he brought Alexander, who was his son by his first marriage to Olympias, to join his court. The kingdom of Macedonia, from being perceived by the city-states of southern Greece as an uncivilised, hardly Greek, state, was becoming the most significant power on mainland Greece. Mindful of their independence and threatened by Philip's growing interference the city-states, fearing autocratic rule, came together in a last attempt to resist Macedonian dominance.

In 338 BC in central Greece the issue between Philip and the Greek city-states was decided. At the battle of Khaironeia, Philip destroyed the armies of the city-states and all resistance to his leadership of Greece. For the first time mainland Greece had been forcibly united and Philip, ironically given the Greeks' suspicion of the Macedonian monarchy, now provided the Greeks with a vision of a Hellenic future. Greece, united under Macedonia, was to be avenged on Persia and all Greek peoples freed from the Great King's rule. The Greeks were to take war to the Near East. The ancient world was about to enter a whole new era.

Alexander the Great

On that momentous day at Khaironeia Philip's son, Alexander, had revealed his military brilliance as he led the charge of the Macedonian heavy cavalry, known as the Companions, and broke the enemy's battle line. Just a couple of years later he was to become king when a disgruntled aristocrat assassinated Philip. Alexander was to fulfil his father's professed ambition of avenging the Persian invasion of Greece by not only conquering but also destroying the Persian Empire.

Alexander crossed over the Bosphorus and in a series of engagements swept the Persian king, Darius III's forces before him. After the Battle of Issos in 333 BC he pressed south to secure the Phoenician littoral and deprive the Persians of their Mediterranean fleet. The Cypriot city-kingdoms quickly submitted to him and supplied 120 warships to help in Alexander's siege of Tyre. Named amongst the Cypriot contingent were Pnytagoras of Salamis, Androkles of Amathus and Pasikrates of Kourion. The Tyrians believed their fortress, literally an island off the coast, to be impregnable. Our main source for Alexander's campaigns, Arrian, writing in the second century AD, tells us that Cypriot engineers helped construct the mole that Alexander built to link the mainland with the island. It took seven months before finally Tyre was taken by assault. Cypriots went on to support Alexander's campaigns across Asia, for example Stasanor of Soloi became governor of the Iranian province of Drangiana and Cypriot shipwrights and sailors were amongst those who built and sailed the fleet under Alexander's admiral Nearchus on the return journey from the Indus to the Persian Gulf.

In Cyprus itself Alexander introduced his own imperial coinage and replaced local weights and denominations. Otherwise, there was little impact from his short reign. Aged only thirty-three Alexander died at Babylon in 323 BC without any clear successor to his throne. His generals then competed against each other to inherit his empire. The 'successors' engaged in a long series of wars in order to lay claim to parts of Alexander's empire. The territories he had conquered soon became fragmented with rival claims and wars. Cyprus, because of its important strategic position, was one of the lands that was much fought over and the historical narrative becomes complex and has the potential to be confusing. It is difficult to weave a coherent story of the Hellenistic period and during this period Cyprus understandably only had a small part as various contenders and armies contested with each other across the Near East.

CHAPTER FOUR

The Hellenistic Period,
323–30 BC

Ptolemy and the wars of 'the successors'

In 321 BC Ptolemy, who had been made satrap of Egypt and was later to be known as King Ptolemy I Soter (the 'Saviour), when threatened by Perdiccas, the regent for a son of Alexander's in Macedonia, formed an alliance with four Cypriot kings, Nikokreon of Salamis, Nikokles of Paphos, Pasikrates of Soloi and Androkles of Amathus. Perdiccas attempted an invasion of Egypt but his expedition failed. Subsequently another one of Alexander's generals, Antigonos, who was controlling Anatolia, Syria and Phoenicia, sent his general Agesilaus to seize Cyprus. Agesilaus was able to form alliances with the cities of Kition, Lapithos, Marion and Kyrenia. Ptolemy then sent his brother Menelaus with a force of thirteen thousand men. By 313 BC with the help of another successor general, Seleukos, Menelaus was able to capture the cities Kyrenia, Lapithos, and Marion and came over to him. It is assumed Kition fell as its king Pumiathon was executed and the Phoenician temple of Herakles-Meqarth was destroyed. It seems clear that the Phoenicians of Cyprus had sided with Antigonos who controlled the mainland of Phoenicia. Ptolemy's victory dealt a severe blow to Phoenician interests in Cyprus.

Although a short-lived peace was concluded amongst the warring successors in 311 BC, a year later the last king of Salamis, Nikokreon, was forced to commit suicide by Ptolemy. He was suspected of being in correspondence with Antigonos and his palace was surrounded. Rather than surrender his brothers fired the building and everyone perished. So ended the Teucrid dynasty of Salamis. A cenotaph erected to the memory of this royal family has been discovered on the edge of the town.

DEMETRIOS POLIORKETES

In 309 BC Ptolemy attacked the Lycians and Carian towns (south-western coast of modern Turkey) under Antigonos' control. He then went on to seize territory in mainland Greece. However, in 306 BC Antigonos' son, Demetrios, known as Poliorketes (the 'Besieger') sailed against Cyprus with a fleet of 190 ships and an army of fifteen thousand men. Outside Salamis Menelaus engaged Demetrios in a land battle but was defeated, losing over a thousand men. Demetrios then started to besiege Salamis. Ptolemy tried to come to his brother's aid, but was defeated at sea. The historian Diodoros gives us an interesting insight into the 'gentlemanly' conduct that could operate among the successors during these wars. During the fighting Demetrios captured Menelaus and Ptolemy's son Leontiskos. Demetrios returned them and other high-ranking prisoners, loaded with gifts, to Ptolemy. However, he did hold on to Lamia, a celebrated courtesan of Ptolemy's. Although considerably older than Demetrios she was said to have exerted a powerful influence over him.

Demetrios' victories resulted in all of Cyprus capitulating to his father's rule. Antigonos then declared himself a king and, not to be outdone, was quickly followed by the other 'successors', including Ptolemy. Antigonos then attempted an invasion of Egypt, but Ptolemy was able to hold the frontier against him. In 301 BC Antigonos himself was defeated and killed at Ipsos by an alliance of the 'successors'. Demetrios, who had survived the defeat, was left to rule Cyprus on his own and around 298 BC Ptolemy even gave him his daughter, Ptolemais, in marriage. However, an expedition against the mainland of Greece went badly for Demetrios and he had to withdraw the fleet and forces that protected Cyprus. Ptolemy seized his opportunity and launched an expedition against Cyprus. All the cities surrendered without a fight except for Salamis where Demetrios' grandmother Stratonike held out. Finally, the city fell in 294 BC and Ptolemy returning Demetrios' compliment of earlier years, returned Stratonike and her grandchildren to Demetrios. Demetrios was fully engaged in defending his territory in Asia Minor and was unable to counter-attack on Cyprus.

Ptolemaic Period

Apart from a short period in the second century BC Cyprus remained under the control of the Ptolemaic dynasty for about 250 years. It was a complex era full of intrigue and dynastic conflicts. The Ptolemaic government's main interest in the island was its supply of copper, corn and timber; the last being a crucial source for maintaining the kingdom's navy. The city-kingdoms were now brought to an end and the island was politically and administratively incorporated into the Hellenistic kingdom of Egypt. The capital city now moved from Salamis, which had by this time begun to silt up, to Nea (New) Paphos in the south-west that was well-suited for communication with Egypt.

For most of the period the island was ruled by a general (*strategos*) who report directly to the king. These generals (*strategoi*) were high ranking and described as 'kinsmen' of the king. The *strategos* had a mercenary force at his disposal and each city had its own commander, usually a non-Cypriot, and garrison. The coinage of Cyprus was controlled by the *strategos* and the mints produced Ptolemaic coins.

Nevertheless, the Ptolemies had an essentially Hellenic perspective and so the Greeks of Cyprus seem to have lived relatively comfortably and been given a certain amount of liberty. They appear to have controlled their cultural and religious activities, forming a federation of semi-autonomous communities, 'the League of Cypriots', and inscriptions give evidence of games, competitions and other festivals. Phoenician influence declined although there is evidence a Phoenician dynast still had power in Lapithos at the beginning of third century BC.

Greek cults flourished with that of Aphrodite being the most important. Her large shrine at Old Paphos reveals how Phoenician deities were assimilated, as there she was equated with Astarte. There is evidence of the other main Greek deities, including the chief Olympian god, Zeus, as well as Apollo and his sister Artemis, Dionysus and Pan. There was also a dynastic cult developed around the deified wife of Ptolemy II Philadelphos, Arsinoe. Her cult seems to have enjoyed great popularity in Cyprus. Cities were founded in her name, including that on the old site of Marion, destroyed by Ptolemy I in 312 BC, and a shrine was built to her at Idalion.

Ptolemy I had died in 283 or 292 BC and his son, Ptolemy II, who had been made joint ruler in 285 BC, inherited the throne. Shortly after his marriage to Arsinoe in 277 BC, his half-brother was accused of raising rebellion in Cyprus and was put to death. However, generally his reign was a time of peace for Cyprus. Ptolemy II was not a warrior in the old Macedonian style. His reign was celebrated more for the splendid court he held at Alexandria (the city founded by Alexander at the mouth of the Nile) and for scientific and cultural advances, rather than for victorious campaigns. In Egypt he built the famous Pharos (lighthouse), museum and library. In Cyprus he founded three cities, including Ammochostos (the later Famagusta), as a replacement for the silted up Salamis. During his reign its seems Cypriot artists and writers flourished. Unfortunately, they tend to have come down to us as just names as their works have been lost.

Under the Ptolemies portraiture became fashionable in Cyprus and votive sculptures from shrines often reflect Hellenistic royal portraits, affecting the poses of gods and goddesses. There are also relatively large numbers of statues of small boys, found in the sanctuaries of Apollo and Aphrodite which are distinctive to the island. The so-called 'temple boys' are sculpted kneeling and holding offerings. Their purpose is unclear and there has been speculation about their role as either temple servants or even possibly prostitutes. The explanation, however, may be simply that they are a record of a first offering by a boy.

ZENO (*c.* 335–264)

It was during this time that one of the most famous characters of ancient Cyprus, Zeno of Kition, was at Athens, developing his philosophical theory, which became known as Stoicism, named after a public building in the city, the Stoa Poikle, where he met with his followers. Zeno, who had started as an adherent of Cynicism, founded his own philosophical school. Its origins have been ascribed to a combination of Hellenic and Phoenician influences which Zeno absorbed in his native Cyprus. Although it can be dangerous to oversimplify a complex set of

A bronze bust (2nd century AD) of one of the most famous characters of ancient
Cyprus: Zeno of Kition who founded his own philosophical school
c. 336–264 BC

ideas, the essential qualities his philosophy can perhaps be best described
as both systematic while theoretical, and enterprising while practical.

Stoicism is probably best known today through its transmission and
transformation during Roman times of its basic ethical doctrine. Its
moral essence has been perceived in a form that argues a human being's
main purpose in life, happiness, is best achieved through all desires being
subordinated to virtue. The means of accomplishing this was living by
reason, *logos*, rather than emotion. It follows that reason, rationality, was
equated with virtue and emotion with irrationality. This has generally
been characterised in an exaggerated form by suggesting Stoics suppressed all emotion, but, in reality, it was rather the belief that, although
it was right to attach some value to natural desires, reason should be the

ultimate moderator of behaviour, that dominated the behaviour of Stoics. Because of its appeal to the intellect it was inevitable that the attraction of Stoicism tended to be limited to the well-educated.

Euergetes I

Ptolemy II Philadelphos was succeeded in turn by his son Ptolemy III Euergetes I in 246 BC. It was during his reign that Ptolemaic Egypt reached the zenith of its power and influence. In Cyprus a high level of affluence is revealed through the remains of public and private buildings, mosaic floors and sculpture. Although these works demonstrate strong Hellenic cosmopolitan influences the native Cypriot quality was not lost. For example, in the medium of sculpture the use of the local limestone as opposed to marble helped preserve a uniquely Cypriot fusion of western and eastern representation. Under the Ptolemies portraits became fashionable and the Ptolemies themselves would affect the poses of gods and goddesses. But again the Cypriot character can be clearly discerned in the portraiture of the time.

The next king, Ptolemy IV, known as Philopator, (reigned 221–204 BC) has gained a reputation as a debauchee. He has been charged with matricide and being dominated by favourites, male and female, who conducted the affairs of state just to their own advantage. Whatever the truth about his personal behaviour, a decline in Ptolemaic power can be observed. Although he was able to halt Seleukid advances with a victory in Palestine in 217 BC, he had been forced to arm the native Egyptians, who spent the rest of his reign raising a series of rebellions.

Cyprus seems to have been left more or less to itself, with honorific inscriptions to governors and officials, testifying to a considerable degree of autonomy. Elaborate rock-cut tombs with niches and extensions radiating off the main chamber also confirm the power and wealth of the Ptolemaic aristocracy in Cyprus. The best examples, known as 'the Tombs of the Kings', are at Nea Paphos, where subterranean tombs reflect similar ones found at Alexandria in Egypt. Some have elaborate peristyled (columned) courts carved in the style of the Doric order of Greek architecture.

Ptolemy V, Epiphanes (reigned 204–181 BC), the son of Philopater, was only five when he came to the throne. Under his rule Egypt was racked by a series of native revolts and Philip V of Macedonia and the Seleukid King, Antiochus III, taking advantage of Eygpt's weakness formed a pact in order to divide up those Ptolemaic territories outside Egypt. Cyprus, however, through the strength of the Egyptian navy remained under Ptolemy's control. This control, nevertheless, seems to have been fairly loose as the powerful *strategos* on the island, Polykrates (203–197 BC), was able to put his own mark on coins minted in Cyprus.

Philometer and his brother Physkon

Ptolemy VI, Philometer (181–145 BC) soon found himself embroiled in a war with the Seleukid Antiochus IV. In 170 BC Antiochus invaded Eygpt and captured Philometer. The Alexandrians then placed Philometer's younger brother on the throne, Ptolmy VII, Euergetes II, nicknamed Physkon because of his 'pot-bellied' appearance. In 168 BC Antiochus demanded the surrender of Cyprus. After some initial resistance the *strategos* conceded and went over to the Seleukids. It was at this moment that the Romans, whose power had been growing in the Mediterranean since their defeat of the Carthaginians, intervened. Courted by both of the Ptolemies and anxious to curb the growing power of Antiochus, the Romans made threatening noises and compelled Antiochus to withdraw his forces from Egypt and evacuate Cyprus, returning the island to Philometer. Soon after the Seleukid Demetrios I Soter attempted to seize Cyprus by winning over the Ptolemaic strategos, Archias. However, the plot was exposed and Archias hanged himself.

In a political game of divide and rule Rome attempted to play one brother off against the other, creating continual instability in Egypt. In 154 BC Physkon, supported by Rome, invaded Cyprus. However, Philometer's forces surrounded Physkon at Lapithos and he was forced to surrender. Philometer decided to free his brother after he agreed to a treaty, which assigned Physkon the territory of Cyrene and guaranteed Philometer an annual tribute of corn. The Romans were not at that point able to intervene and the famous Senator Cato in a speech recognised the magnanimity and generosity of Philometer's actions.

Two years later Philometer joined a coalition against Demetrios I. For a few years this coalition was entirely successful, but changing alliances and manoeuvrings undermined stability in the region. Philometer attempted to establish some security within the Seleukid territories and supported Demetrios II, the young son of his former enemy Demetrios I. Although victorious in a battle just outside Antioch he suffered in a mortal wound and died in 145 BC. Of all the Ptolemies, given the complex machinations of the dynasty, Philometer emerges with the best press. He is characterised as reasonable and good-natured and his acts testify to a generosity of spirit in a subtle and corrupt era.

On Philometer's death Physkon wasted no time and seized his chance. He descended on Alexandria from Cyrene, married his brother's widow Kleopatra II and killed Philometer's young son whom the Alexandrians had proclaimed as their next king. A year later in 144 BC he also married Kleopatra's daughter, Kleopatra III. In 131–0 BC the Alexandrians supported Kleopatra II in driving out Physkon, who took refuge in Cyprus. Then it is said, that fearing his eldest son might replace him Physkon sent for him and had him executed. In what can only appear as an extreme act of barbarity he had his head, hands and feet sent as a birthday present to the mother. Physkon later returned to Alexandria in 127 BC where he ruled until his death in 116 BC. It is difficult to make an objective assessment of Physkon's rule as it seems the Greek sources damn him as an 'evil-doer', but there is evidence that he was sympathetic to the native Egyptians and received their support against the Greek population.

Lathyros

Physkon's will was complex and divided the Ptolemaic territories up amongst the family, sowing the seeds of future strife. It was also to be later claimed by the Romans that he bequeathed part of his kingdom to Rome. Cyprus, during the later part of his rule, had virtual independence with the *strategos* exercising sole control over the island. This was partly due to a serious deterioration in security in the eastern Mediterranean because of uncurbed assaults of the pirates out of Cilicia (the southern shore of modern Turkey). These attacks resulted in Cyprus having to fend for itself so that the island became isolated from its theoretical rulers in Egypt.

Of Physkon's two sons by Kleopatra III, Ptolemy VIII Soter II, nicknamed Lathyros, ruled in Alexandria, and Ptolemy IX Alexander I was sent to govern Cyprus. Lathyros, however, was forced by his mother to divorce his sister Kleopatra IV and marry another sister, also called, Kleopatra, known as Selene. Kleopatra IV went to Cyprus where she raised an army and then went on to Syria where she married the Seleukid Antiochus IV, taking her army as a dowry, only eventually to be killed in one of the intrigues of the Seleukids.

In 108 BC Lathyros was driven out of Alexandria and Alexander I was invited back from Cyprus by his mother, who had always preferred him to Lathyros, to rule Egypt. Lathyros then took over Cyprus. It is during Lathyros' rule that, according to the first Book of Maccabees (a history of the Jewish people from the Old Testament), Jewish settlements, which later become very populous, are first mentioned. At this time Lathyros was considered a friend by the Romans who had established bases in Pamphylia and gave provincial status to Cilicia in 103 BC.

In 89 BC Alexander I was expelled from Alexandria in a rebellion and in the following year perished in a sea battle off the shores of Cyprus. Lathyros immediately returned to Alexandria where he reigned with his sister Berenike. Cyprus was once more united with Egypt as part of one kingdom. In 86 the Roman general Licinius Lucullus (whose gardens in Rome were later to become a byword for elegance and luxury), who was seeking ships to operate against the Cilician pirates, was to visit Cyprus. On Lathyros' death (in 80 BC) Berenike assumed the government, but Alexander I's son, Ptolemy X Alexander II, with Roman support, returned to Egypt. Alexander II had been taken to Rome by the Roman dictator Sulla as a hostage. On entering Alexandria he instantly married his, now elderly, cousin Berenike and within twenty days had her murdered. The people were so enraged by his behaviour they rose up and he was killed in the subsequent riot. With his death the legitimate line of the Ptolemies came to an end. So it was that the seeds sown by Physkon's will were reaped.

With there being no legitimate heir the Romans claimed that Alexander had bequeathed his kingdom to Rome. The Alexandrians, however, decided to divide the kingdom between the illegitimate male children of Lathyros. The eldest Ptolemy XII, Philopater Philadelphos Neos Dionysios, nicknamed Auletes ('the piper') ruled Egypt, while the younger, for whom we have no name other than Ptolemy, took over Cyprus. Auletes had to spend the rest of his reign bribing the aristocracy in Rome to stay on his throne. His half-brother, Ptolemy, in Cyprus was to prove less co-operative with Rome's aggressive tactics.

The Romans

When Ptolemy was asked to pay a ransom for the Roman tribune, Publius Clodius Pulcher (renowned as the sworn enemy of the famous orator Cicero), who had been kidnapped by the pirates of Cilicia, he only offered a derogatory amount. Clodius was released anyway (it is said in disgust at the small amount offered) and gained his revenge on Cyprus by passing a law in Rome which proposed annexing the island. The income from the island would provide the Roman treasury with enough money to pay for the free bread (corn dole) that was given to the citizens of Rome. In 58 BC Marcus Porcius Cato, known as Cato the Younger, was appointed the first Roman governor of the island. Ptolemy was unable to resist the might of Rome, and, despite being offered the priesthood of Paphian Aphrodite by Cato's supporter Candidus Crassus, as compensation for the loss of the throne, committed suicide.

At a time of extreme venality at Rome it is recorded that Cato, the epitome of the Roman Stoic, and therefore of high moral stature, raised some 7,000 silver talents by selling off Ptolemy's effects. All the proceeds from the sale were lodged in the treasury at Rome and the only thing that Cato retained for himself was a bust of Zeno, the founder of Stoicism. Cyprus was now incorporated into the Roman Empire as part of the province of Cilicia.

Amongst the early governors of the expanded province was Marcus Tullius Cicero, the famous Roman orator. It had not been Cicero's wish to leave Rome but he was to take up office overseas in May 51 BC. His lieutenant Quintus Volusius was despatched to administer affairs in Cyprus. He advised Cicero about the exorbitant rate of interest being charged by Marcus Brutus, who was to become one of the leading assassins of Julius Caesar, on a loan Brutus had made to the city of Salamis. It was a common practice among Roman aristocracy to lend money at high rates of interest to city authorities who had difficulty in meeting Roman taxes. Brutus, who was praised in the writings of Plutarch for his nobility, was none the less a 'true' politician and was quite prepared to make a financial killing out of the provincials in Cyprus. Cicero tried to have the amount reduced but was foiled by Brutus' delaying tactics, so that the issue was left in abeyance until Cicero's term of office came to an end.

Cicero, although he had tried to help the Cypriots in this particular case and seemingly failed, wrote in 49 BC to Caius Sextilius, who had been sent to take up a government post in finance on the island. In his letter Cicero recommends all the inhabitants to Sextilius, especially the people of Paphos, implying in his advice that it would be to Sextilius' own advantage to treat the Cypriots properly.

KLEOPATRA AND ANTONY

It would not be long before the Ptolemies also had to yield Egypt to Roman might. Auletes, despite having been exiled in 58 BC, returned to Alexandria in 55 BC, finally dying in 51 BC. He was succeeded by his son, Ptolemy XIII and daughter Kleopatra VII, the notorious Kleopatra as described in Plutarch's vivid accounts and who was later immortalised by William Shakespeare. Kleopatra's destiny became inextricably bound up with Rome after Julius Caesar visited Alexandria in 48 BC. Her brother Ptolemy XIII tried to resist Caesar but was driven out of Alexandria and later drowned in the Nile. Another younger brother, Ptolemy XIV, was then forced to marry Kleopatra. He was made king of Cyprus by Caesar, but was subsequently murdered, it is said, by Kleopatra – his sister and wife.

After the assassination of Julius Caesar, Mark Antony, as a token of his love, gave the island to Kleopatra. She is shown on coins of Cyprus holding her child, whom she claimed was fathered by Julius Caesar, called Ptolemy XIV, Philopater Philometer Caesar, but better known as Caesarion. After Mark Antony's victory over the conspirators who had assassinated Julius Caesar, at the battle of Philippi in northern

Greece, Kleopatra had her *strategos* on Cyprus, Serapion executed by Mark Antony, probably to tighten her control on the island, and replaced by a freedman of Julius Caesar, Demetrios.

A year after his final defeat at Actium, by Julius Caesar's nephew and adopted son, Octavian, Mark Antony committed suicide. Kleopatra, in order to avoid the humiliation of a Roman Triumph, where she would have been paraded by Octavian as a captive before the Roman mob, followed Mark Antony's example and killed herself. The rule of the Ptolemies came to an end, Egypt became a Roman dependency and the island of Cyprus was returned once more to direct Roman rule.

CHAPTER FIVE

Roman Cyprus,
30 BC–AD 330

Augustus

Octavian, in settling the affairs of the Empire after the civil war with Mark Antony, included Cyprus, along with Cilicia, in the province of Syria, under the command of his supporter Marcus Valerius Messalla Corvinus. In his retirement Corvinus took to writing about history and religion, but, although it is known he was widely read in the ancient world, unfortunately, none of his works have survived. Later, possibly 29 or 27 BC, the surviving son of Marcus Cicero, who had committed suicide after being proscribed (put on a death list) by Mark Antony, became governor of the province. It is not known what he did in Cyprus, but the younger Cicero was famous for his temper and it is said he once threw a goblet of wine in the face of Octavian's chief lieutenant, Agrippa.

In 23 BC, as part of a further reorganisation of the Empire, Octavian, who had assumed the title Augustus, detached Cyprus from Syria and made it into a separate province. It was put under senatorial control rather than that of the emperor. In theory it meant that the Roman Senate selected the province's governors. However, an inscription of Publius Paquius Scaeva, as governor of Cyprus, demonstrates that Augustus was prepared to nominate his choice for senatorial provinces and suggests the senate essentially acted as a rubber stamp confirming his candidate.

The status of the island as a senatorial province does indicate that Cyprus was not considered by the emperor as militarily sensitive and there were no legions stationed there which could be used by any ambitious claimant to the imperial throne. The island was clearly perceived as peaceful and stable. Paphos remained the capital of Cyprus and was the residence of the governor, whose title was *proconsul*, indicating that he had previously held the post of *consul* at Rome and was, technically, appointed governor by the senate. For the purposes of administration and the dispensation of law, the island was divided into four districts: Lapithos in the North, Salamis in the East, Amathus in the South, Paphos in the West.

PAX ROMANA

In reality the Roman period in Cyprus heralded no great changes from rule under the Ptolemies. The island's reputation for a high level of prosperity and good living was not only sustained but also increased. As part of their normal practice across their vast empire the Romans put investment into developing the infrastructure of the island, for example, by building new roads – one road went all the way around the coastline. An ancient map dating from around fourth century AD, but surviving in a 13th century copy, known as the Peutinger Table, shows a well-developed road system and numerous Roman milestones have been found across the island. The cities also thrived, perhaps with rather greater local autonomy than previously under the Ptolemies. In Cyprus the Roman Government supported the local aristocracy, as the natural and appropriate ruling class, and encouraged urban pride and competition amongst the municipalities. This was standard policy, as Rome exercised its rule throughout its territories by wooing the wealthy through granting privileges and steadily 'Romanising' the upper classes. The aristocracy gained much through the *pax Romana,* peace under Roman rule: stability and peace brought affluence and opportunity. Individuals were anxious to demonstrate their wealth and power through patronage and philanthropy. The wide-spread practice, across all parts of the Empire, of recording a person's achievements with inscriptions either on public monuments or on tombstones testifies to the significance attached to achievements and benefactions being remembered.

During the Roman period large building programmes took place, with impressive public edifices, including *fora* (the main public square in

The theatre at Soloi built during Roman rule in the 2nd century AD

an ancient city), gymnasia and theatres being erected; for example, there are impressive remains still surviving at the sites of Salamis, Soloi and Kourion. For the modern visitor to Cyprus the vast majority of the visible archaeological remains belong to the Roman period and it is difficult not to be impressed by the scale and quality of the civic facilities that have survived the ravages of time. The cultural tradition, however, was still strongly Hellenistic, with Greek forms of art and architecture, as well as the Greek language being dominant.

There are some fine mosaics from the period found at Paphos, Kourion and Salamis. At Paphos in 1962 excavations were started at what turned out to be a splendid Roman villa, which has been dated to the third century AD. It is on a large scale with twenty-two rooms grouped around a pillared courtyard. It was probably destroyed by an earthquake as nothing survives above ground level. However, in fourteen of the rooms are some magnificent mosaics in an excellent state of preservation. The scenes mainly depict stories from Greek mythology, such as Apollo and Daphne. In an adjacent villa there are equally fine mosaics of an earlier period. This villa is known as the Villa of Theseus, as one scene shows the Athenian hero slaying the Minotaur of Crete, while Minos' daughter Ariadne, who helped Theseus kill the

Minotaur, is looking on. It is possible that this splendid villa was the residence of the Roman governor of Cyprus.

Archaeological evidence also suggests that Cypriot goods were exported widely throughout the Roman Empire. Since the suppression of the Cilician pirates by the Romans, the East Mediterranean had been secured through the *pax Romana* and agricultural exports such as wheat, olive oil and dried fruits could now be freely traded throughout the Roman world. In particular the elder Pliny, who was to meet his death when the volcano Vesuvius, in the Bay of Naples, erupted in AD 79, praises the quality of Cypriot wine.

The copper mines were worked throughout the Roman period as part of imperial property. It seems that the mines were contracted out under the supervision of an imperial official. For example, there is a reference that in 12 BC half the production of the Soloi mines was leased to King Herod the Great of Judaea for 300 talents. Along with Soloi the other important mining centres of Marion, Golgoi, Amathus and Tamassos were enlarged during the period. The Roman slagheaps, consisting of several million tons, are scattered across the foothills of the Troödos. Unlike those from earlier times, Roman slag is shiny black and it has a different colour and nature from earlier times because of the Romans' superior smelting technique. Modern miners have often traced copper ore by prospecting near the Roman slag heaps, finding old shafts, galleries and foundries, with remains of ancient timber supports and oil lamps, penetrating to great depths in the mountain sides.

RELIGION

Loyalty to the Roman emperor was maintained through the Imperial Cult, a religious practice that the Romans had adopted from the Hellenistic world. Alexander the Great had encouraged belief in the divine ruler, borrowing from oriental concepts of kingship, in particular the Persian perception of their monarch, the King of Kings. Worship of the Roman emperor became widespread, especially across the Hellenistic communities in the eastern part of the Empire. The emperors used the Imperial Cult as a means of focusing and securing the political loyalty of their subjects. Worship was a means of enhancing the per-

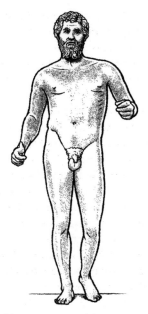

The over life-sized bronze statue of the Emperor Septimius Severus
(AD 193–211) from Kythrea. Depicted here as an athlete it exudes the might and
power of a Roman emperor

sonality cult associated with the emperor. A remarkable example of an
imposing image of the emperor is a bronze sculpture of Emperor
Septimius Severus (AD 193–211) found at Kythrea, and now in the
Archaeological Museum in Nicosia. Over life-sized the sculpture
represents Emperor Septimius as an athlete. The grizzled portrait of this
tough military usurper from Leptis Magna, Libya, in North Africa, who
had gained the imperial throne through civil war, looks quite incon-
gruous fixed on a naked athlete's body. It is hardly a beautiful work of
art but it exudes the might and physical power of the ruler of the
Roman Empire. Septimius was eventually to die of natural causes, rare
during this period of the Empire, while at York, after having campaigned against the Caledonians in Scotland.

One of the main functions of the Community (*Koinon*) of Cypriots, a federation of cities, which survived from the Hellenistic period, was the maintenance of the Imperial Cult as well as arranging other religious festivals. The Community represented both the political and cultural expression of Cyprus within the Empire. It passed honorary decrees, recognising the munificence of public benefactors, and even issued its own local copper currency, which is further evidence of the strength of Hellenism on the island as the coins were inscribed in Greek.

Aphrodite still held her supreme position among the deities on Cyprus and her games and festivals were celebrated as in Hellenistic times. The geographer Strabo describes such celebrations at Old Paphos. In 15 BC Augustus had rebuilt the temple of Aphrodite there after it had sustained damage following an earthquake. Later the historian Tacitus wrote about the right of asylum being practised at her temple as well as some sanctuary sites of other deities on the island. Both the Roman authors Tacitus and Suetonius mention that Emperor Titus visited her sanctuary, where he admired the wealth of her temple and where his success was prophesied, on his way to Palestine to repress the Jewish rebellion in AD 69.

Jewish Rebellion

Peace on Cyprus was shattered during the reign of Emperor Hadrian in AD 116 by another Jewish rebellion. Following a rising in Cyrene in North Africa the Jews in Egypt, Palestine and Cyprus rebelled. It seems their main anger was directed against the Greek population in those provinces. The most serious incidents during the rebellion occurred on Cyprus. Quite why the revolt was so ferocious on the island is unclear, but as there were essentially no troops on the island it seems the rebellion was able to spread quickly and take hold. Led by someone called Artemon, interestingly a Greek name, the Jews inflicted terrible massacres on their Greek neighbours. At Salamis over 200,000 gentiles are said to have been killed. Emperor Hadrian sent to the island the commander Lucius Quietus, who had been one of Trajan's, the preceding emperor, cavalry commanders in the successful war against Parthia (later Quietus was to fall from grace and be executed by

Hadrian). After he had suppressed the rising all the Jews were expelled from the island and forbidden to return.

During Roman rule the island suffered from several serious earthquakes, and in 15 BC nearly the whole of Paphos is thought to have been destroyed. Another natural disaster, but brought to the island by man, was the great plague carried back by Lucius Verus' troops from their campaign in Mesopotamia in AD 164. This outbreak spread throughout the Roman realm and is thought by some historians to have had a devastating effect on the manpower of the Empire, weakening its military strength and ultimately helping to lead to the Empire's collapse in later times.

Christianity

During the Roman period Christianity was introduced to the island. The first documentary evidence of Christianity in Cyprus comes from the *Acts of the Apostles* where we are told Stephen who was later to be martyred by stoning, came and preached to the Jewish communities. In *c.* AD 45 St Paul accompanied by St Barnabas, a Jew from Cyprus, who replaced Judas Iscariot as an Apostle, landed at Salamis. It was claimed that at Paphos the Roman proconsul himself, Sergius Paulus, was converted after being convinced by St Paul blinding a Jewish rival appropriately named Elymas Bar-Jesus. Afterwards it was said that St Barnabas, after a disagreement with Paul, returned to Cyprus with Mark, but was stoned to death by a mob at Salamis. Tradition makes St Heraklides of Tamassos the first bishop and the Greek Cypriots of Larnaca claim that St Barnabas consecrated Lazarus, the brother of Mary and Martha of Bethany, bishop of Kition. Outside these traditions there is little archaeological evidence to assess the strength of Christianity in Cyprus prior to Emperor Constantine's conversion and the adoption of Christianity as the official religion of the Empire at the beginning of the fourth century AD.

In the third century the Empire suffered a good deal of instability and, rather than expanding the imperial territories, the lands of the Empire came under threat so that soldier emperors spent much of their time defending its frontiers. A major onslaught came from the incursions of the Goths (Germanic tribes from across the Danube frontier). In AD 269 a raiding party of Goths even landed on Cyprus, but appear to have done little damage as they were overtaken by sickness.

Diocletian and Constantine

The Empire was stabilised at the end of the third century by Emperor Diocletian (AD 284–313), who came from the Province of Dalmatia and built a remarkable palace which has given its name to the modern day city of Split in Croatia. Diocletian attempted to create a system of imperial succession (known as the Tetrarchy, 'the rule of four') which would help put an end to the civil wars that arose from rival claimants contesting the throne. In the end his dynastic system was to fail but a more lasting reform was his reorganisation of the provinces of the Empire. He grouped them into larger units, called dioceses. Cyprus came within the Diocese of Oriens, which was based at Antioch in Syria.

Diocletian's reign came to an end amidst a flurry of civil wars between competing successors. The final confrontation was to be between Constantine who had become supreme in the West and Licinius who controlled the eastern part of the Empire. During the conflict Licinius in AD 324 collected ships from Cyprus, but his naval forces were defeated by Constanine's son Crispus – who was later to be executed by his own father. Constantine was ultimately victorious and he once more reunited the Empire under his sole control. There is no evidence that Cyprus suffered in any way during the civil war. However, there is an odd story from a few sources about an insurrection on the island in AD 334 led by a certain Calocaerus. According to the sources he was sent as governor, and introduced a special breed of cats to Cyprus in order to deal with a plague of snakes that had resulted from a drought on the island. These cats are mentioned in mediaeval sources as being cared for by the monastery of St Nicholas near Akrotiri. Calocaerus seems to have had an obscure origin, and in one account he is referred to as a camel driver (this is perhaps just a standard insult). The nature of the revolt is obscure but he seems to have wished to seize power for himself in Cyprus. He was soon captured by Dalmatius, another of Constantine's sons, who had him burnt alive in the forum at Tarsus.

Writing much later Lactantius, a bishop of the Church, records that during his campaign in Italy against his rival, Maxentius, Constantine was miraculously converted to Christianity. Initially this resulted in a new toleration of a religion that since its inception had suffered intermittent, but vicious, bouts of persecution from the imperial authorities. Later Constantine's support developed from promotion of Christianity to its recognition as the official religion of the whole Empire. Constantine's espousal of Christianity, often termed 'the triumph of Christianity', was to have a profound effect, not just upon the Empire but on entire world history. It has been argued from a non-religious perspective that it was Constantine who ensured the survival of Christianity and the blossoming of a relatively small sect into a major world religion.

CHAPTER SIX

The Byzantine Period,
AD 330–1191

The Triumph of Christianity

Constantine commemorated his own triumph in AD 330 by rebuilding the city of Byzantium, and inaugurated it as his new Christian capital in the eastern part of the Empire as a rival to Rome. Byzantium was strategically in a superb position not only commanding the straits of the Bosphorus (the entrance to the Black Sea), but also being at a crossroads for travel from north to south and east to west. The city flourished and was soon called Constantinople ('the city of Constantine') after its founder. (It was, during the time of the modern Turkish state, in 1930, when Constantinople was renamed Istanbul.) The establishment of this new capital in the eastern half heralded the separation of the Greek speaking part of the Empire from the Latin dominated West, and the evolution of a Hellenised Christian realm that has come to be known as Byzantium. Precisely when the Byzantine period begins is a matter for debate as there is no one clear historical event which immediately transformed the eastern half of Roman Empire into the Byzantine Empire. The key criteria of what modern historians describe as Byzantium relate to the emergence of a state underpinned by an Hellenistic, Greek speaking Christian culture, focused on the city of Constantinople, which came to dominate the East Mediterranean for a thousand years.

It is not known how strong the Christian population in Cyprus was when Constantine adopted Christianity, but it is clear once it was the official religion of the Empire the whole island was quickly converted. A leading protagonist of the new faith was Helena, the mother of

Constantine. She went on a pilgrimage to the Holy Land, where she not only founded churches in Bethlehem and Jerusalem, but also discovered the site of Jesus' crucifixion along with fragments of the True Cross (the cross on which it was believed Jesus was crucified). On her return from the Holy Land she is said to have visited Cyprus where she miraculously put an end to a severe drought that had been afflicting the island for more than thirty years. She founded several churches on the island and legend says she established the monastery at Stavrovouni, where she left a holy relic, a fragment of the True Cross.

COUNCIL OF NICAEA

In AD 325 at the first Ecumenical Council, summoned by Constantine, at Nicaea there were three bishops from Cyprus. Although his attendance is far from certain, one of these bishops is supposed to have been St Spyridon of Tremithus. He, it is said, survived the persecution, instituted by Emperor Galerian in AD 304 and later in 1453 his remains were taken from Constantinople, just before the city was captured by the Turks, to Corfu, where he became that island's patron saint. Sometime shortly after AD 330, according to a biography written by St Jerome, St Hilarion is believed to have fled from Gaza, Palestine, visiting Sicily and Epidauros (Dubrovnik), until finally settling in Cyprus. He was a hermit and lived near Paphos until he died at the age of eighty. His body was then smuggled back to Maiuma in Palestine. Another influential bishop of Salamis was St Epiphanios, who wrote polemics against heresies and attacked the teachings of Origen. He even went to Constantinople to dispute with the famous cleric John Chrysostom, but died on ship as he was returning to Cyprus.

Further evidence of the growing size and strength of the Church in Cyprus comes from the Council of Sardica (modern Sofia, Bulgaria) in AD 343, where twelve Cypriot bishops were signatories to the decrees refining canonical law and granting provisions to the Bishop of Rome as a bishops' court of appeal. Then Theophilos, the archbishop of Alexandria from AD 384/5, who collaborated with Emperor Theodosius in persecutions of non-Christians and the destruction of the ancient temple, the Serapeion, in AD 394, wrote to the church in Cyprus, mentioning that there were then fifteen bishops in Cyprus.

Christianity can be seen as a key element in the religious and culture changes that heralded the transformation from the ancient to the mediaeval world. The confidence in the rational and material world, which is manifest in classical art, literature and philosophy, was replaced by introversion that focused on the metaphysical or the immaterial dimension. Mediaeval asceticism – austere abstinence – rejected bodily functions, and life on earth was of no significance in comparison to the afterlife in an ethereal realm of either heaven or hell. Byzantine art did not attempt to replicate the physical but to indicate the hieratic – fixed by religious tradition, the 'virtual' world of the spiritual. The emperor, often referred to as the thirteenth Apostle, took on theistic (superhuman) powers as God's vice-regent on earth. Byzantium shifted from the more heterogeneous expression of, if not secular, polytheistic – many gods – classicism towards the absolutism of a theocratic – ruled by God – state, and the persecutions that had been practised against Christianity were now, ironically, instigated against all other religions. Christianity, theologically akin to gnostic (religious sects seeking divine truth) beliefs, was itself to be riven by a series of heresies, which were in turn extirpated with all the harshness and cruelty the state could exercise.

Overtly pagan practises were outlawed, including some of the inhuman practices that had existed across the Roman Empire: for example, gladiatorial contests along with crucifixions were abolished. However, slavery, torture and mutilation easily co-existed with Christian ethics of charity and peace. In Cyprus, as in other parts of the Empire, Christianity had mainly appealed to the urban proletariat and ancient religious practices were still maintained in the countryside (the word for non-Christian, *pagan,* literally means 'a country dweller'). So, for example, although the worship of Aphrodite was banned, dances and rites in her honour still survived, gradually to be incorporated into the island's Christian culture. (A similar tolerance and absorption of pre-Christian beliefs and ceremonies can be observed in the Churches of South America.)

AUTOCEPHALY OF THE CHURCH OF CYPRUS

The key issue for Cypriots that emerged during fifth century AD was the independence of their Church from the Patriarchy of Antioch in Syria.

The city of Antioch (now Antakya in Turkey) had been founded in 300 BC by Seleukos I on the left bank of the Orontes. It had flourished, its wealth deriving from its position as a commercial depot for the eastern Mediterranean, and it became the capital of the diocese of Oriens. Antioch claimed the right to appoint the bishops of Cyprus and in the early fifth century Alexander, the Patriarch of Antioch, wrote to Pope Innocent I to complain that the Cypriots were ordaining their own bishops. A canon from the Council of Nicaea, claiming that Antioch was entitled to appoint the archbishop of Cyprus was cited, but was seen as a forgery. Nevertheless, the Pope ordered the Cypriots to obey Antioch, but they ignored his judgement. Hostile incidents between Antioch and Cyprus then followed with Theodore, the Archbishop of Cyprus, being slapped in the face when he visited Antioch.

When Theodore died the new Patriarch of Antioch, John I, persuaded the Count of Oriens, Flavius Dionysius to order the governor of Cyprus to prevent, using force if necessary, the election of a new archbishop by the Cypriot bishops. The whole issue was to be brought before the Third Ecumenical Council, which was due to meet later at Ephesus in AD 431. In complete defiance of Antioch the Cypriot bishops (suffragans) elected Rheginus to the position of archbishop, and he and a few colleagues, Sapricius of Paphos, Zeno of Kourion, Evagrius of Soloi and the Protopapos Caesarius, set out for Ephesus to plead their case. More is known about the Council of Ephesus than previous general councils because it is the first with extant original acts. Ephesus had been called by Emperor Theodosius II to settle a Christological dispute relating to the teaching of Nestorius, who was supported by Antioch, and the divine nature of Christ and hence the divinity of the Virgin.

Most of the decisions at the Council, which went against the Antiochene position, had been made before John I's party arrived at the Ephesus. Nestorius' teachings on the divinity of Christ were rejected and, although Sapricius died on arrival at Ephesus, the remaining Cypriots convinced the Council that the tradition was one that allowed Cypriots to choose their own archbishop without interference from Antioch. The Council appeared to endorse this argument by confirming that the church authorities in Cyprus should consecrate their bishops according to the existing established customs.

A gold coin showing the Emperor Zeno (AD 474–91)

Ephesus, however, was not the end of the dispute and nearly forty years later the then Patriarch of Antioch, known as Peter the Fuller, pursued the issue with Emperor Zeno (AD 474–91), who had placed him in office. Peter argued that as the Cypriot Church had been founded by Antioch and because Antioch was an Apostolic see, Cyprus should be under his authority. To counter Peter's claim the archbishop of Cyprus, Anthemius, had a providential dream which led him to the burial place of the apostle St Barnabas. The body was found in a coffin lying in a cave and on his breast a copy of the Gospel of St Matthew. The apocryphal story was that St Barnabas always carried with him a copy of the Gospel, transcribed in his own hand and that St Mark had placed it on his dead body.

Anthemius travelled to Constantinople where he presented the emperor with the Gospel. Zeno, was clearly impressed and the Patriarch of Constantinople summoned a synod which confirmed the independence (autocephaly) of the Cypriot Church. The archbishop of Cyprus was also given the privilege of carrying a sceptre rather than a staff, signing his name in purple – normally the sole right of the emperor – and wearing a purple cloak. These symbols are seen by some as suggesting temporal control over the island, but in reality the palace still appointed a governor. Antioch also still had to provide the chrism (oil of consecration) for the archbishop, and this practice lasted until 1860. (Since 1864 the chrism has come from the Patriarchy of Constantinople.) Although never achieving the status of a patriarchate, the autocephaly of the Cypriot Church has remained unchallenged up to the present day and has played an important role both in defining identity and providing political leadership for the Greek Cypriot community.

Outside church history of the island we know little of what took place from the fifth to the seventh centuries. The name of one governor is known – Epiphanius – who was the father of St John the Almsgiver (*c.* AD 560–619). He was bishop of Amathus and, as his name implies, was famous for the support he gave to all, including the poor, refugees and those down on their luck. In his will he said he found the treasury of his church full and left it empty. Cyprus seems to have remained relatively prosperous while the Syrian mainland not only suffered earthquakes but also devastation during a war against Persia. Twice during the reign of Emperor Justinian (AD 527–565) severe earthquakes hit Antioch and in AD 540 the king of the Sassanians (a Persian dynasty) sacked the city. Perhaps because of the instability in Syria in AD 536, Justinian did remove Cyprus from the jurisdiction of the prefect of Oriens, and along with five other provinces placed the island under the control of a newly created *quaestor exercitus*. About 3,000 Persian captives are said to have been settled on the island by Justinian and later the future emperor Maurice, near the end of Justin II's reign (AD 565–578), sent thousands of prisoners from Greater Armenia to Cyprus.

Justinian's reign also did bring one important benefit to the island. In AD 533–4 silk moth eggs were reportedly smuggled out of China by some monks and silk manufacture was established within the Empire. Cyprus was one of the areas where the new industry began to flourish. Cypriot silks became famous and islanders were able to benefit from the wealth of this trade. It is also likely that the island generally increased its trade with the West after Justinian's reconquests in North Africa from the Vandals and Italy from the Ostrogoths.

Islam and the Arabs

In the reign of Heraclius (AD 610–641) the whole political situation in the Near East was to change. A new Persian offensive resulted in the capture of Jerusalem and the loss of Egypt. Even Constantinople came under siege, but managed to resist. During this time it is probable that the mint at Antioch was relocated to Cyprus. A new aqueduct for the city of Salamis (then named Constantia) was completed. Heraclius also attempted to introduce his theological doctrine of Monotheletism into Cyprus. This doctrine, though it recognised the two natures of Christ – divine and human – argued there was only one will. Heraclius supported this position as he hoped to be able to bring the Monophysites, who only recognised the divine nature of Christ, back together with the Orthodox, who taught the double nature of Christ, divine and human. Heraclius wrote to Arcadius, the archbishop of Cyprus, articulating the doctrine of Monotheletism, but to little avail. In reality the attempt at a compromise only increased the hostility between the two sides and there is no evidence that Cyprus ever adopted the doctrine.

After years of difficult fighting within the borders of the Empire Heraclius entered Mesopotamia and completely defeated the Persians. The war, however, left both the Persians and Byzantines exhausted and the Arab tribes, inspired by the new religion of Mohammed, rose up, destroyed the Persian Empire and swept away Byzantine resistance in the eastern provinces in a remarkably short time. By AD 639 all of Palestine and Syria was under the control of the Caliph Uthman and probably in AD 649 Muawiya, the governor of the newly-conquered territory and the future Caliph, gathered a fleet of 1,500 ships and invaded Cyprus. The expedition seems to have been bent on raiding rather than conquest. Salamis was besieged and sacked, with a large number of the inhabitants being massacred. The booty was said to have filled seventy ships – which, even if an exaggeration, suggests the level of the wealth that had built up in the island. The city was so thoroughly despoiled that it never really recovered.

Muawiya and his second-in-command travelled with their wives; the latter's wife was Umm Haram, whose mother was a close relation of

Mohammed. According to tradition the older lady fell off her horse and died and was buried at the site of Hala Sultan Tekké – which is still a sacred site for Muslims – by a salt lake just outside Larnaca. On learning that a Byzantine fleet was on its way to the island Muawiya withdrew, but he was to claim that he had imposed an annual tribute, which never seems to have been paid, on the Cypriots. In AD 653–4, he sent another force, under one of his commanders, this time to capture the island. Many of the inhabitants were killed and the city of Lapithos captured. A garrison of 12,000 troops was stationed on the island.

Caught up in his struggle with Ali for the Caliphate, Muawiya signed a three-year truce with the Byzantines, during which he was required to pay 1,000 solidi (gold coins), one slave and one horse per week to the emperor. However, once he became caliph Muawiya renewed his attacks on Byzantium and during the years AD 674–8 actually besieged Constantinople. After suffering heavy losses the Arab forces finally withdrew and, the now ageing Muawiya, was compelled to conclude a thirty-year peace, agreeing to pay the emperor annually 3,000 solidi, fifty prisoners and fifty horses. Although there was no specific mention of Cyprus in the treaty, it looks as if the Arab garrison's position became untenable and it was withdrawn about AD 683. The treaty with the Byzantines was reconfirmed both in AD 685 and then with a new Caliph, Abd al-Malik, and the Byzantine Emperor Justinian II in AD 688. This treaty stipulated that the revenues from Armenia, Georgia and Cyprus should be shared. The island was to be neutralised with neither Arabs nor Byzantines stationing troops on Cyprus.

Despite the treaty Justinian II decided to resettle the Greek population of Cyprus on the Anatolian mainland. He built a new city near Cyzicus on the southern shore of the Sea of Marmora, named New Justinianopolis for the archbishop, John, and his flock. The Church Council at Trullo (AD 691) confirmed the autocephaly of the Cypriot Church and the diocese of the Hellespont, where the new city was sited, was also included in its control. (The archbishop still has the honorary title of primate of that city today.) The transfer to New Justinianopolis did not work and one shipload of emigrants from Cyprus, including a number of Muslim prisoners, was shipwrecked with a huge loss of life. Some Cypriots then fled to Syria to avoid being transported to the new city. In AD 698 after Justinian II had been deposed Tiberios III returned the settlers to Cyprus and negotiated with the caliph a return to the island for the refugees from Syria.

There may have been another clause in the agreement of AD 688, referred to in his correspondence by the patriarch of Constantinople, Nicholas I Mysticus (AD 852–925), which required the two communities (Greek and Arab) to help each other if attacked from the outside. It seems that Cyprus remained essentially demilitarised for nearly three hundred years apart from a brief period when Basil I sent a force to occupy the island in late ninth century. Certainly, when the English pilgrim St Willibald, a future Bishop of Wessex, visited Cyprus in AD 723, staying at Paphos and Constantia, he describes the island as shared between Greeks and Saracens (Arabs) and he seems to have had no problems in travelling freely. It has to be assumed that officials from the Empire and Caliphate were able to operate among their own communities, and it also appears that Byzantine and Arab fleets used the strategically important facilities of the island.

In AD 743 a raid was made on Cyprus by the forces of Caliph Walid and a number of Christians were carried off. However, Walid's son Yazid III, a few years later allowed them to return. In AD 747, during the reign of the Emperor Constantine V, the Caliph Mervan II amassed a large fleet of over a thousand Arab ships from Egypt with the intention of attacking Byzantium. A Byzantine squadron, sailing from the Pamphylian coast caught them unawares off the coast of Cyprus and won a devastating victory, destroying the fleet.

Iconoclasm

In the early eighth century the religious movement known as Iconoclasm, which comes from the term for *image destroyer*, gained sway in Byzantium. The movement was based around a controversy over the status of icons. The Iconoclasts deprecated the worship given icons by the Iconophiles (*lovers of icons*) and had a puritan approach to religious art – possibly a view influenced by aniconic (non-figurative art) Islam, which in its purest form is against any natural representations. The Isaurian Dynasty (AD 717–802), founded by Leo III, supported the

Iconoclast cause and by the 760s acts against the Iconophiles were being enforced. Monks and nuns were the staunchest supporters of the icons and were persecuted for their devotion. There are stories of them being driven out of monasteries and being forced to marry, while icons and any human representations of Christianity were destroyed. In 770s monks and nuns who had refused to marry, after having been cruelly blinded, were sent in exile to Cyprus. Others fled the persecutions by escaping to Cyprus, which perhaps because of its special status seems to have been spared the excesses of Iconoclasm. At the Second Council of Nicaea AD 787 Iconoclasm was set aside and it was the archbishop of Cyprus, Constantine, who proposed the formula that icons should be respected but not worshipped.

Abbasid Caliph Harun al-Rashid (AD 786–809)

From the late eighth to early ninth century Byzantium was in a state of weakness and this was exploited by a series of Arab raids on Cyprus. In AD 773 after a raid the Byzantine governor was captured and carried off. Then the aggressive Abbasid Caliph Harun al-Rashid (AD 786–809) almost continuously attacked Byzantine territory, twice raiding Cyprus. In the second raid many Christians, possibly including the archbishop of Cyprus, were taken as captives. Despite these raids many Christians during this period also fled to Cyprus because of the Muslim persecutions against them in Syria and Palestine. Under the Emperor Basil I (AD 867–886) Cyprus seems to have been designated, under the governor Alexius, an Armenian, a *theme* – a territorial unit administered by *strategos*. The origin of the term *theme* and the date when it was introduced into the Empire are both disputed. However, it does appear that probably by the end of the seventh century most of Byzantine territory was organised into these relatively large units under a military commander who also acted as civil administrator and judge. The designation of Cyprus as a *theme* seems to have been short-lived and only lasted for about seven years.

There is not much known about the overall economic state of the island during this period. The few accounts from travellers suggest a moderate prosperity. The silk industry continued to be developed and the export of produce to the Syrian mainland is recorded. The Cypriots seem to have had to pay taxes both to the Byzantine authorities and the Caliphate.

In AD 905 the Byzantine admiral Himerius defeated an Arab fleet in the Aegean, and five years later he stopped off at Cyprus on his way to raid Laodicea, where he is said to have killed some Muslim officials. The next year, in AD 911, Himerius led a large armada against Crete, described in the *Book of Ceremonies* of Constantine VII, but it went badly and on his return his fleet was destroyed off Chios by a Greek renegade called Damian, who then went on to raid Cyprus. The Patriarch of Constantinople, Nicholas I Mysticus (mentioned above) wrote to the caliph in protest about Damians's raid on the Christians of Cyprus.

During the tenth century the Muslim world began to fragment and Fatimid Egypt annexed Palestine and parts of southern Syria. After having retaken Crete for Byzantium in AD 961, the future emperor Nicephorus Phocas conquered Cilicia on the mainland of Anatolia. He then defeated the Egyptian fleet in a naval battle off the coast and sent one of his generals, Nicetas Chalcutzes, to occupy Cyprus.

NICEPHORUS PHOCAS

A measure of the turn around in fortune for Byzantium was that in AD 961 generals of Nicephorus Phocas captured Antioch; this patriarchal city had been in Muslim hands for over three hundred years. Nicephorus Phocas pushed his conquests further into Syria, and received the nickname 'White Death' from his vanquished Arab foes. His successor and one time supporter John Tzimisces, gained the throne by murdering Nicephorus, but continued to increase the strength of the Empire.

The consequences of this Byzantine revival for Cyprus were that the island was not just fleetingly occupied by the Empire, but that the islanders were once again fully under its control. There have been, however, debates both about the advantages and disadvantages of once more being governed from Constantinople, and about the ethnic character of the island after centuries of Arab settlement. And in both cases the evidence is not clear-cut. The argument about ethnic identity relates to the balance on the island between Semitic peoples from Syria

The Byzantine church of St Barnabas and St Hilarion at Peristerona,
10th century

and Palestine and Indo-Europeans from Greece. It does seem that some
Arabs emigrated back to the mainland of Syria and others appear to
have been absorbed in the Christian community.

The advantages of Cyprus once more being part of a Christian
community and the additional security provided by the imperial forces
stationed on the island are said to have been offset by the more rigorous
collection of taxes and the loss of independence some islanders had
enjoyed. The leadership of the autocephalus church of Cyprus had
enjoyed autonomy and status as not only the spiritual voice of the
Christian community, but also the political representatives of the
Greek-speaking people. The archbishop had been regarded as the head
of the Christian community and any resident Byzantine officials had,
comparatively, had little control. The new Byzantine governors
seemed to represent a challenge to the position of the archbishop and a
tension arose between the religious and secular powers.

THEOPHILUS EROTICUS

Added to this sense of hostility between the two authorities, Cypriot
Church and Byzantine State, governors on the island, now with their

own armed forces, were sometimes tempted to defy the ruling emperor and through rebellion try to create their own opportunity for greater power. There is the odd case of Theophilus Eroticus (an apt name for the governor of Aphrodite's isle). As governor of Serbia in AD 1040 he had failed miserably to put down a revolt. However, instead of being ignominiously dismissed, probably because his family was friends with the emperor at the time, Michael IV, he was transferred to become governor of Cyprus. Shortly after his appointment Michael IV died and his nephew Michael V came to the throne. When in AD 1042 there was a coup and Michael was deposed and blinded, Theophilus Eroticus attempted to stage a revolt. However, one of the senior imperial officials on the island, Theophylact, not only refused to join him but, seemingly, before he was imprisoned by Theophilus, warned the new Emperor Constantine IX Monomachus, of the revolt. The emperor sent a squadron of ships to the island and the revolt was easily put down and Theophilus taken in chains to Constantinople. There he was treated in a bizarre and humiliating, if not violent, manner. He was, apparently, led around the hippodrome where the chariot races, a major passion for the citizens of Constantinople, were held, dressed as woman and, after all his possessions had been confiscated, he was allowed to go free.

The eleventh century was a critical period for the Byzantine Empire. The recovery and strength exhibited at the end of tenth century was replaced by weakness and disintegration after the death of the last strong ruler of the Macedonian Dynasty, Basil II (AD 976–1025). The threats to the Empire came from a resurgent West and the rise of new power in the East. Cyprus was to play an important role in the events of the period because of its strategic position.

The governors of Byzantine Cyprus were in many ways key agents for overseeing the interests of Byzantium in its relations with the caliphates of Syria and Egypt; for example, in AD 1027 a treaty with the Fatimids had allowed the emperor to rebuild the Church of the Holy Sepulchre which had been destroyed by the Muslims in AD 1009. When finally the work started in AD 1045 it was the governor of Cyprus who was charged with making the arrangements for rebuilding the Christian quarter in Jerusalem. When Bishop Lietbert of Cambrai and his party of pilgrims journeyed to the Holy Land they were kept on the island. Although they were probably placed there because of the dangers of Western Christians travelling in Syria at the time it was interpreted as an attempt by the Byzantine authorities to sabotage the visit. This is perhaps not surprising given the situation at the time between the Churches of the East and West.

East West Schism

For centuries East and West had been evolving along different lines and the relations between the two Churches reflected this. The political development of independent states in the West was quite contrary to the political culture of the universality of the Byzantine state. The competition for Christian souls among the Slavs of the Balkans between Rome and Constantinople was a recognition of their estrangement. When the Slavs of Russia chose Constantinople in preference to Rome it was clear that recognition of the Pope's position as *primus inter pares* (first among equals) no longer held sway in the East. In fact, a definite hostility towards Rome can be observed in Byzantium. Although there was an attempt to establish a peaceful division of authority in AD 1025 the two Churches could not agree terms.

In the end matters were brought to head by an uncompromising Pope, Leo IX, and a headstrong Patriarch of Constantinople, Michael Cerularius. At a time when the Byzantine star was waning and the West's help would be needed to stem the advances of Islam, these political considerations were put to one side and doctrinal and liturgical differences were allowed to dominate relations. In the end the Pope sent his legate Cardinal Humbert to Constantinople, who in an extraordinarily aggressive move placed a Papal Bull, excommunicating the Patriarch and his chief followers, on the altar of the cathedral church of Hagia Sophia on 16 July AD 1054. Any hope now of drawing back from a complete schism between the Christian Churches was lost. Even those, including the Emperor Constantine IX Monomachus, who were either lukewarm or opposed to Michael Cerularius' attitude to Rome, rallied to his support. A synod was called and, in a decision of reciprocity, the Eastern Church excommunicated the Papal legates.

Although at the time the behaviour of the two Churches was part of a wider political stance, the significance of this schism was to be far deeper rooted, disastrous for Christendom and has still not entirely been healed (although the anathemas were annulled in 1965).

Manzikert

In the East a new power was emerging which was not only to change the political shape of the Middle East but also ultimately destroy Byzantium. This new force was the Turks. The name Turk has been used in a general way to describe those peoples originating from the region of Turkestan. As a result of the Arab conquests in the eighth century across the region of Transoxiana most of the Turkic tribes were converted to Islam. In the early mediaeval period many Turks migrating as nomads or as warriors – often acting as mercenaries for the Arab rulers – reached Eastern Europe and the Mediterranean and so came into contact with Byzantium. In the eleventh century a powerful dynasty, the Seljuks, arose among the Ouz tribes. A leading chief of the Seljuks, Tuğril Bey (AD 1038–63), overran all of Persia and then came to the support of the Caliph of Baghdad, who was beset by unorthodox Muslims, the Shi'ites. As a reward Tuğril Bey was appointed Sultan of Baghdad. His successor and nephew, Alp Arslan, expanded the Seljuk conquests and soon took on the weakened Byzantine Empire, destroying the Emperor Romanus IV's army at Manzikert in AD 1071. It was a blow Byzantium was never fully to recover from, and migrant bands of Turks soon pushed westward settling in Anatolia and others penetrated southward into Syria and Palestine. The impact of these incursions was not just the immediate one of disrupted communications with Constantinople and the threat of invasion as a Turkish fleet began to capture the Aegean islands, but long term, with the eventual dominance of the Turks in the region having long-lasting consequences for the island of Cyprus.

ALEXIUS COMNENUS

In the West the soured relations with Byzantium paved the way for Norman adventurers, under their brillant Duke, Robert Guiscard, to complete the conquest of Southern Italy – the fall of the last Byzantine town, Bari, taking place, coincidentally, in 1071, the year of the defeat at Manzikert. Byzantium appeared to be on the point of complete collapse, as swathes of territory were lost and revolt and usurpation became the familiar pattern at Constantinople. However, Byzantium was not yet ready to disappear and at this critical moment Alexius I Comnenus (AD 1081–1118), nephew of the Emperor Isaac, came to the throne and his reign opened a new period in Byzantine history. His daughter, Anna, wrote a detailed account of his reign which, fortunately, has survived, so there is a first hand account for historians of this troubled but restorative period. Through Alexius' skill as a statesman, a combination of leadership and diplomacy, he steadied the situation and Byzantium was able to survive. However, the Byzantine Empire was now much reduced in size and was never able to return to times of its former glory. Nevertheless, with a reorganised army Alexius' generals recovered the Aegean islands and much of the Anatolian coast, but the hinterland of Anatolia was permanently lost to the Turks.

In AD 1093 Rhapsomates, the governor of Cyprus along with the governor of Crete, Caryces, and with the expectation of help from the Turkish Emir of Smyrna, Tzachas, rebelled against Alexius. The emperor quickly responded by sending a fleet, commanded by his brother-in-law, John Ducas to suppress the rebellion. When the force approached Crete the people rose up against Caryces and in the words of Anna he was 'cruelly murdered'. Sailing on to Cyprus a force of imperial troops, under the command of a certain Manuel Butumites, disembarked at Kyrenia, and although Rhapsomates had moved his militia to a camp above the town he missed his opportunity to attack. When he did finally march his forces down from the hills, some of them went over to the other side. Rhapsomates, clearly having lost any confidence in his ability to resist, fled towards Limassol. However, he was captured at Stavrovouni and sent back to Constantinople where presumably he met an unpleasant end. A new military governor, Eumathius Philocales, was appointed and Calliparius, 'not a nobleman', according to Anna, was put in charge of the financial and judicial matters of the island.

Both Manuel Butumites and Eumathius Philocales reappear in the pages of Anna as staunch lieutenants of Alexius. There is a story that Butumites, while he was in Cyprus, suffered an attack of sciatica. He was cured by a monk, Esaias, who was then encouraged to found a monastery at Kykko. Under Butumites' patronage Esaias visited Constantinople where he was said to have also cured Alexius' daughter of the same complaint. As a reward the emperor gave him an icon of Mary, thought to have been painted by St Luke, which has become the island's holiest icon. In AD 1097 Philocales was involved in an attack to recover Laodicea on the Syrian coast. It seems after serving one term as governor Philocales returned later to Cyprus to hold office a second time.

It was probably after Philocales last time as governor, in AD 1112 that the archbishop of Cyprus, Nicholas Muzalon, wrote a long poem, describing the miseries of the Cypriot people. The poem that goes on at length about the exorbitant taxes the islanders had to pay, also attacks the governor and those of the clergy who supported him. In what has been described by some as 'exaggerated ranting', the poem describes the torture and starvation the clergy had to suffer. Other evidence would actually suggest the island at this time was quite prosperous and wealthy enough to export foodstuffs. There are also grounds for believing that Muzalon was a miserable character who had become embittered in old age. When he later became patriarch of Constantinople, he seems to have been so unpopular because of his temperament that, apparently, his contemporaries were delighted when his election was declared uncanonical and he had to step down from being patriarch.

The First Crusade

In AD 1071 the Turks had conquered Jerusalem wresting the city from Fatimid control. Oppressive action by the new rulers of the Holy Land against the Christian clergy and the harsh treatment of pilgrims to the Holy Land helped stir up a sentiment that had been growing in the West. Appeals from Byzantium to the Pope for help in stemming the Muslim tide added to the sense that a war to recover the Holy Land was required. In reality the forces that came from the West were independent of, and ultimately hostile to, the interests of Byzantium. By the end of the year AD 1096 the First Crusade had reached Constantinople and in AD 1099 the city of Jerusalem was to fall to these western knights. The Emperor Alexius, after extracting an oath of allegiance, had provided transport and supplies and Cyprus was to play its part in keeping the Crusaders in provisions and military equipment.

The difference in purpose, however, between the Crusaders and Byzantium did not enhance their feelings towards each other, but soured relations. The Byzantines had requested help to recover lost lands from the Muslims, the Crusaders had come with the stated intentions of freeing the Holy places, but were, in fact, as much freebooters bent on carving up territory for themselves. So, inevitably, the relationship between these 'allies' against Islam was fraught with tension and hostility. The Byzantines perceived the Westerners, who they referred to as Latins, as uncouth and violent and the Crusaders believed the Byzantines to be duplicitous and devious.

Bohemund

When in AD 1099 a fleet conveying the archbishop of Pisa, Daimbert, who had been appointed by the Pope as his legate in Palestine, started to raid the Greek islands in the Ionian Sea, Alexius organised a military response. After a naval clash with the Byzantines the Pisans landed on Cyprus intent on raiding, but the governor Philocales was easily able to drive them off. The Byzantine fleet in pursuit stopped over in Cyprus and there Butumites was selected as an emissary to the Norman Bohemund, the son of Robert Guiscard, who had seized Antioch and was where the remaining Pisans had sailed. The Byzantines wanted to establish some form of truce, but Butumites' mission was unsuccessful and he had to return to Cyprus empty handed.

However, despite these examples of hostility to Byzantium, particularly Bohemund, some of the Crusaders did remain loyal to their oath to Alexius. Raymond Saint-Gilles, Count of Toulouse, fought hard for the Emperor and in AD 1102 ships were sent from Cyprus to aid the Count's siege of Tripoli. Unfortunately, Saint-Gilles died of an illness before he could take the town, which he had promised to hand over to Alexius.

At the same time it seems that the Byzantine authorities were not entirely unsympathetic to the Muslims under attack from the Crusaders. Perhaps this sympathy reflected the past stable, if not necessarily friendly, co-habitation of the island. It was also in their political interest to play the Crusaders off against each other. The Byzantines were, rightly, suspicious of the Crusaders' motives so there were sound benefits, when it suited, in keeping in with the other side. Thus, when Baldwin captured Beirut in AD 1110, the Emir and many of the inhabitants fled to Cyprus seeking refuge. This episode also reinforces the tradition of Cyprus being a place of refuge, which applied to the Muslims as much as to the Christians.

There is also evidence of Maronite Christians fleeing Syria and settling in Cyprus, and in AD 1137 an Armenian community was transported to the island by the Byzantines. After a brilliant campaign, the Emperor John Comnenus, who had succeeded his father Alexius, defeated Leo the Prince of Lesser Armenia. Lesser Armenia was the name given to territory in Cilicia where Armenians had settled in their flight from the Turks as they absorbed Anatolia following Manzikert in AD 1071.

The establishment of the Crusader states in Syria and Palestine and the constant traffic from the West did give Cyprus opportunities for developing trade. In AD 1123 the Doge of Venice, Domenico Michiel put in at the island. The Venetians became the most active of the Western traders in the East Mediterranean and they gained trading privileges in return for naval help to the Byzantines. In AD 1148 the Venetians were given commercial privileges in Crete and Cyprus in return for helping the Emperor Manuel, the grandson of Alexius, fight the Normans in Corfu. Evidence of increased wealth can be seen in the architectural and artistic activity on the island, as illustrated by the elegant frescoes in the church at Asinou, which were commissioned by Nicephorus, probably the son of the governor Catacalon.

Renaud de Châtillon

In AD 1156 a French adventurer, Renaud de Châtillon, who had become a Prince of Antioch through marriage, allied himself with the Armenian Prince Thoros II in planning a raid on Cyprus. Although King Baldwin III of Jerusalem warned the Byzantines the fleet sent from Constantinople arrived too late, and Renaud raided the island with a large force. The Byzantine militia was unable to resist and the Byzantine governor, another John Comnenus, was captured at Nicosia, which had now become the capital city of the island. There is a description of all the pillage that followed and Renaud sailed for the mainland laden with booty. The raid was a measure of the attitude of some of the Crusaders not only to Byzantium but to their own opportunities for gain. Eventually, the Emperor Manuel having brought his army to the gates of Antioch, was able to extract a humiliating apology from Renaud. In AD 1158 Cyprus was raided again, this time by the Emir of Egypt. Once more much booty and the governor's brother, who may have been John Ducas, the emperor's cousin, was captured. This perhaps explains why he was very soon after returned in some style as if the raid had been a mistake; it has been suggested that in fact there had been no official sanction for the raid.

St Neophytos

In AD 1166 Andronicus Comenus, the future dynamic but unstable emperor, was appointed governor of Cilicia with control over Cyprus. He seems to have spent his time extracting large amounts of money out of the island while he seduced the emperor's sister, Philippa, of Antioch, and then ran off with his cousin Theodora Comnena. A year later in AD 1167, a man of very different character from Andronicus, St Neophytos, who had been living his life as a hermit on the island, established his 'Enclosure', a monastery some miles north of Nea Paphos. The monastery housed around a dozen monks and was run on the strict lines still found at Mt Athos, in Greece today – no females, not even female animals (chickens no doubt, as on Athos, were an exception). During his life St Neophytos wrote prolifically, often criticising the authorities, but he was immensely popular with the people and his rock-cut and painted chamber became an important place of pilgrimage.

Isaac Comnenus

The successes of the Comenene Dynasty came to an end in AD 1176 when the Byzantine army was heavily defeated by the Seljuk Turks of Iconium. The Emperor Manuel had been fighting on all fronts, the Latins in the East and in the West, particularly Italy, against the Serbs and Hungarians in the Balkans and the Turks in Anatolia. The resources of the Empire had become too stretched and with the loss of control in Anatolia to the Turks, Cyprus found itself isolated. Following the Emperor Manuel's death the Empire slid into a rapid decline once more with the Comene Dynasty coming to an end, followed by a series of weak emperors. In AD 1184 Isaac Comnenus, the great-nephew of the Emperor Manuel, sailed to Cyprus. Isaac had been governor of Cilicia but had been captured by the Armenians and handed over to the Latins at Antioch. The emperor had ransomed him and then, apparently after forging documents, Isaac claimed to be governor of Cyprus. Once established he proclaimed himself emperor of the island, minting coins showing him dressed in the imperial garb. The sources are all hostile to Isaac and he is portrayed as a tyrannical ruler accused of murders, maimings and sexual abuse of wives and virgins. The emperor in Constantinople sent an expedition against Isaac but it came to nought. Isaac was able to overcome the expeditionary force on land and the fleet was defeated by Isaac's ally the admiral Margarito of Sicily.

Richard I, 'The Lionheart'

In AD 1187 Saladin the Sultan of Egypt defeated the Latins at Hattin and went on to capture Acre and Jerusalem. Papal support for the enemies of Byzantium in the West and the constant depredations upon imperial territory of the Crusader Kingdoms in the East had persuaded Constantinople to take an anti-Latin stance. Therefore, Saladin's conquests were seen as an opportunity more than a threat. However, the news from Syria and Palestine in the West motivated the Third Crusade in which Philip Augustus of France and Richard of England played key roles. In AD 1191 Richard set sail from Sicily for Palestine, but three of his ships were driven by a storm to Cyprus. Two of the ships were wrecked but the third, containing Richard's sister Queen Joanna of Sicily and his betrothed Berengaria, the daughter of the king of Navarre, anchored off the coast at Limassol. Isaac invited the women ashore, but they refused, fearing to be taken hostage. Isaac had been in communication with Saladin and he no doubt hoped to use the royal women as bargaining chips in any dealings with the Crusaders. Isaac then brought troops to the coast and refused to allow water or provisions to be taken on board. Soon after Richard arrived with his forces and Isaac fled. Sources suggest that not only were the Latin merchants pleased to welcome Richard, but also the Cypriots who had suffered under the tyrannical rule of Isaac.

At first Isaac sought to negotiate with Richard and came to his camp, offering provisions, finance and his own daughter as a hostage for his good behaviour. Perhaps having assessed Richard's forces as less formidable than he feared he later decided to repudiate the agreement. Richard was immediately joined by some of the Crusaders who had already landed in Syria, including Guy de Lusignan, who had a claim to the kingdom of Jerusalem through his wife. On 12 May AD 1191 Richard married Berengaria in the Chapel of St George in Limassol. The following day the rest of the English fleet joined Richard. Isaac then fell back on Famagusta. However, he realised he would not be able to hold the town against the superior Crusader forces. He then fled to Nicosia, but sent his wife, an Armenian princess, along with his daughter to Kyrenia, so that if necessary they could escape to the mainland. Meanwhile Richard sailed to Famagusta and prepared to march on Nicosia. Having collected all the troops he could muster Isaac decided his best defence was to meet the English army in battle. An engagement took place outside the village of Tremithus and Isaac's forces were routed. Isaac fled to Kantara and Richard entered Nicosia, where he fell ill for a short time. Meanwhile Guy de Lusignan took Kyrenia, capturing Isaac's wife and daughter before they could escape.

Although Isaac's remaining forces held the castles of St Hilarion, Buffavento and Kantara, it was only a matter of time before they would be reduced. Richard recovered from his illness and began the blockade of the castles. Isaac, assessing the situation as hopeless, decided to surrender, his only condition being that he was not put in irons. It is said that he was brought before Richard in silver chains. A vast amount of booty was taken and all the islanders were asked to give up half their possessions. Richard realised what a valuable base Cyprus would be for pursuing operations against Syria and Palestine. A Crusader garrison was left on the island and two officials, justicars, the Englishmen Richard de Camville and Robert of Turnham, were appointed to organise the sending of supplies to the Crusaders in Palestine. Isaac was taken along with his wife and daughter as captives. The two women were attached to Queen Joanna's household, but Isaac was handed over to the the Knights of St John of the Hospital (Hospitallers), spending time in prison at Acre and Margat near Tripoli. Eventually, around AD 1194 he was released and went to the Seljuk court at Iconium where he plotted against the Byzantine Emperor Alexius III. It is alleged he was eventually killed there by poisoning. Cyprus soon found there was little gain from their change in rulers. Isaac may have been tyrannical and cruel, but the Westerners soon revealed themselves indifferent to the fate of the islanders.

CHAPTER SEVEN

The Frankish Period,
1191–1489

After Richard had sailed with his army for Acre, a relative of Isaac, who had become a monk, proclaimed himself emperor and rose in rebellion. It cannot have been very serious because he was quickly seized by Robert of Turnham and hanged. Despite Richard's recognition of Cyprus as a useful base for operations in the Holy Land he clearly thought he could not afford the resources to hold on to the island so he sold it to the Knights Templars for 100,000 dinars of which 40,000 was immediately paid and the rest raised as a tax on the islanders. The Templars were also faced by a rebellion as they tried to exact taxes from the islanders. There were only twenty-nine knights with a few foot soldiers, so their leader Bouchart took refuge in the castle at Nicosia. However, he made a surprise sally and his men proceeded to massacre the inhabitants of Nicosia. It was said the streets ran with blood and a stone was identified as marking the point where the flow of blood reached. Such were the Templars' depredations on the people that many fled into the mountains. The Templars' position on the island was unsustainable and they negotiated with Richard to take back Cyprus.

Guy de Lusignan

In 1191 after the Crusaders captured Acre, despite Richard's support, Guy de Lusignan failed to be given the title of king of Jerusalem. Most of the nobles preferred Conrad, Marquis of Montferrat to Guy. In the following year, as compensation, Richard gave Cyprus to Guy, as a fiefdom, and he willingly repaid the Templars the money they had

The Lusignan abbey of Bellapais built during the Frankish period in the
13th century

given Richard. Even after Conrad was murdered by the Muslim sect,
the Assassins, the throne of Jerusalem did not go to Guy but to Henry of
Champagne, who had married Princess Isabella, the legal heir to the
throne. When Guy died in 1194 Richard made no claim on Cyprus, as
technically those rights now were with Henry, king of Jerusalem, and
the Byzantine government was too weakened to mount any recon-
quest. Thus began the Lusignian period in Cyprus which was to last
until 1489. It was a time of relative stability and prosperity for the
island, but the Western hierarchical feudal system imposed on Cyprus
by its new rulers ensured little benefit reached the native people. The
Frankish nobility controlled every governmental institution on the
island, but their courtly life was one of political manoeuvrings and
rivalries, conspiracies and murder. Despite their constant feuding the
Frankish rulers of Cyprus became notorious for their luxurious living.

LIFE UNDER THE LUSIGNANS

The Frankish period of Cyprus saw the island become an important
entrepôt for trade with the Middle East. The Syrian ports became the
land terminals for trade caravans coming from as far as China. Trade

ships also arrived at the island from Egypt with spices and other exotic goods being carried across the Indian Ocean and the Red Sea. Famagusta was to grow into the greatest emporium in the eastern Mediterranean and was said at one stage at the end of thirteenth century to have as many as 365 churches – one for each day of the year. The capital of Cyprus, called by the Franks Nicosia, as they were said to be unable to pronounce the Greek name Lefkosia, expanded considerably – the circuit of the Venetian walls represents a considerable shrinkage from its size under the Lusignans.

AIMERY (1194–1205)

Guy had never taken the title of king of Cyprus as he still hoped to recover the crown of Jerusalem. In 1194, with his death, his brother, Aimery, succeeded. In 1197 Henry gave up his claim to Cyprus in exchange for Jaffa, which Aimery controlled. He was then able to regularise his sovereignty by paying homage to the Holy Roman Emperor, Henry VI, as his liege, and in return he received the title of king of Cyprus. Not long afterwards Henry died and Aimery also gained the kingship of Jerusalem by marrying Isabella, Henry's widow. However, the Latins were under pressure from the Sultan of Egypt, al-Malik al-Adil, and Aimery's responsibilities as king of Jerusalem brought the fighting to Cyprus, with raids from the Egyptian fleet. In retaliation Aimery sailed against the Egyptian Delta and returned with considerable booty. In around 1200 Aimery established the Abbey at Bellapais for the Augustinians, who had previously controlled the Church of the Holy Sepulchre untill the fall of Jerusalem in 1187.

The Fourth Crusade

In the year of 1204 Byzantium suffered a shattering blow. The Fourth Crusade, which had been organised by Pope Innocent III ostensibly to attack Muslim Egypt, was diverted by the Venetians, who provided the ships for the Crusaders, and sacked Christian Constantinople. The city, which had not fallen for over eight hundred years, was mercilessly despoiled and plundered, and on 15 April Count Baldwin of Flanders was crowned Latin Emperor of Constantinople and the Byzantine

Empire divided up amongst the conquerors. Aimery, realising that the promised help from the West would not be forthcoming, concluded a treaty with the Sultan that secured him some territory in Palestine. In the following year Aimery died, it is said from overeating fish at one meal. The general view seems to be that Aimery was a prudent and strong ruler, very different from his weak and vacillating brother Guy. His son Hugh I (1205–18), by Eschiva of Ibelin, succeeded him.

Hugh I (1205–18)

Hugh was only a child at his accession and Walter de Montbéliard, Constable of Jerusalem, and the husband of Hugh's eldest sister Burgundia, was entrusted by the High Court (*Haute Cour*), a body comprising of all the nobles, with the regency. The kingdom of Jerusalem, however, now passed to Queen Isabella, who had been four times married and thrice widowed, but she soon died afterwards. Despite her importance in determining the throne of Jerusalem, little is known about her other than she was considered very beautiful. Her daughter by Conrad, Maria of Montferrat, succeeded to the throne of Jerusalem, with Isabella's half-brother, John of Ibelin, the ruler of Beirut, as regent.

Walter de Montbéliard went to aid the Christians in Adalia when they were besieged by the Sultan of Iconium, Ghiyas ad-Din Kaikhosrau, but the Latin garrison, including forces from Cyprus was forced to surrender in 1207 and Walter, defeated, returned to Cyprus. When he came of age Hugh accused Walter of embezzlement and, rather than face his peers, Walter fled the island with his family and a large sum of money. Hugh I joined the Fifth Crusade of 1217 which invaded Egypt, but threw away its early successes by delay and indecisiveness. Eventually, having achieved nothing the Crusaders dispersed. On his return Hugh went to Tripoli to celebrate the marriage of his half-sister Melisende with Bohemund IV, the ex-Prince of Antioch. On 10 January 1218 Hugh suddenly died, leaving the throne to his eight-month-old son Henry, under the regency of his young widow Alice, the daughter of the earlier king and queen of Jerusalem, Henry of Champagne and Isabella.

Henry I (1218–1253)

Henry I (1218–1253), known as Henry 'the Fat', was, as this nickname suggests, to prove committed to good living, good natured, but lazy and lethargic. This was perhaps a result of the long regency of his mother. Alice was Regent for over fifteen years and during this time she was supported by her two uncles, Philip and John d'Ibelin, as *bailli* (sheriffs). The aristocracy of the island generally benefited from the long regency and easy rule of Henry as they could pursue their own agendas with few constraints from the crown. However, the negative aspect of such a light rule meant there was not much in the way of concerted effort to develop the security of the kingdom. In fact Alice, in one of her first acts, allowed Cyprus to become a hostage to fortune through a treaty with the Genoese. Perhaps because of the weakness of the Cypriot navy, she conceded extensive commercial privileges to Genoa which, it is generally agreed, were to prove damaging and ultimately disastrous for the island.

The first crisis Alice faced was when Leopold VI, duke of Austria, who had been a member of the Fifth Crusade, attempted to take over the kingdom. Alice was put under the protection of the papacy by Honorius III and it was probably at this moment her uncles associated themselves with her regency. Certainly Alice's relationship with Philip d'Ibelin, the second son of Queen Maria Comnena, were fraught. In 1223 he openly thwarted her plan, recommended by the Cardinal Pelagius, that the tithes of the Orthodox clergy should be handed over to the Latin Church. It is said that in a fit of pique she sailed to Tripoli and there married Bohemund V, in a futile attempt to replace Philip with her new husband.

However, in 1227 Philip died and the High Court of Cyprus now invited his brother John, the ruler of Beirut to take his brother's place. He was also immediately faced with a threat from the Holy Roman Emperor, the notorious Frederick II Hohenstaufen, who claimed the regency of Cyprus on account of the homage paid by King Aimery to Fredrick's predecessor, Henry VI (see above). In 1225 Frederick had married Yolande, the heiress of the kingdom of Jerusalem, and he now claimed the kingdom of Jerusalem in the name of his son, Conrad IV.

In July 1228 Frederick arrived at Limassol and summoned the Cypriot court to meet with him. Frederick tried to bully John d'Ibelin into recognising him as regent, but although the nobles in Cyprus honoured the Emperor as suzerain he was not received as regent.

Frederick left five of his adherents with a force of Lombards to rule Cyprus, but John d'Ibelin skilfully manoeuvred diplomatically and militarily against them. The castles of St Hilarion, Kantara and Kyrenia changed hands and in the battle of Agridi (near Kyrenia) the Lombards were defeated. Although Kyrenia held out for ten months, eventually, with the help of the Genoese, John d'Ibelin prevailed and the imperial forces capitulated in 1233. Three years later John of d'Ibelin died and his son, Balian d'Ibelin, Constable of Cyprus, took his place as protector of Henry I. A decade later the Pope, Innocent IV released Henry from the oath of fealty that he had been forced to swear to Frederick.

In 1244 Jerusalem fell to an attack of the Khwarismian Turks, who had been driven out of Iran. Later that year a Latin force, including a Cyprus contingent of three hundred, was wiped out in Gaza by a combined force of Egyptians and Khwarismians. Such was the loss on the Latin side that there were barely enough men left to garrison the Holy Land. In that same year the French King Louis IX (canonised after his death as St Louis) had fallen seriously ill. King Louis vowed that should he recover he would lead another Crusade from the West. The Pope had been calling previously for a Crusade against the growing power of the Mongols. In fact he saw an opportunity to convert the Mongols to Christianity and with their alliance he hoped not only to free Jerusalem but totally drive Islam out of the Holy Land.

In 1248 after careful preparation King Louis reached Cyprus where he wintered his troops. King Henry the Fat, who was now twenty-one, agreed to take part in this Seventh Crusade. In the following May the two kings set sail from Limassol and sailed straight to Damietta in Egypt. At first all went well and King Henry was present when Damietta fell to the Crusaders. The Latin Archbishop of Nicosia had accompanied the expedition but he was to die in Egypt. In the following year the Cypriots distinguished themselves in the battle of Bahr-al-Saghir. However, the campaign was in deep trouble and in the spring of 1250 Louis' army surrendered. Although Louis stayed in the Holy Land for another four years, nothing came of the hoped alliance with the Mongols, and he decided to return to France, calling in on Cyprus once more on his way home.

HUGH II (1253–67)

Henry the Fat, meanwhile, had married for the third time. His first wife had been Alice of Montferrat. When she died he had married Stephanie of Lampron, from the royal house of Armenia. On her death he married Plaisance, the daughter of Bohemund V of Antioch. Before Henry's death in 1253 she bore him a son, Hugh II (1253–67), who like his own father was to succeed when only a few months old. The queen was clearly a woman of strong character and is referred to 'as one of the most valiant women in the world'. The High Court recognised her as regent and she shortly afterwards formed a union with Balian d'Ibelin, the nephew of Henry the Fat's advisor of the same name, whose father John Arsur was Constable of Jerusalem. However, the Pope, Alexander IV, objected to the union on the grounds that it was a relationship forbidden within the prohibited degrees of incest by the Church. Eventually in 1258, she separated from Balian, and managed to persuade Bohemund VI of Antioch, some of the knightly orders, and the Pisans and Venetians, who were in conflict with the Genoese, the Spaniards and the Hospitallers, to recognise Hugh as heir to the kingdom of Jerusalem. Not that the title in reality meant much at the time, as the Egyptian Sultan was steadily eroding the Latins' hold on the Holy Land.

HUGH III (1267–84)

In 1261 Plaisance died and she was succeeded as regent by her cousin Hugh of Antioch, the son of Prince Henry of Antioch and Isabel de Lusignan. Six years later Hugh II also died, aged fourteen and with him the original line of the Lusignans. Hugh of Antioch adopted his mother's name and, despite rival claims, including the Hohenstaufen, the High Court recognised him as Hugh III (1267–84). For much of his reign he was absorbed by the affairs of Syria and the Holy Land where he attempted to play a mediating role amongst the squabbling Latins. Once more there was an opportunity to co-operate with the Mongols against the Muslims but the Christians were so divided that they allowed their internecine struggles to distract them from their main enemy.

At this time the most active Muslim forces were the Mameluks, Turkish slaves, who had seized the Sultanate of Egypt. They were steadily reducing Christian strongholds one after another throughout the Holy Land. Hugh III attempt to help in the resistance but his small Cypriot force was essentially ineffective. In 1271 the Sultan Baibars even attempted an attack on Cyprus. Disguising his fleet as Christian ships, flying the cross, he planned an attack on Limassol. However, the fleet was wrecked and 1800 surviving crew members were captured. In the following year Hugh campaigned with Prince Edward of England, who captured Nazareth, but his force was too small to have much of an impact, so that in the following year he agreed a truce with Baibars. Later in 1272, after a failed assassination attempt, Edward sailed back to England, originally with the intention of returning with a larger army, but on reaching Britain he found his father, Henry III had died and the rest of his reign was spent securing his kingdom.

In the meantime Hugh found himself in conflict with the Templars, who supported the claim of Charles of Anjou to the kingdom of Jerusalem. Hugh, in anger, left Syria in 1276 and on reaching Cyprus seized Templar property in Paphos and Limassol. He then destroyed their fortress at Gastria and confiscated their revenues from the island.

The Sultan Baibars died in 1277 and was succeeded by Kalaun. In 1281 a combined force of Mongols and Armenians nearly destroyed Kalaun's forces at Homs, but, despite the success of the Armenians during the battle, when Timur was wounded, the Mongols' nerve failed and they withdrew. This expedition by the Mongols was, ironically, probably the last chance to save the Latin territories of the East, but short-sightedly, most of the Latins had refused to give support to the Mongols. Allegedly, Hugh did attempt to bring reinforcements, but the Cypriot contingent arrived too late for the battle.

HENRY II (1285–1324)

Three years later in 1284 Hugh died while at Tyre and was succeeded by his eldest son, John I (1284–85), who was about seventeen and considered delicate. He was crowned king of Cyprus on 11 May and then crossed to Tyre to be crowned king of Jerusalem. He also died young and only reigned for a year. He was succeeded in the summer of 1285 by his brother Henry II (1285–1324), aged fourteen. Although Henry II reigned for forty years his rule was ineffective and disastrous for the Lusignans. He suffered from epilepsy and lacked the respect of his subjects because of his infirmity. Nevertheless, in 1286 at Tyre he was crowned king of Jerusalem. However, the title was essentially meaningless as the Mamelukes under their Sultan al-Malik al-Ashraf captured Christian stronghold after stronghold in Frankish Syria. In 1291 Acre, Tyre, Sidon, Beirut and Haifa all fell. At the siege of Acre Henry himself fought bravely but once the land walls were taken had to flee in one of the last Christian ships to escape to Cyprus.

In 1299 the Mongol khan of Persia, Ghazan, invaded Syria and was joined by an Armenian force. The Latins failed to send help, again due to internecine squabbling between the Templars and the Hospitallers. The Mongols defeated the Mameluks outside Damascus and went on to take the city. However, the following year Ghazan had his own problems with attacks from another group of the Mongols from Russia and withdrew his army to Persia. The Christians were unable to exploit the Mongol successes and both a small force sent from Cyprus to Syria and a raiding expedition against Egypt, led by Henry himself, came to naught.

The reduction of Latin Syria had the adverse effect of increasing the power of the Genoese and Venetians, whose navies were vital to the continuance of Cyprus as an outpost of the West in the Eastern Mediterranean. There is no doubt their control of the sea was crucial to the prosperity of the island, but neither power had any long term interest in the security of the Lusignan state. The hostility between the Genoese and the Venetians may have helped distract them from their greedy depredations on the island, but in reality, as the historian George Hill argues, both Italian nautical powers behaved like a 'parasitic growth' that damaged the future of Cyprus. Both in 1292 and 1294 the Genoese defeated the Venetians in naval actions off the coast of Cyprus. The latter engagement was a response to a raid by the Venetians on the Genoese living on the island. King Henry II tended to favour the

Venetians as a counterweight to the dominance of the Genoese and probably as a result the Genoese resorted to a form of piracy against Cyprus. In 1302 a major Genoese raid resulted in the sack of Episkopi.

By the beginning of the fourteenth century only the small island fort of Ruad outside Tripoli remained in Latin hands, and in 1303 Ruad finally fell and Henry, who was ill at the time, was unable to send any help. Cyprus became the refuge for the fleeing Latin population from the mainland and perversely Cyprus was able to benefit from the demise of the Latin East. It became the main trading centre with the Middle East and at the same time its rulers no longer had to invest in supporting military efforts in Syria or Palestine. The fourteenth century was a period of considerable prosperity for all of Cyprus, but particularly Famagusta, which became the major deep-sea port for the island. The riches that the aristocracy and merchant classes accumulated were massive and became the subject of critical comments, such as from the German traveller Lindolf von Suchen who visited the island in 1350. The level of wealth was such that even the native islanders, who had been made subject to the Latins, seem to have gleaned some benefit. However, in general, because of the strict hierarchical nature of Lusignan society the lower orders lot was not an easy one.

Lusignan Society

The Lusignans had established a strictly ordered society in Cyprus as evidenced by a written constitution, the *Assizes of Jerusalem*, which is often described as setting out the archetypal feudal state. The ruling class was an élite group of French speaking Europeans, mainly of French lineage, which dominated a subject population of predominantly Greek-speaking islanders, with a few Armenian and Syrian settlers. The land was divided between the king, the nobles and Latin religious orders. The nobles held their land as fiefs and in return rendered the king military service. The original group of Lusignans who accompanied Guy is said to have numbered no more than five hundred (three hundred knights and two hundred mounted sergeants). The principal constitutional body was the High Court (*Haute Cour*), which combined legislative, judicial and executive powers, and was made up of all the barons. The High Court acted as a peer court for its members and the king could not punish any noble without its assent. There was a lower court (*Cour des Bourgeois*) for the other non-noble Latins).

The subject classes were divided into three groups with names in Greek. Those who held the tenure of their land free from feudal dues, either through purchase or grant, were known as free men (*lefteri*). The second class was known as *perperiarii* (the standard Byzantine coin was known as *hyperperon*), because, by agreement with their feudal lord, they paid an annual tax of fifteen hyperpera rather than giving labour. The lowest and most numerous class was the *paroikoi* ('those living around without rights'), or serfs, who were completely subject to their lords in all legal matters, paying poll-tax, giving two days labour and a third of their crops. There are conflicting perceptions as to the natives' lot, but it seems clear that the Lusignans made no effort to integrate with the indigenous islanders, so it must be suspected that, even allowing for modern sentiments of nationality, the Cypriots resented the domination by foreigners from the West.

Clear evidence of the complete insensitivity of the Lusignian rulers was the treatment of the Orthodox Church of Cyprus. At the outset of their rule the Lusignans had invited the Pope to establish the Latin Church on the island with authority over the Orthodox Cypriot Church. In 1196 Nicosia became the seat of the Latin archbishop and three other sees were established at Paphos, Limassol and Famagusta. The Latins treated the Orthodox as schismatics and in 1220 ousted them from the main churches forcing them to live in the countryside. However, the main Orthodox monasteries were maintained and became the heart of Orthodox Christianity for the island. In 1260 the Pope promulgated the Bulla Cypria directing the remaining four Orthodox bishops (reduced from the original 13) to swear fealty to the Latin archbishop, hand over all revenue and not to replace the Orthodox archbishop.

In 1306 Henry's younger brother Amaury staged a coup and gained the support of the High Court. Amaury was named 'governor' and just over three years later Henry was forced to flee Cyprus for refuge in Armenia. However, Amaury's sole rule did not long last as he was murdered by his own favourite, Simon de Montolif. Henry returned from exile amidst a splendid pageant to rule for another fourteen years. The verdict seems to be that he was not a strong king but did not deserve the allusion in Dante's *Paradiso* (XIX, 145–8) to him being 'a beast who brought lamentation to Nicosia and Famagusta'.

HUGH IV (1324–59)

Henry died in 1324 and was succeeded by Hugh IV, the son of his brother Guy. His reign was a relatively peaceful one and he was known for his love of hunting and literature. The main threat to Cyprus during his reign was from continued piracy. Cyprus had no real navy of its own and so was subject to the raids of the Genoese and, in particular now the Catalans. There were other troubles for Cyprus: devastating floods in 1330, a vicious outbreak of fighting between the Genoese and Venetians in Famagusta in 1345, and an outbreak of the Black Death which killed perhaps as much as half the population in 1348.

On the mainland of Asia Minor the Ottoman dynasty of the Turks was steadily growing in strength. Their expansion posed a threat to the tribute that Hugh received from the mainland coastal cities that faced Cyprus. Cyprus joined the Venetian league and twice defeated the Ottomans in naval engagements in 1334 and 1338; and in 1343 as member of the Holy Union under the leadership of Pope Clement VI, helped capture the important town of Smyrna. Hugh's son Peter also travelled to the West, although this was against his father's wishes, to whip up support for a new crusade to check the Ottoman's growing power. Forgiven for his disobedience Peter returned and was crowned by Hugh in an attempt to forestall any claim on the throne by Peter's nephew.

PETER I (1359–1369)

On succeeding to the throne Peter pursued his aim of raising a new Crusade. His first expedition was against Cilicia where he captured the town of Adalia, and according to one source he massacred all the citizens. However, Peter was short of resources and between 1362 and 1365 he went on a tour of the West in an attempt to raise support for his next Crusade. Although he was welcomed by the courts of Europe there was little enthusiasm for another Crusade. Peter came to England in the winter of 1363, where it is said the Master of the Vintners gave him a banquet in the City of London, attended by the kings of England and Scotland. The English king, Edward III, honoured him with a tournament at Smithfield and when Peter was robbed on his way back to the coast, Edward compensated him with lavish gifts, including a ship named *Catherine*. However, despite this warm hospitality Edward wanted no part of a Crusade and no support was forthcoming.

In France Peter met with Edward's son, the Black Prince, in Acquitaine, and travelled to Rheims where he attended the anointing of the French king Charles V. He then went on to visit the Holy Roman Emperor in Germany, and the kings of Poland and Hungary. He finished his travels at Venice, which was the one power that offered him support. Peter had helped the Venetians repress a rebellion by their Cretan subjects and in recognition of that service they now promised ships and men. On his return to Cyprus he assembled 140 ships for a daring expedition against Alexandria in Egypt. In October 1365 the Cypriot forces captured the city and plundered it for three days and then returned to Cyprus laden with booty. Peter has been criticised for not following up his success in Egypt, but it is probable, given his financial difficulties, that the main purpose of the raid was to replenish his treasury.

No doubt because of his previous visit, the report of his success became notorious throughout Europe. Guillaume De Machaut celebrates the event in the epic *La prise d' Alexandrie* and in 'The Monke's Tale', in *The Canterbury Tales*, Peter is extravagantly praised and Chaucer's knight also claims to have taken part in the sack of Alexandria. Writing later, the French poet Villon, in his *Ballade des Seigneurs du tempe jadis*, proclaims the 'renown' acquired by Peter. However, the Venetians were anxious about his success lest it might damage their trade with the Muslim rulers of Egypt and Syria and they stymied any further efforts to bring reinforcements from Europe. Nevertheless, Peter was able to take Tripoli from the Mameluks. He even challenged the Emir Yalbugha to individual combat in order to decide the issue between the two sides, but it was not taken up. Famed for these acts of individual daring, the Pope Peter V referred to Peter as an 'athlete of Christ'.

However, it seems Peter was known for another athleticism, because despite his devotion to his wife, Eleanor of Aragon, whose nightgown he was said to take with him on campaign, he also had at least two mistresses. It seems his sexual appetite, which perhaps drove him to cuckold some of his Cypriot nobles, as well as an increasingly dictatorial manner, not only alienated his court but his family as well. In 1369 a plot was hatched against him, which appears to have included his own brothers. After one of his mistresses, the appropriately named Echive de Scandelion, left his chamber, a group of nobles burst in and stabbed Peter to death – it was significant that the commander of his cavalry, James de Nores, castrated the dead body of the king, seemingly making a very clear statement.

PETER II (1369–82)

Peter's son also called Peter, succeeded his father at the age of fifteen. His uncle, John of Antioch, acted as regent. Peter II's reign was to prove a complete contrast to his father's as his character was the antithesis to his father's, he was weak and lethargic. Although he was little pressed by the Muslims, his lack of resolution was to leave him at the mercy of the quarrels between the Genoese and Venetians.

In 1372 when Peter was about to be crowned king of Jerusalem at Famagusta a row broke out between the Genoese and Venetians as to who should have precedence. At previous coronations the Genoese had claimed the right to hold the right-hand rein of the king's horse as he left the cathedral. On this occasion the Venetian consul seized the reins through the use of force. A riot broke out in which the Franks took the side of the Venetians and Genoese property was looted and some lives lost. There was a general distaste for the Genoese who had shown themselves arrogant and piratical.

In Genoa there were claims of a massacre and a force was assembled to punish Cyprus. The Venetians were unable to help and in 1373 the Genoese fleet arrived at Cyprus demanding compensation. Although refusing the Genoese demands Peter and his supporters showed no clear leadership and Paphos, Nicosia and Famagusta all fell to the Genoese. Through a blatant breach of faith the Genoese were able to hold the king captive so that despite considerable resistance in the end the Cypriot Franks had to come to terms with Genoese demands. These consisted of exorbitant payments of tribute and fines – Famagusta was held onto by the Genoese until 90,000 gold florins were handed over. This last exaction seems to have signalled the end of the prosperity of the island.

Peter I's widow, Eleanor of Aragon, in spite of his apparent infidelities, seemed determined to use the opportunity of the weakness of the Cypriot nobility to reek revenge on her husband's murderers. The Genoese were happy to help in hunting them down as it suited their purposes to eliminate the Frankish establishment. Even Peter II's regent, John of Antioch, was murdered by Eleanor on assumption of his complicity in Peter I's death. It is said he was invited to dinner, and clearly unsuspecting any murderous motive, he accepted. After the meal a covered dish was brought in and when the top was removed it contained the bloodstained shirt of her husband. This was a signal for her Genoese supporters to rush in and slay him. Whether it was because of her vindictiveness against those she presumed had conspired against her husband or her strong dislike of her son's wife, Valentia Visconti, the daughter of the duke of Milan, or a combination, Peter felt compelled to move against his mother. In perhaps the only decisive act of his reign he sent Eleanor back to Aragon. At the age of twenty-nine, and now known, like his earlier predecessor Henry I, as 'the Fat', he died without an heir.

JAMES I (1382–98)

Peter II was succeeded by his uncle James I. At the time of Peter's death James was actually a prisoner in Genoa, having been taken captive in the typically treacherous manner of the Genoese. James was released in 1382 provided he permanently conceded Famagusta and a stretch of sea around the city to the Genoese, that Kyrenia was pledged to Genoa and he made a payment of 852,000 florins. James' son by Heloise of Brunswick, Janus (named after the mythical founder of Genoa), was held hostage to ensure he stuck to the terms of the deal and was only allowed to return to Cyprus in 1392.

The crippling constraints imposed upon Cyprus by the Genoese resulted in high taxes and the continued weakness of the kingdom.

Somewhat ironically in 1393 James took the title of king of Armenia on the death of the last Armenian king, Leo VI, who died in exile. After three hundred years the Mameluks had brought Cilician Armenia, as a sovereign state, to an end in 1375. However, some respite was brought to the island when the French gained ascendancy over Genoa in 1396.

A French traveller described James as a handsome man, who enjoyed hunting, and was known for his fulsome hospitality. In 1392 he had entertained the English knights Henry Percy, nicknamed Hotspur, and Henry Bolinbroke, the son of John of Gaunt and the future Henry IV. The two Englishmen were later to quarrel and Hotspur was killed at the Battle of Shrewsbury in 1403, when the Percies attempted to overthrow Henry IV.

JANUS (1398–1432)

James was succeeded by his son Janus. He is described as tall and good looking, but like a couple of previous Lusignan kings of Cyprus, he was also known for his corpulence. In 1399 he was crowned not only king of Cyprus but also of Jerusalem and Armenia. However, his main concern was to re-establish the crown's authority over Famagusta and erode the influence of the Genoese. In 1402 and 1404 with the aid of the Catalans and Venetian canon he tried unsuccessfully to capture Famagusta, and in 1421 there were further disturbances in Nicosia involving the Genoese.

The Cypriots and Catalans also raided Egypt, but in 1414 a treaty was agreed with a mutual exchange of prisoners. With the accession of the Sultan Barsbai the situation changed and in 1425 he planned a major raid on Cyprus. Under the command of Taghribardi al Mahmudi a force of 180 ships plus five thousand men invaded Cyprus. The Genoese and Venetians refused to send help to Janus. At a battle outside Khirokitia Janus' forces were defeated and, fighting bravely to the last, he was forced to surrender. The countryside was ravaged and virtual anarchy broke out. An Italian mercenary leader, named Sforza, led a band of mainly Spaniards, who plundered the countryside. The indigenous Cypriots now seized the chance to rebel against the Latins, and a man called Alexis proclaimed himself king.

Janus' brother Hugh, who was archbishop of Nicosia, had managed

Kolossi castle which was the headquarters of the Order of St John of Jerusalem, the Knights Hospitallers in the mid 15th century

to escape with most of the royal family and treasure to Kyrenia. Once the Mameluke forces had left with their spoils, he was able with the help of the Hospitallers, whose fortresses at Episkopi and Kolossi had held out, to bring some order to the island. By 1427 Janus had been ransomed and Alexis captured and hanged. However, Janus had been humiliated by the Sultan by being forced to ride a lame donkey in a triumphal procession in Cairo, and many of the captives taken from Cyprus were tortured to death if they refused to convert to Islam. When Janus returned to Cyprus he was a broken man and handed over his powers to Hugh. In 1432 Janus became paralysed by a stroke and he died the following year.

JOHN II (1432–58)

Janus was succeeded by his only son John who was eighteen-years-old. Peter Lusignan, the Count of Tripoli, acted as Regent and Constable during his early years. John is described as tall and handsome like his father, but he is accused of weakness and the Pope, Pius II, condemned him as 'cowardly and vile in spirit' and 'living the life of sloth, gluttony and lust'. He is best known in popular tradition as a man ruled by the women in his life. His first wife was Medea of the Palaeologi of

Montferrat and his second was Helena, daughter of Theodore II Palaeologina, the Despot of the Morea (in the Peloponnese) and granddaughter of the Byzantine Emperor Manuel II. He also had a mistress, Marietta of Patras, who gave birth to James who was to be John's successor. Perhaps not surprising Helena hated Marietta and it is said bit off her nose in a fight. This fight was witnessed by John who is reported to have been flattered by this display of jealousy and the contest for his affection.

It is significant that these three women had Greek connections, and Helena, despite a reputation for a strong will and excessive influence on her husband, was much loved by the islanders because of her devotion to the Orthodox Church – her relationship with John is still celebrated in folk song. Probably because of the nature of John's household the evidence suggests an improvement in the status and condition of the Greek population of Cyprus. Certainly, the wealthier and better-educated Greeks derived advantage from John's reign. For example, the historian Machaeras, acted as the king's ambassador to the court of the sultan of Iconium, although he also deplored what he saw as the contamination of the Cypriot form of Greek by the introduction of French words.

Cyprus was still under pressure from the Genoese and Mamelukes and had to pay tribute. With the help of the Catalans, John made several unsuccessful attempts to recover Famagusta. The Genoese, nevertheless, were finding the government of Famagusta a liability. The population appears to have rapidly declined and a German pilgrim, Stephen von Gumppenberg, who visited the city in 1449–50 describes fine buildings situated amidst much empty space. In 1447 the Genoese, in order to cut their losses, handed over the city to the Office of St George. Two years later a tax that had been imposed on foreign merchants was removed, but it seems to have had little impact and the decline of Famagusta continued.

The Mamelukes had raided the island in 1434 and in 1440 the Egyptian fleet anchored at Cyprus on its way to attack the Knights of St John's main base on Rhodes. John also had problems with the Venetians over the recovery of 'debts' and the taxing of 'White Venetians' – these were essentially Syrians who had been granted Venetian citizenship, whom the king saw as legitimately liable to tax as they had never even been to Venice. In 1448 Gorhigos (Corycus), which had been ceded to Cyprus by the Armenians in 1360, the last remaining stronghold on the mainland of Asia Minor, fell to the Grand Karaman, the Turkish ruler of Konya. Although oblivious at the time of its long-term consequences, in 1453 the capture of Constantinople by the Ottoman Mehmed II heralded a new era for Cyprus and the East Mediterranean.

John's only legitimate offspring was his daughter Charlotte, who was another firebrand who seems to have intimidated her father and her second husband Louis, count of Geneva, and son of the duke of Savoy. The queen, Helena, had disapproved of this match because Louis was Charlotte's first cousin and such a union transgressed the canons of the Orthodox Church. However, Helena died before the wedding and shortly afterwards King John followed her.

CHARLOTTE (1458–60)

Charlotte was recognised as queen by the High Court and Louis was granted rights of succession should there be no heirs. However, Charlotte had a rival for the throne in James, the bastard son of Marietta. James was very different from his father in that he was energetic, ambitious and ruthless. He had already shown that he was prepared to murder in the pursuit of power. He had been appointed archbishop of the Latin Church in Cyprus by John, but had not received recognition from the Pope. He had then been implicated in the assassination of Thomas of the Morea – it is said Charlotte put him up to the killing as part of a struggle for influence between the Latins and Greeks. Deprived of his position by King James he had, never-theless, returned to Cyprus from Rhodes where he had previously fled. He then organised the killing of some of the queen's adherents and seized the episcopal palace. The High Court, presumably concerned about the queen's influence then agreed to reinstate James as arch-bishop.

With his father's death James took an oath of allegiance to Charlotte, but he was soon to attempt to usurp her power. His plot was betrayed and he fled to Egypt where he was well received by the sultan who saw an opportunity to bring Cyprus under his rule. He recognised James as king of Cyprus, on the basis that the sultanate had suzerainty over the island. In 1460, supported by an Egyptian fleet of eighty ships, James returned to Cyprus where he gained immediate popularity by freeing large numbers of serfs. Charlotte and Louis retreated to Kyrenia. Then the Mameluke forces began to besiege the fortress, but when winter came most of the troops were withdrawn to Egypt. James was now in difficulty, as most of the Latin barons supported Charlotte, and he also had Savoy, Genoa, the Pope and the Hospitallers ranged against him. Fighting and manoeuvring went on until in 1463 when James, with Catalan and Sicilian support, was able to make a breakthrough: Kyrenia was surrendered through the treachery of its commander who was rewarded by being made Constable of the island, and Famagusta, faced with starvation, was handed over by the Genoese.

JAMES II (1460–73)

James now controlled the whole island, but he faced immediate danger in that he had killed most of the Mameluke soldiers that had not left the island in the winter of 1460. The sultan, it seems, accepted James explanation that they had been plotting against him. However, James was the target of an assassination attempt instigated apparently by the wife of the murdered Mameluke commander, Janibeg. The attempt failed when James was able to wrestle his attacker into the water at the harbour in Famagusta. Charlotte and Louis still pressed their claim to the throne from Rhodes, but they could gain no practical help. There was a peasants' revolt, which ended in failure, in their favour in 1472, and when Charlotte died in 1485 she ceded her inheritance to Savoy.

James' position was not secure and he sought support from the Venetians, who had become the dominant trading power in the region. The Venetians were concerned about the growing strength of the Ottoman Empire, which threatened their trade routes and looked to Cyprus as a suitable base to protect their interests. In 1468 James married Catherine Cornaro, a Venetian of noble descent, and it was agreed that Venice would inherit Cyprus should there be no heirs. In 1473 James died of dysentery and Catherine who was pregnant became regent.

JAMES III (1473–74) AND CATHERINE CORNARO (1474–89)

Catherine gave birth to a son James, but he only lived for a year. The Venetians had to send a fleet to protect Catherine. Not only were Charlotte's supporters plotting to overthrow her, but there was also a party that supported the claims of Ferdinand II, the Aragonese king of Naples, to the Cypriot throne. Ferdinand II had murdered Catherine's uncle, Andrew Cornaro, who was acting as her principal adviser. Once Venetians landed they gained popular support and took control of the whole island. One of the first acts of the Venetians was to banish the Catalans, Neapolitans and Sicilians along with members of the Lusignan royal family, like John II's mistress Marietta of Patras and James II's illegitmate children.

In 1479 there was an attempt to remove Catherine which was led by a discontented Venetian, Mark Venier. The plot was instigated by

Catherine Cornaro, a Venetian lady of noble descent who married James II in 1468

Charlotte's supporters and was backed by Ferdinand, who was prepared to send a fleet to Cyprus. The conspiracy, however, was betrayed and the Venetians captured Mark Venier and his followers who were all hanged. Now the Venetians, for all intents and purposes, ran the kingdom, appointing two officials, who were described as counsellors, to act in their name. Ten years later there was another plot which involved attempting to persuade Catherine to marry Don Alonzo of Naples. Two of the conspirators were captured on Cyprus, one killed himself and the other was executed some years later. In the same year the Venetian fleet had to make a grand demonstration to ward off an attack from the Ottoman Sultan Beyazit.

No doubt as a result of this plot, and the growing Ottoman threat to the island the Venetians decided they should take over direct rule of Cyprus. Catherine's brother, George Cornaro, possibly because of threats to the family back in Venice, was used to try to persuade her to abdicate. Eventually after some resistance she agreed and sailed for Venice. In 1489 her formal abdication took place in St Mark's Cathedral and she retired to an estate at Asolo and a pension of eight thousand ducats a year.

CHAPTER EIGHT

The Venetians,
1489–1571

In order to govern Cyprus Venice established a lieutenant and two counsellors, who were known as the three rectors, and the army was commanded by a captain. Their term of office was limited to two years. As a republic ruled by an oligarchy of powerful families, Venice never allowed individuals to acquire too much power, but such short stays in office tended to encourage office-holders in their colonies to make quick gains through corruption. Venice had gradually assumed control of territories vital to its trade interests in the East Mediterranean: in 1206 it had seized Crete, in 1207 the Cycladic Islands, in 1215 Euboea, 1386 Corfu, in 1483 all the Ionian Islands, and now Cyprus in 1489.

Venetians taxes proved heavy, and most of the resources from sale of salt went back to Venice. Little was spent on defence, despite their exposed position, to the gathering power of the Ottomans, of the island. The remaining Lusignan nobles and the Greek population suffered from Venetian corruption and inefficiency. The High Court had been abolished and the nobles were sidelined, the Greeks were exploited having to work for the Venetians two days a week as well as pay an annual tax. It has been suggested that partly because of the inefficiencies of Venetian rule and the gradual severance of their trade routes by the Ottomans that the population dwindled during the period from half a million to just over 100,000.

In 1481 Leonardo da Vinci is said to have come to the island in order to purchase fine cloth for Milan cathedral. The embroidery of Lefkara still shows the influence of Italian needlework. Apart from the important salt industry Cyprus was still producing wine, flax, hemp, indigos and saffron. The perception is that the Venetians used Cyprus more as base for their operations rather than an island they wanted to invest in. However, various travellers still write about a lifestyle amongst the Cypriot upper classes that reflected the feudal model: a love of hunting, music, and contests of arms. The lower classes, the indigenous Greeks, apart from the exploitation by the Venetians mentioned above, are described as enjoying dancing and poetry, as well as games.

The Ottoman Turks raided the north of the island in 1500 and again in the following year, but the Venetians were able to negotiate a treaty with the Sultan Beyazit I in 1503. However, this was only a short respite, for Selim I, Beyazit's successor, renewed Ottoman expansion and in 1517 his army conquered Egypt. He immediately demanded from the Venetians five years of tribute that was owing to the Mameluks. Cyprus was now virtually isolated and the Venetian position extremely difficult, so that after some negotiation they conceded and in 1519 agreed to the payment. The next year, 1520, Suleiman, nicknamed the Magnificent, became sultan and began a massive Ottoman expansion through the Balkans, even forcing the Austrian throne to pay tribute. His piratical admiral Hayrettin Barbarossa roamed the Aegean harassing Venetian possessions. In 1539 Limassol was raided and the Venetians were forced to renegotiate a treaty with the Ottomans.

The pressure increased on the Venetians, when in 1562, a plot was hatched by the Greeks to rise up against them. The cousin of the despot of Moldavia, James Diassorin, conspired with a Greek captain of horse, Megaducos, to seize the island with Turkish help. Through one of their agents in Constantinople, the plot came to the attention of the Venetian authorities. Although they were able to capture and execute Diassorin it was clear not only were a large number of Greeks involved in the attempted coup but also the Frankish nobility. The fact the islanders were prepared to conspire with the Ottoman Turks showed what little loyalty or association they felt for the Venetians.

In 1566 Selim II became sultan and one of his advisers, Joseph Miques, a Jewish banker, who was rabidly anti-Venetian, now worked to persuade the sultan to invade Cyprus. Selim II, felt the need for a victory over Christian forces to redeem the defeat of his father in 1565 at the siege of Malta, where a massive Turkish force had eventually been checked by the tiny garrison of the Hospitallers and had been forced to make a humiliating retreat. In 1569 there was a terrible explosion in the arsenal at Venice, thought to be the work of Miques' agents and, with Venetian forces weakened, the Ottomans demanded the handing over of the island. Despite completely inadequate defences, a disgruntled Cypriot population and a peace party in Venice willing to sacrifice the island for trade concessions, in the end the Venetian government refused the Sultan's demand.

The Ottoman Conquest

On 1 July 1570 the Turkish forces under Lala Mustapha Pasha, the Beylerbey of Damascus, sailed past Paphos and landed on the south coast. It is not precisely known what the size of his army was, but it estimated from later accounts when his forces swelled to about 100,000 at the siege of Nicosia, that the invasion was conducted probably with between 20,000 and 40,000 foot soldiers, and 3,000 to 4,000 horse. The Venetians had probably as little as 3,000 to 4,000 foot and 3,000 horse to oppose them. The incompetent Venetian commander Nicholas Dandolo, despite the pleadings of Astorre Baglione, the experienced soldier from Perugia, refused to oppose the landing. An attack at that point could have seriously weakened the Turkish forces and might even have halted the invasion.

The Venetians with the help of the Papacy and King Philip of Spain, under pressure from the Pope, tried to organise an expeditionary force to relieve the island. However, because of intrigue, mainly around Philip's dislike of the Venetians, the expedition became impossibly delayed and in the end after reaching the southern coast of Asia Minor turned back. Meanwhile Mustapha marched on Nicosia. Although the Venetian fortifications around the city had been begun in 1567 by Julius Savorgnan, the work was still incomplete at the time of the Turkish siege. Some of the most vital elements like the moat had not been finished. When this lack of preparation was added to the incompetence of the Lieutenant Dandolo it is not surprising that the Turks met little serious opposition. The Turkish canon hammered at

A Venetian engraving of the Turkish siege of Nicosia in 1570

the unreveted walls and the garrison was steadily reduced to less than four hundred by the end. One of the commanders, Piovene of Vicenza, made a daring sortie which could have been a turning point. However, Dandolo, instead of sending support to Piovene when he captured two Turkish siege forts, prevented a sally to support him by the cavalry by closing the city gate shut, so that the hopelessly outnumbered Piovene and his band were eventually surrounded and cut down.

The final assault took place on 9 September. The remaining defenders fought bravely but the odds were now hopeless and once the walls fell only a remnant of the defenders retreated into the lieutenant's palace. Mustapha offered them clemency if they surrendered, but as soon as they agreed to his proposal he had them all massacred, including Dandolo, who had hoped for special treatment. Dandolo's head was sent to Famagusta, as a warning of what was to come. Nicosia was totally sacked, and it was said a ship was loaded not only with immense treasure but also with a human cargo of young men and women as a gift to the sultan. The story goes on to say that a Cypriot woman, rather than be humiliated by being forced to enter the sultan's harem, blew up the ship by setting fire to the powder magazine. The Turkish army, with reinforcements, now numbering 200,000 marched on Famagusta.

THE SIEGE OF FAMAGUSTA

The defence of Famagusta is an epic tale of resistance by an inferior force against overwhelming odds. The commander of the garrison, Marcantonio Bragadin, was from a noble Venetian family, and he was ably supported by Astorre Baglione. With forces of little more than 3000 regular Italian foot, 4000 Greek militia, 300 horse and 90 guns Bragadin had to face 200,000 Turkish troops, including about 6,000 horse, and 145 guns – four of the guns were known as basilisks and could throw immense balls of over 90 kilos (200 lbs). The siege lasted from 16 September 1570 until 1 August 1571. Although it was to end in disaster for the Venetian defenders it was to soak up a huge amount of Turkish resources, more than 80,000 were killed during the siege, which consequently relieved, for twenty years or so, the Ottoman pressure on Europe.

Mustapha first established a series of forts, along with a network of zig-zag trenches big enough for cavalry to ride through. The defenders constantly attacked these forts and trenches. Baglione, ably supported by another legendary commander, Nicholas Donato, led twenty-six sorties during the length of the siege. At the end of January 1571 a Venetian commander, Mark Quirini, reached Famagusta with a dozen galleys. He was able to capture one and destroy three Turkish ships and break through into the harbour. Although he had been able to bring munitions and supplies there were to be no reinforcements and by mid-February Quirini sailed for Crete with the women and children. At the end of March a new Turkish admiral, Ali Pasha, replacing Piale Pasha, arrived with thirty more warships.

By May Mustapha was ready to launch a massive bombardment, but the Venetian reply was equally vicious, until the defenders began to run short of munitions. No doubt under political pressure, because of the length of the siege and the sultan's memories of Malta, from the Porte (the Ottoman government) a despatch was sent to Constantinople claiming Famagusta was not defended by ordinary men but giants. By the end of the month false hope was raised for the defenders by a ship arriving from Crete with the promise of help. The besieging forces now concentrated on trying to undermine the wall and on 21 June a huge explosion destroyed part of the walls, but the following assault was thrown back with huge Turkish losses. Another Venetian ship arrived with the promise of reinforcements shortly. However, it turned out to be another false promise. For the next few days the Turkish forces made continuous assaults on the breach in the walls. We are told the defenders fought without sleep, and the clergy and those women, who had stayed with the defenders, continually supplied the troops in the front line with munitions and water.

By July the Turks had built a fort that overtopped the Venetian arsenal and had spread poison on the main ravelin (a salient that defended the main gate) – an early example of chemical warfare. Once this was captured the besiegers were able to mount guns that could fire directly into the heart of the city. Resistance was inevitably weakening, but, nevertheless, attack after attack was repulsed, but the defenders having eaten all the animals in the city were running out of supplies. Mustapha ordered further attacks through the breach. After resisting three major assaults in six hours, which cost the besiegers 5,000 dead there were only seven barrels of powder left and virtually no food. On 1 August Bragadin decided to seek terms. Initially, Mustapha complimented the defenders on their magnificent resistance and promised safe passage. On 5 August, the surrender was acknowledged in writing, sealed by the sultan, and the defenders put themselves in Turkish hands.

THE TORTURE AND EXECUTION OF BRAGADIN

It is then recorded that at a given signal a massacre of the defenders began, Bragadin and the leading commanders were brought before Mustapha, who flew into a rage accusing the Venetian commander of torturing and executing fifty Turkish prisoners. Bragadin apparently denied this charge, but Mustapha then railed at him for killing 80,000 of his troops and had him bound and his nose and ears chopped off. At this point Braglione, who then castigated Mustapha for breaking his word, was immediately beheaded. The city was completely sacked and those surviving were sent off as trophies to Constantinople. The torture of Bragadin, however, was to continue. He was forced to carry sacks of earth and kiss the ground when he passed Mustapha. On 17 August he was hoisted in a chair on the yard of one of the Turkish ships. He was a pitiful sight with festering wounds from the mutilations. He was then brought down and flayed alive, only dying when the knife reached his waist. All this he apparently bore unflinchingly. Parts of his body were then put on display and his skin was cured, stuffed and paraded on a donkey. The impact upon Venice and the West was, as several writers have pointed out, truly shocking and it was no coincidence that the great Venetian painter Titian chose as his subject the mythical scene, *The Flaying of Marsyas,* in 1576, as an immortal reminder of such terrible cruelty. The skin was sent to Constantinople as a trophy for the sultan, where it was stolen by a Venetian in 1581 and placed in an urn in the church of SS Giovanni e Paolo in Venice. The inhuman treatment meted out to Bragadin is not only an insight to the inhumanity of the times, but perhaps also to the frustration that the long siege of Famagusta had caused in the Turkish ranks.

The failure by Western Christendom to relieve Famagusta, and hence to defend Cyprus was linked to a far greater assault the Sultan Selim was planning against the Christian West. Just two months after the fall of Famagusta the sultan's fleet mounted a massive attack. It was met by ships of the so-called Holy League: an alliance brought together by the Pope. The fleet, which mainly consisted of Venetian galleys, fought the Turks at the battle of Lepanto, off the coast of western Greece. The total destruction of the Turkish fleet has been seen as one of the crucial engagements that preserved European Christianity from the Muslim Turks, but it had come too late to save Cyprus. Even so, when Mustapha returned to Constantinople, the despondency of the Porte put his triumph in Cyprus into the sober context of the defeat at Lepanto.

Although there were several attempts during the sixteenth and seventeenth centuries to regain Cyprus for either those with Lusignan connections or Venice, none of them was effective and they all came to nothing in the end. However, they did on several occasions draw support from the Greek population of the island that generally resulted in massacres of the local population by Turkish troops; for example in 1572, 1578, 1607 and 1617.

CHAPTER NINE

The Ottoman Period, 1571–1878

The Government of Cyprus

The Ottomans were to rule Cyprus for just over three hundred years, but during that time the island was to play little part in mainstream history. Cyprus' rulers in Constantinople treated the island as a backwater and put virtually no investment into this part of their empire. There are really no buildings of any consequence surviving from the Turkish period in Cyprus. The impression over the period of Ottoman rule is that of a lethargic and corrupt administration presiding over the decaying and romantic ruins of bygone times. However, it was not an easy time for the ordinary people. Although the regime was not particularly oppressive the government of the island did reflect the steady decline of the Ottoman Empire, which was both neglectful and occasionally savage.

Initially, recalling past connection with Cilicia, Cyprus was incorporated into a province (a *Pashalik*) that included the mainland territories (*sanjaks*) of Alaya, İçil, Zulkadir and Tarsus. The governor, the first one being the conqueror Mustapha Pasha, received the position of Berleybey, and was a pasha of the highest status, that of 'three tails', which was a reference to three horses' tails on his standard, recalling the nomadic days of the Turks. His official residence was in Nicosia.

Particularly important for the future of the island, however, was the introduction of Turkish settlers, who were encouraged to emigrate from the mainland to Cyprus. Land and houses had also been given to the veterans of the conquering army as well as Turks from Anatolia, the central area of modern Turkey, who now made their new home in

The Haidar Pasha mosque after the drawing by Archduke Luigi Salvatore, 1873

Cyprus. It seems that probably there were about 20,000 Turks, including a garrison on the island in the sixteenth century, living alongside the Christian population. The Christians, who numbered about 85,000, included Armenians, Maronites, and Catholics, as well as the majority, Orthodox, Greek speaking population, were required, under Turkish law, to pay a poll tax.

The Ottoman system of empire was based on continuous warfare against non-muslims, and conversion to Islam was the only means of integration, otherwise Turkish subjects, *rayahs* ('cattle' – the possessions of the sultan), were left to run their own affairs within their own community, a *milet*. These non-Muslim communities had to pay tax, which exempted them from military service and allowed them to practise their religion. The leaders of the *milets* were required to ensure order and obedience to the Ottoman authorities among their people. The largest *milets* within the empire were the Orthodox Christians. After the conquest of Constantinople Mehmet II had recognised the Patriarch of Constantinople as the titular head of the Orthodox Chrisitians. The Ottomans, in fact, relied on their Greek subjects to administer their empire while they focused on military matters. It is, therefore, not surprising that the Ottoman equivalent of head of the civil service, the Grand Dragoman (meaning literally 'interpreter') of the Porte was always a Greek. In Cyprus it was entirely consistent that the archbishop was identified as the leader of the Cypriot Orthodox community, and a Greek was dragoman to the Ottoman government of the island.

The Orthodox Church

In comparison to the Latin Church, the Orthodox gained much from the Turkish conquest. The Roman Catholic Church was abolished and the only Latin ecclesiastic to survive was the Archbishop, Mocenigo, who had fled to Venice. Of the Latin nobles, only a few were able to buy back their lands, some converted to Islam, but most seem to have been absorbed into the Orthodox Church. The autocephaly of the Cyprus Church was recognised and its bishoprics were restored and the church authorities were accorded secular powers. The use by the Ottomans of the archbishop as the head of the *milet* led to the increased political power of the Orthodox Church as the representative of the largest community on the island. It was the Church and particularly the archbishop who challenged the corruption and oppression of the Ottoman authorities. At the same time the archbishop, alongside the dragoman, was responsible for much of the day to day administration of the island and the collection of taxes.

Under Ottoman rule the ordinary people were initially to benefit from a lower levy of taxation and the abolition of the Latin feudal system. The farmers who had been serfs now had rights over their land and could pass on the title to their descendants. However, as well as suffering from the natural disasters of plague and locusts the challenge of supporting the corrupt Ottoman administration became a severe burden and large numbers of islanders fled to Crete, Corfu and southern Greece. A census taken around 1640 reveals that the island's population had shrunk to a mere 25,000. Steps were taken by the Ottoman government to reduce the burden on the islanders and encourage those who had left to return – in 1641 emigrants were offered tax relief for a year if they returned. However, the evidence of travellers in the seventeenth century paints a depressing picture of a potentially rich island appearing depressed and neglected with large tracts of land abandoned.

Nearing the end of the seventeenth century, probably for economic reasons, it was decided to abolish the province. Cyprus itself was reduced to the status of an island territory, like the islands in the Aegean, and placed under the control of an admiral, the Kapudan Pasha, who had a governor of lesser importance to administer the island. These governors (known as a *müsellim*) had to bid for the post that only lasted a year so they determined to make their wealth during their term through extortion. According to one account their relatively junior status created tension with the senior officials (*Aghas*) in Nicosia. These administrators controlled the collection of taxes and this gave them considerable influence at the Porte to undermine the *müsellim*. Rivalries and politicking led to unrest and revolt. In 1673 one of the Ottoman officials, Mehmed Ağa Boyacioğlu, rebelled and managed to control Cyprus for seven years. Apparently, he was careful to still send taxes to Constantinople, but eventually the sultan dispatched troops from the mainland and Boyacioğlu was tracked down and executed. The rebellion of Boyacioğlu was, it seems, treated with complete indifference by the Christian population.

Some years later, possibly as result of the conflicts between the officials, control of the island was given to the grand vizier, the chief political minister of the sultan, who tended to use the revenue from the island as a source for his private income. The grand vizier appointed a *müsellim* who also had the role of tax collector (*muhassil*) to ensure he squeezed the maximum income out of the island. This arrangement did not last long and in 1745 Cyprus became an independent province, again under a pasha of three tails. The British consul from Aleppo, Alexander Drummond who visited the island at the time, was complimentary about the new pasha, Abu Bekir, who, he noted, built, at his own expense, an aqueduct for the town of Larnaca.

ÇIL OSMAN AĞA

Shortly after 1750 the island was once more returned to the control of the grand vizier with the appointment of a *müsellim*, who combined governance with the role of tax collection. Over-taxation and the resulting misery is a constant theme for the Cypriots. According to the account of the archbishop Kyprianos, one of the worst of the *muhassils* (tax collectors) was Çil Osman Ağa who bought the post for a considerable sum in 1764. He was not only determined to recoup his investment, but make a huge fortune from the post, so he doubled the amount of tax the Christians had to pay and even increased the tax on the Muslims. A complaint was made to the grand vizier who dispatched one of his own staff with an official order (*firman*) to return the tax rate to the original rate and repay the amount gathered in excess of that. The leaders of the Christian community along with senior Turkish officials were summoned to hear the grand vizier's judgement at the governor's residence (*saray*).

During the procedure part of the floor where the Christian ecclesiastics were stood collapsed, sending them into the basement. The area where Çil Osman Ağa was sitting was fine and soon stories spread that the beams supporting the floor had been sawn through deliberately. An attempt was then made on the life of the grand vizier's official by giving him poison, but an antidote was administered in time to save him. Both the Greek and Turkish leaders were appalled at these outrages and the governor was summoned by the Muslim religious leader (*molla*) to appear before him. When he refused the Cypriots reacted angrily and Çil Osman Ağa's troops fired on the gathering crowd outside the governor's residence. The mob then stormed the building, killing Çil Osman Ağa and another eighteen of his officials, looted and burnt it down to the ground.

The Turkish authorities that had survived the riot persuaded the sultan that the fault lay with Çil Osman Ağa and a moderate new governor, Hafiz Effendi, was appointed. Although no severe punishment was inflicted on the Cypriots they were required to pay extra taxes in reparation for the governor's residence and blood money for the relatives of the Turkish officials who had been killed when the residence was stormed. Although the Christians agreed to terms set by the new governor, the Turks refused and a rebellion was started, led by the Turkish commander, Khalil Ağa, of the fort at Kyrenia. Many of the Turkish Cypriots supported Khalil and the rebellion lasted over a year. The Christian community suffered from the conflict, ravaged by both the rebels and government forces. In desperation the archbishop sailed to Constantinople, pleading with the Porte to send forces to restore law and order. Eventually, a force was sent from the mainland and Khalil was shut up in the fort at Kyrenia. In the end he was tricked into giving himself up and then in violation of a safe conduct he was executed and two hundred heads of his followers sent to the sultan to signal the end of the rebellion.

Russo-Turkish War 1768–1774

The Ottoman Empire was under growing pressure from Russia, and when the Russo-Turkish war of 1768 broke out Cyprus was to feel the consequences. In May of 1769 the Turkish fleet was destroyed by the Russians at Çesme and the Turks lost control of the East Mediterranean. Cypriot trade was disrupted and the island's inhabitants had to find extra resources to support the increased number of troops which were sent to protect the island from possible Russian attack. Three hundred soldiers had been sent but the governor Ismail Ağa refused to pay or feed them so the Cypriots were forced to pick up the costs, but were not exempted from the normal tax payments. In reality, although there was a vague plan to destroy the Ottoman Empire and restore Byzantium, the practical goal of the Russian monarch, Catherine the Great, was the annexation of the Crimea, and Cyprus was never seriously threatened.

Haci Baki

In 1771 the infamous Haci Bakir became the head of the treasury (*defterdar*) of the island. Much scandal and myth surrounds this character. It is said he was a one-eyed illiterate woodcutter from Klavdhia in Cyprus, who after a reckless time spent as part of an irregular militia, found favour through a liaison with a member of the harem of the governor of Antalya on the mainland. Expelled from Antalya for corruption he returned to Cyprus where he became a magistrate at Larnaca. Again he was dismissed, this time by the dragoman, Christophakis, for extortion, but Bakir took his revenge by having the dragoman murdered. Despite his criminal past he later gained the post of *defterdar*. However, he had not put aside his murderous behaviour and he soon had the dragoman of the time, Haci Joseph, who threatened to get in his way, removed and it is said he then poisoned two successive tax collectors.

Despite his outrageous record he still managed somehow to persuade the authorities to appoint him governor in 1777. Initially he seems to have been quite constrained and was thought of as a good administrator, but it was not long before he was back to his old extortionate habits. In 1783 the archbishop and his bishops eventually managed to convince the grand vizier to dismiss him. However, Bakir himself then went to Constantinople where he was able to persuade the grand vizier's successor to reappoint him to the governorship. Finally, the leaders of both the Muslim and Christian communities journeyed to Constantinople to block his reappointment. It is said he was then sent to Aleppo where he died through plague while working for the customs office. So notorious was his time as governor that he has slipped into folk-memory as the archetypical tyrannical governor.

Hajigeoghiakis Kornesios

At the end of the eighteenth and the beginning of the nineteenth century the leaders of the Orthodox Church seem to have had considerable influence on the administration of the island. Since the 1750s the archbishop as the leader of the *milet* had been responsible for the collection of the taxes and in the early 1800s it is reported that the Greek dragoman, Hajigeoghiakis Kornesios, was the most powerful and wealthy person on the island. The Greek leaders have been condemned for their relentless exaction of tax from the ordinary people, but at the same time the repressed Greek population undoubtedly looked to them for protection from the oppression of the corrupt Turkish officials. Nevertheless, like the rest of the Ottoman Empire at this time Cyprus was in a pretty parlous state.

In 1804 the Muslim population again attempted rebellion and many of the Greeks emigrated. Troops were sent from the mainland and the

The powerful Greek dragoman, Hajigeoghiakis Kornesios (1779–1809)
holding a diploma with the sultan's cipher

leaders of the rebellion were captured and impaled. Just two years later
a Turkish adventurer, named Altiparmak, from Tarsus on the mainland,
raided the island, was joined by some of the former rebels and started
attacking the Christian population. He was captured and flayed alive.
Then in 1808 another dissident Turkish officer from Antalya seized the
fortress at Limassol. After a short siege he too was captured and executed. In 1809 Hajigeoghiakis, himself, had to flee the island, such was
the anger at his depredations. He escaped to Constantinople where the
grand vizier had been informed of his abuse of power, but promised not
to hang him, and then with what passed for the humour at the time,
had him beheaded instead.

The Greek War of Liberation

At this time on mainland Greece, with the support and help of
European powers, influenced by the romance of Classical Greece,

insurrection against the Turks was being fomented. In 1821 the Greek War of Liberation was instigated by a group of leading Greeks who formed a society, the *Philike Hetaireia* (Friendly Society), and they included the Greeks of Cyprus in their plans for rebellion. Agents had been sent in 1818 to sound out the Greek Cypriot leaders. The archbishop, Kyprianos, promised money and supplies if a Greek force could be sent. (In fact in 1821 the Greek naval commander Kanaris was re-supplied when he called in on the island.)

It was clear Turkish rule on the island was under threat, because although Cyprus had the disadvantage of being a long way from mainland Greece, the island government was inefficient and the garrison small. However, the Turkish authorities were aware of what was happening and the governor, Mehmed Silahsör (nicknamed *kücük* Mehmed = little Mehmed), requested additional troops from the mainland. In April 1821 the governor started disarming the Christians – even taking away butchers' knives. He had already asked the sultan's permission to execute nearly five hundred of the leading Christians, but for broader political reasons the sultan had hesitated for the moment. The governor, however, began killing Christians of lesser importance and in early July he received permission to carry out the execution of the Greek leaders. The sultan, threatened by the deteriorating situation in Greece and the fear of a general uprising of Greek-speaking people across the empire, had carried out the execution of the Patriarch of Constantinople. After hanging the patriarch, his body was cut down after three days, given to the Jews, the traditional enemies of the Orthodox, and his body was dragged through the streets of Constantinople in a final humiliation.

On 9 July three Cypriot bishops were beheaded and the archbishop, Kyprianos, was hanged in front of the governor's residence. The following day the abbot of Kykko and other ecclesiastical figures were killed. Churches, monasteries and Greek houses were now robbed and looted. Christians were ordered to pull down the upper storeys of their houses as only Turks were allowed to have houses with upper floors. Across the island persecutions continued, so that the French consul in Limassol reported that in early August only two Greeks were left in the town. With a worsening situation the sultan called on the pasha of

Egypt, Mehmet Ali, to send military forces to the island to restore order, but they were so badly disciplined that many Greeks just fled the island. It is said that Kücük Mehmed made so much money out of theft and confiscation of the property of the massacred that he was able to bribe his way into another year of office.

Although the Greek fleet had made a couple of forays against Cyprus in 1823 and 1826 it was not powerful enough to have any impact. However, in 1827 Admiral Codrington with a combined fleet of British, French and Russian ships destroyed the Turkish navy at Navarino. This decisive engagement ensured the independence of Greece, and with the formal Treaty of Adrianople two years later, which ended the conflict, Mehmet Ali's troops withdrew from Cyprus. The success of the Greeks to establish their own nation for the first time in their history fuelled the desire for a union of Greek-speaking people (*enosis*). In 1830 when Capo d'Istria came to power in Greece he constantly espoused the cause of *enosis* with Cyprus.

However, despite three revolts breaking out in 1833, the Ottoman government was able to maintain its hold on the island. The first rebellion was led by Nicholas Theseus, but seems to have had more to do with resentment over tax, and it was not supported by the arch-bishop. In the end, with the help of the French consul and the poet Lamartine, Theseus was able to flee Cyprus. The second insurrection does seem to have had a firm link with the idea of *enosis*. It was organised by a monk, known as Joannikos, who was said to have fought for the Greeks in the War of Independence. He established himself in the Karpass where he was joined by some Albanians, who were ex-prisoners and on their way home from Egypt. Eventually, he and his followers, who were poorly armed, were captured and executed. Finally, in that year there was a rebellion organised by a wealthy Turkish landowner from Tremithusa, Giaur Imam. He seems to have been driven by some personal insult but was able to rouse support on the basis of the continual extortion of the Turkish authorities. His revolt lasted for about three months and both sides committed unspeakable atrocities against the innocent ordinary people.

For the European powers the Ottoman Empire now represented a major problem. Across its territories, especially in Europe, subjugated peoples were dreaming and planning independence. The dismantlement or fragmentation of 'the sick man of Europe' threatened instability and conflict amongst those European powers. Whereas some powers worked to destroy the Ottoman Empire others sought to sustain some form of balance of power by propping up the Ottoman Empire. (In 1854 Britain and France were to ally themselves with Turkey, in attempting to check Russian expansion into the Balkans, by attacking the Russians in the Crimea.)

Pressure all round was exerted on the sultan to reform the outmoded and corrupt Ottoman government. In 1839 the Sultan Abdul Mecid I issued a degree with a series of reforms. In the following year a new governor, Talat Effendi, was sent to Cyprus to introduce reforms, especially with regard to the system of taxation. However, the vested interests of the Turkish officials and others who had benefited from corruption meant that there was resistance to any tampering with the existing system. Although the governor brought in troops from the mainland he was so intimidated that the proposed reforms were postponed. However, changes as to the method of collection were established so that the taxes went directly to the government and the archbishop and other ecclesiastical officials were no longer involved.

In 1846 Greece established a consulate in Cyprus and this soon became the focal point for the movement for *enosis*. Just the next year the Ottoman governor, İsmail Adil Pasha, ordered the removal of a Greek flag at the consulate. A few years later, pamphlets, urging *enosis*, were found in the archbishop's palace. They belonged to a Greek schoolteacher who was expelled along with other compatriots from Greece. In 1867 the Ottomans were so concerned about political pamphlets, claiming Cyprus and Constantinople for the Greeks, which had been sent from Athens by Erato Karyke, an authoress who had taught in Nicosia, that a Turkish warship was put on patrol to stop any other material reaching Cyprus.

The British

British imperial concerns in the East Mediterranean during the eighteenth and nineteenth century were mainly concerned with their hold on India, and Cyprus began to emerge as a factor in the government's thinking. During the Napoleonic Wars British fleets had undermined French efforts to control the Mediterranean, and its strategic importance had been duly noted. In 1799 the commander, Sydney Smith, of the *Tigre*, an eighty-gun ship of the line, had raised the siege of Acre, thereby preventing Napoleon marching from Egypt via Turkey. Sydney Smith then put down a mutiny in Cyprus and met with the archbishop of the time, Chrysanthos.

After the defeat of Napoleon the British began to sense a danger to India from Russian ambitions. The threat Russia posed was not only to the Bosphorus, but also came from the Tsar's rapid expansion beyond the Caucasus into Central Asia, bringing the Russian Bear up to the frontiers of India. Cyprus would probably have played a part in the development of a land route to the Indian sub-continent for the British through Mesopotamia, but the idea was dropped because the government did not want to clash with French interests in Syria. In 1849 the British Admiralty conducted a survey of the island but because of a lack of a deep-water port necessary for the large warships of the time Cyprus was rejected as a possible base. Nevertheless, Cyprus had the potential of a *place d'armes* (a military base). The British were among those European nations determined to prop up the Ottoman Empire as a counter to Russian expansion, but they lacked a base from which to operate as the Crimean War (1854–5) had demonstrated. A further factor in the need for the British to have a presence in the East Mediterranean was the opening of the Suez Canal in 1869, which significantly reduced the sea route to India. By 1875 the British had acquired a controlling share in the canal, but still had no military base.

The Russo-Turkish War

Although the Crimean War had checked Russian expansion into the Balkans for a while the Tsar's ambitions, as the liberator of the Orthodox Christians, to wrest the Balkans from Turkey especially the Bulgarians who had suffered appalling atrocities (famously condemned by Gladstone) at the hands of the Turks, remained. The 'eastern question' – what to do about the Ottoman Empire – continued to be a conundrum for the European powers. The weakness of the Ottomans was as much of a threat to peace as their strength had once been. After the Germans defeated France in 1870 the Russian Tsar, Alexander II, took the opportunity to ignore the terms of the Treaty of Paris, which at the end of the Crimean War had imposed restrictions on Russian activity in the Balkans.

After the Turkish defeat of Serbia and Montenegro, Russia, as defender of the Orthodox Christians declared war on Turkey in 1877, and advanced through Bulgaria eventually reaching the Turkish defences before Constantinople. Although Alexander II had been indecisive, by March 1878 a treaty was concluded at San Stefano, which annexed large swathes of the Ottoman Empire. However, the British, although they had not interfered in the fighting, felt their position threatened by the Russian advance and had despatched a fleet to the Bosphorus. The other European powers were also alarmed by the extent of the Russian gains. The Austrians, who also had claims in the Balkans, threatened to attack the Russians in the rear, so reluctantly the Tsar agreed to a new treaty that was drafted at the Congress of Berlin in June of that year.

THE CYPRUS CONVENTION 4 JUNE, 1878

However, before the terms of the Congress had been settled, Benjamin Disraeli, who was the Conservative British Prime Minister at the time, proposed a secret convention to the sultan. Britain wanted to keep Russia from seizing Constantinople but there was no support in the country for allowing Turkey to hold on to its European possessions. Therefore, the focus of the Convention was on preserving the Ottoman Empire in Asia. The British undertook to support the sultan militarily if the Russians retained Batoum, Ardahan and Kars (cities in Caucasian Armenia), which had been captured in the war and if there was any attempt by the Tsar to take any more Ottoman territory. In return the sultan had to provide protection for his Christian subjects ('military consuls' would report on his performance), reform his government and lease Cyprus to Britain. The British would pay the Porte whatever was the excess of revenue over expenditure in the island. The excess was to be calculated by the average of the last five

A *Punch* cartoon in 1878 showing the British prime minister, Benjamin Disraeli, carrying the Turkish sultan across the Congress of Berlin

years. However, if Russia restored Kars and the other territory to the Turks, Britain would immediately withdraw from Cyprus.

To all intents and purposes the British actually gave the Sultan an ultimatum with just forty-eight hours to consent to the proposal. With no other options the Ottoman Government signed the Convention. When Britain disclosed the agreement just a week before the Berlin Treaty was signed, the French were furious at what they felt was underhand manoeuvrings by the British. However, without the concession to the Russians of the cities in north-eastern Turkey the Tsar would not have accepted the Berlin Treaty, and without the acquisition of Cyprus it is unlikely popular opinion in Britain would countenanced an alliance with Turkey. On 8 July, the day after Britain revealed the terms of the Convention, a British fleet under Lord Jon Hay appeared before Larnaca. On 11 July the administration of the island was formally acceded by the Ottoman authorities to the British.

CHAPTER TEN

The British Period, 1878–1960

The Handover

On 12 July 1878 Lord Hay journeyed to Nicosia and met with the Turkish Governor Ahmed Bessim Pasha. In the afternoon the Union Jack was raised in front of the Turkish barracks and Hay made a short speech in which he promised fair and just rule for the island. A Greek Cypriot, George Kepiades, a historian of the 1821 massacre, responded by expressing the delight of the Cypriots at the prospect of liberty. The passing of power to the British was almost without incident – there is a report of a Turkish officer drawing his sword when baited by a Greek Cypriot – and the administration of the island was easily transferred. The island had little crime and the existing Turkish police force, the Zaptieh, was merely reorganised and retrained by the British.

Although a contingent of four hundred Indian troops was immediately posted to the island from Malta, Cyprus was not destined to become a big military base for the British, although that seems to have been the intention behind the Convention. In 1880 the Conservatives were defeated in the elections and Gladstone became Prime Minister. He loathed the Ottoman Empire and had never favoured the Convention. He ended the system of 'military consuls' and appears to have ignored Cyprus, neither investing in, nor withdrawing, from the island. In 1882 the British, having secured their hold on the Suez Canal, occupied Egypt and the port of Alexandria was much better suited, with its fine harbour and plenty of surrounding land, as a military base than Cyprus. The island was to fall into relative neglect under the British – it is true, a neglect that was more benign than that under the Ottomans.

A wood engraving of 1878 showing the Union Jack being hoisted in Nicosia

On 22 July 1878 the first British High Commissioner, Sir Garnet Wolseley, landed at Larnaca. There was a mood amongst Cypriots that the oppression, corruption and inefficiency of Ottoman bureaucracy had come to a final end. Wolseley was addressed by Archbishop Sophronios, who welcomed the change in rule and celebrated a new life 'of truth, duty and liberty'. The bishop of Kition, Kyprianos, added to these sentiments by pleading that Britain would act as it had with the Ionian Islands and unite Cyprus with Greece. The British who had acquired the Ionian Islands during the Napoleonic Wars had ceded them to Greece in 1864. This act was seen as a precedent for *enosis* for Cyprus with the Greek Motherland. Greek nationalism since the War of Independence on the mainland had cherished the vision of uniting all Greek-speaking parts of the Eastern Mediterranean. At its most extreme there were Greek nationalistic hopes of reviving the Byzantine Empire with its capital at Constantinople (the so-called *Megali Idea* = the Great Idea), and a consequent reduction, or even elimination, of the Turkish State. These revanchist dreams were to be harshly exposed to reality after World War I when the Greeks were defeated in Anatolia and with the Turkish capture and destruction of Smyrna. The subsequent peace treaty of Lausanne in 1923, resulted in an exchange of populations between Greece and Turkey and was the virtual end of 2,500 years of Greek presence on the littoral of Asia Minor.

'ENOSIS'

During the British rule of Cyprus the demand and hope for *enosis* among the Greek Cypriots was consistently strong, even though this desire was often disregarded and underestimated by the British government. The evidence is quite clear that, despite the view sometimes voiced that the islanders were content with British rule, the Greek Cypriot majority consistently and determinedly demanded the end of British rule and union with Greece – constantly bombarding the British government with pleas and petitions (in diplomatic language, known as 'memorials') for *enosis*. The fact, initially, that Cypriots were officially described as subjects of the Ottoman Empire meant that the British government had a convenient argument for not engaging with the debate about the Greek Cypriots relationship with Greece. However, after World War I when Cyprus officially became a Crown Colony the situation was to change.

Gladstone, at first when Britain had occupied Cyprus, did appear to offer support for *enosis* and in a couple of speeches voiced his view that the island should be unified with Greece. However, he took this position when he was in opposition and when he became prime minister, as noted above, he did nothing to help achieve *enosis*. Later, when the island of Crete, through the action of the European powers, gained independence from Turkey in 1898, Greek Cypriot expectations were further aroused. Crete did achieve *enosis* with Greece in 1908, but the Turks living on the island paid a terrible price. Claims and counter-claims have been made about how many Turks were killed or left Crete of their own accord. Whatever the truth about massacres of the Turkish population by the Greek Cretans, there was no intervention from the European powers and the island was, to use that modern expression applied to the practice in the break-up of Yugoslavia, 'ethnically cleansed' of Turks. The fate of the Turks in Crete was to provide a fearsome prediction for Turkish Cypriots opposing the Greek Cypriots' demands for *enosis*. It has been suggested by some that Turkish Cypriots were not always hostile to *enosis* but that is simply to ignore the facts.

WINSTON CHURCHILL

The Greek Cypriots' historic connection with Greece seemed to have been recognised by Britain when Winston Churchill, Parliamentary Secretary of the Colonial Office, visited the island in 1907. Churchill endeared himself to the *enotists* by stating that it was only natural for the Cypriots because of their 'Greek descent' to wish for union with their mother country. He went on to say: 'Such a feeling is an example of the patriotic devotion which so nobly characterises the Greek nation'. He, however, also commented that '... the opinion held by the Moslem population of the island, that the British occupation of Cyprus should not lead to the dismemberment of the Ottoman Empire ... is one His Majesty's Government are equally bound to regard with respect'. Unsurprisingly, therefore, there were no moves by Britain to accommodate the Greek Cypriots' aspiration. However, at the end of 1912 Lloyd George, in the presence of Churchill and Louis of Battenberg (who changed his name later to Mountbatten), proposed to the Greek Prime Minister, Eleftherios Venizelos, that Cyprus be exchanged for a base at Argostoli, in Cephalonia (one of the Ionian Islands). On the island itself the knowledge of the discussions generated considerable excitement among the Greek Cypriots and alarm among the Turkish

Cypriots. However, at the time not all of Venizelos' ministers wished to be so closely allied with Britain and the offer went no further.

World War I

At the time Lloyd George was talking to the Greek Prime Minister, the Greek king, Constantine, was, in reality, more pro-German and was at odds with Venizelos' sympathies. When in the summer of 1914 World War I started with the Austrians' attack on Serbia, Venizelos, despite being opposed by Constantine, immediately offered Greek forces to support the Entente against the Central Powers (Germany and Austria), by going to the Serbs' aid. However, the British Foreign Secretary, Edward Grey, was chiefly concerned with thwarting an alliance between Turkey and the Central Powers so that Greece's offer was not taken up. However, by November 1914, Turkey had joined Germany and Austria so that the British immediately annexed Cyprus. It also became apparent that Bulgaria might soon join the Central Powers. Having failed to prevent Turkey allying with the Central Powers, Grey now focused on trying to prevent Bulgaria joining the War. Grey negotiated with Venizelos to prevent this happening by drawing Greece into the conflict, but after various machinations his plans came to nothing. King Constantine, espousing neutrality for Greece, forced Venizelos to resign. Although Venizelos returned to power after elections in 1915, Constantine unconstitutionally dismissed him once more. It was at this point that Britain offered to Venizelos' successor as Prime Minister, Alexander Zaimis, the cession of Cyprus to Greece in return for Greek military support for both Serbia, whose army was broken and on the retreat, and for the British and French forces who had landed at Salonika. No doubt due to pressure from Constantine the offer was not taken up and Zaimis himself soon resigned. By the middle of 1917 Venizelos had forced Constantine to go into exile and the Greek army joined the Entente, eventually helping them to over-whelm the Austrian, Bulgarian and German forces on the Salonika front. However, Britain did not repeat the offer of handing over Cyprus to Greece. It was only later that Greek Cypriots were to learn of this missed opportunity for *enosis*.

SYKES-PICOT AGREEMENT

In 1916 there had been demonstrations both in Limassol and Larnaca demanding *enosis*, but Britain and France had already come to an agreement in May of that year which reinforced Britain's hold on the island. A secret agreement had been negotiated between Sir Mark Sykes, a British diplomat and his French counterpart, François Georges-Picot, to divide up the Middle East after the defeat of the Ottoman Empire. Britain's main aim was to ensure a secure passage between Egypt and British India, while France wanted to be pre-eminent in Lebanon, Syria and Southern Anatolia. As part of the deal Russia would be allowed a free hand in Armenia and northern Kurdistan. In fact, the Bolsheviks after the revolution published the terms of the agreement, causing much international dismay and Arab anger. As part of the so-called Sykes–Picot Agreement Britain undertook not to leave or release Cyprus without French permission – Cyprus in unfriendly hands would have made France's position in the Middle East virtually untenable.

Post–World War I

After the end of World War I in 1918 Archbishop Cyril III went to London to plead the Greek Cypriot's cause. He was received favourably by members, like Ramsay MacDonald, of the Labour Party. It also seems that the British government had not entirely abandoned the idea of the cession of Cyprus to Greece. In 1919 at a meeting of the Council of Four (Britain, France, Italy and the USA) Lloyd George is reported as having said to Woodrow Wilson, the US President, that it was his 'intention to give Cyprus to Greece'. However, the *enosis* cause was undermined by some Cypriots concerns about the situation in Greece, as voiced in Michael Pantelouris' letter attacking 'the incompetence and corruption of the Greek Government'. Added to those concerned about the condition of Greece there were members of the British government who were anxious about the strategic situation in the East Mediterranean at the time and did not wish to abandon Cyprus because of its value as a military base.

When in 1920, following the rejection of the Treaty of Sèvres by Mustafa Kemal (Ataturk) and the Turkish Nationalists, Greece went on the offensive in Anatolia, the British authorities prevented Cypriots from joining the Greek army and demonstrations on the island followed. In 1922 after Greece was defeated by Mustafa Kemal a new treaty (Treaty of Lausanne) was agreed. Greece and Turkey agreed an exchange of their minority populations (as mentioned above) and Turkey formally recognised the British annexation of Cyprus. Turkish Cypriots were encouraged to leave Cyprus, and there was apparently a proposal that the minority populations of Smyrna and Cyprus might be exchanged. However, despite the idea being supported by Fridtjof Nansen, the Norwegian explorer, who worked with the League of Nations helping refugees, such a formal exchange did not happen. The defeat of Greece dampened down the clamour for *enosis* amongst the Greek Cypriots for a short time, and when Ramsay MacDonald did become Prime Minister in 1924, his government, which relied on Liberal support, was short-lived and Cypriot self-determination was not on his agenda.

Crown Colony

In 1925 Cyprus was proclaimed a Crown Colony and this led to further protests and appeals. Greek Cypriot demands were based on two approaches. The more extreme still sought union with Greece, but at the same time there was a more moderate view which argued for constitutional reform, requesting a more democratic voice within the bounds of British rule. A few years after the British occupation of Cyprus, a Legislative Council had been established. Originally this Council had three Muslim members, nine were non-Muslim, six civil servants were appointed and the British governor had a casting vote. The nature of the membership of the Council reveals the manner of British control, which maintained 'divide and rule' between the Greek and Turkish Cypriots. In 1925 as a response to Greek Cypriot pressure for greater representation in the Council, the Greek Cypriot representation was increased to twelve, but at the same time the number of civil servants on the Council was increased from six to nine, thereby maintaining the same balance of power.

Riots of 1931

In 1929 Ramsay MacDonald became Prime Minister with the election of a second Labour government and, following the delivery of a long memorandum demanding *enosis*, a delegation led by Nicodemus Mylonas, the bishop of Kition, went to London. Once more the British government's answer was unresponsive and on his return Nicodemus worked throughout 1930 to strengthen the *enotist* cause. He founded a 'National Radicalist Union', whose motto was '*enosis* and only *enosis*'. The Legislative Council was then boycotted by the Greek Cypriots and in October, 1931 Nicodemus made a dramatic speech at Limassol, denouncing British rule and calling for civil disobedience. The next day the chief priest of the Phaneromeni church in Nicosia, Dionysios Kykkotis, kissed a Greek flag and declared *enosis*. A crowd then marched on Government House, smashed its windows and torched the building to the ground. This sparked off further riots, which some argue were probably pre-planned, across the island. Two Royal Navy ships were sent with troops from Egypt to restore order and ten 'ringleaders', including Nicodemus were deported. Six rioters had been killed, some sixty plus wounded, including thirty-eight policemen, and over two thousand were imprisoned for a short period.

The riots of 1931 were followed by a series of repressive measures from the British colonial authorities: the constitution was suspended, political parties were banned, the press was censored and even the flying of the Greek flag was prohibited. The authorities had in the past taken a liberal view of education on the island and, contrary to the usual British colonial policy of encouraging English, Greek was the language used for the majority and Turkish for the minority. Greek Cypriot schools, therefore, tended to follow the official Greek curriculum so that the history and literature that Cypriot children studied was that of Greece, the Motherland. Naturally, the patriotism and loyalty of Greek Cypriot children became focused on Greece. Now, in elementary schools English was made compulsory and the teaching of the Greek curriculum was discouraged through the use of financial disincentives.

It seems that there was a view amongst some member of the British Establishment that the development of a Cypriot national identity might weaken the *enotist* cause. The first element in this approach was to attempt to de-hellenise ('de-Greek') the Greek Cypriots, the second was to encourage a Cypriot nationalism. In reality, as Ronald Storrs, the governor of the time recognised, the policy was impractical. The Greek Cypriot nationalists perceived Cypriot nationalism as a British trick created in order to prolong British rule. It has been claimed that because Greek Cypriots saw British colonial rule at this stage as more an assault on their cultural identity than their political liberty that the *enosis* movement was very different from other nationalist opponents of British colonial rule. Other British colonies, somewhat later, were to meet opposition from their anglicised subjects, demanding political independence and social reform, but in Cyprus the clamour amongst the Greek Cypriots for union with Greece was in essence solely based upon ethnic descent, racial continuity and religious affiliation.

For the remainder of the decade leading up to World War II most of the agitation for *enosis* took place outside Cyprus. Nicodemus was to die in exile in Jerusalem in 1937 and Kykkotis died in Alexandria in 1942. Two of the other deportees, the Loizides brothers, were to be very active in promoting the cause. Savvas became a member of the Greek parliament and tirelessly campaigned for *enosis* whilst a member of the Greek delegation to the United Nations. In London a Cypriot committee organised by Zenon Rossides continuously lobbied for *enosis* and gained the support of such British luminaries as Arnold Toynbee, Harold Nicholson and Robert Byron.

World War II

The outbreak of World War II and the Italian invasion of Greece in 1940 changed the atmosphere for Greek Cypriots. Greece and Britain were allies and Greek Cypriots joined the cause with over 30,000 serving in the British armed forces. The prohibition on the Greek flag was forgotten and there were hints from Churchill and others that union with Greece might be achieved at the end of the War. When the Italians were facing defeat at the hands of the Greeks the Germans invaded Greece in 1941 and after the capture of Crete in May it seemed that Cyprus might be the next place to fall. In fact, the daring parachute attack on Crete had cost the Germans heavy casualties – German paratroopers were never again used in such an offensive context – and Hitler was then far more concerned about the Barbarossa campaign, the German invasion of the Soviet Union, than attacking the lightly-defended island of Cyprus.

Cypriot support for Britain led to a lifting of the tough control on local politics and from 1941 the prohibition on political parties ceased. First the communist, Progressive Party of the Working People (AKEL) was formed, soon followed by others, the Cypriot National Party (KEK), supporting the *enosis* position, and the Pan-Agrarian Union of Cyprus (PEK). In 1943 municipal elections were held for the first time in twelve years in the chief cities and AKEL gained control of both Limassol and Famagusta. Generally, during the period the issue of *enosis* was not to the forefront. Any protests and disturbances against British authority were mainly based on the economic difficulties of the time. In March 1944 there was a major strike for an increase in wages – known later as 'the labourers strike'. The strike lasted for twenty-three days and was brought to an end when the government gave assurances it would carry out an enquiry into the levels of pay in relation to the cost of living.

POST WORLD WAR II

As the end of the War began to come into sight, the future of Cyprus was once more addressed by the British government. However, the tensions in the East Mediterranean in relation to Israeli and Arab nationalism in Palestine, Egypt and the other Arab states, cast a strong shadow over British thinking. The strategic importance of Cyprus as a military base assumed an importance that explains British determination to hold on to the island. When Sir Cosmo Parkinson was sent by the British Government to the island to gather opinions about Cyprus' future in August 1944, it was clear that his hands were already tied. A Greek Cypriot delegation presented him with a plea for union with Greece, but Parkinson argued that he was not empowered to discuss the subject of *enosis*.

LORD WINSTER

In 1945 the Labour Party came to power in Britain, sweeping Churchill out of power and setting a new political and social agenda – which included self-government for territories of the Empire and in some cases de-colonialisation. In the following year Lord Winster, who had been a Labour member of parliament, was appointed governor with a remit of reintroducing a democratically-elected Legislative Council in Cyprus. The Secretary of State for the Colonies, Arthur Creech Jones announced a series of 'constructive measures' for Cyprus: these described a more liberal political regime, a programme of economic development, a repeal of the legal constraints on the election of the archbishop and an amnesty for those exiled after the 1931 riots. However, there was no mention of *enosis*.

Greek Cypriot resentment was heightened when Italy ceded Rhodes and the Dodecanese islands to Greece, and while other parts of the British Empire were gaining independence (including Transjordan [later to be renamed Jordan] in 1946, India and Pakistan in 1947 and more controversially Israel in 1948). Greek Cypriots were in no mood to accept Creech Jones' proposed reforms without the promise of *enosis*. Even the moderate Greek Cypriot newspaper, *Eleftheria* (Liberty) famously declared in its leading article that Cyprus would reject even the most perfect constitution if it did not include *enosis*. In August 1948 the British Government abandoned the constitutional proposals and Lord Winster resigned to be replaced by Andrew Wright, a career diplomat.

Church plebiscite 1950

In 1949 Archbishop Makarios II, who had been bishop of Kyrenia, succeeded Archbishop Leontius. Makarios was considered right wing and opposed the communists. Before the end of 1949 he proclaimed that the Cypriot Church would hold a plebiscite on *enosis*. The voting took place between 15 and 22 January 1950. The voting consisted of signing a page of a register under the heading 'I demand enosis'. If you opposed you had to sign a different page. All those eighteen years old or over, including women, were eligible to vote, but civil servants, schoolteachers and other government employees were excluded. Of 224,757 Greek Cypriots on the electoral roll 215,108 voted in favour. This amounted to 96 per cent out of 79 per cent of the electoral population. Unsurprisingly, the British authorities challenged the procedures of the referendum and essentially ignored the result.

The organisers of the plebiscite were to claim that a number of Turkish Cypriots went to make up the large percentage in favour of enosis. However, in reality, but unrealistically, many Turkish Cypriots at the time of the plebiscite, were demanding that if Britain were ever to relinquish sovereignty the island should be returned to Turkish rule. In reaction to the political actions of the Greek Cypriots the Turkish Cypriots had merged two parties into the Turkish National Party. Following the plebiscite there were student riots in Ankara and there was great pressure on the Turkish Government from the media, prompting the Minister for Foreign Affairs, J Sadak, to demand in a press conference that Britain should never cede Cyprus to Greece.

Makarios III

In October 1950 Michael Christodoulos Mouskos was elected Archbishop Makarios III at the age of thirty-seven, four months after the death of his predecessor Makarios II. Born into a peasant family on 13 August 1913 in the village of Pano Panayia in the Paphos district, Michael Mouskos had entered, as a novice, the Kykko Monastery. After he had been ordained as a deacon, at the age of twenty-six, he had gone to Athens to study theology and some law. In 1946 he had been selected to attend Boston Theological College on a two-year scholarship. In 1948 while he was still in the USA he was elected bishop of Kition. On his return to Cyprus he became a key figure in organising the plebiscite in 1950. After becoming archbishop he made his first appeal to the United Nations, early in 1951, for *enosis*. In that same year George Grivas made his first post-war visit to the island where he met with Makarios. Makarios and Grivas were the two key advocates for *enosis* and both were to have a profound influence on the contemporary history of Cyprus.

George Grivas

George Grivas was born on 23 May 1898 and came from the small village of Trikomo, twelve miles north of Famagusta. He came from a well off family: his father was a grain-merchant who owned the largest house in the village and was relatively pro-British whilst at the same time supporting *enosis*. Grivas had four sisters and one brother who qualified as a doctor. He went to school at the Pancyprian Gymnasium, as Makarios did later, and did well at school, winning several athletics prizes. In 1916 he went to Athens and was admitted to the Greek military academy and later took part in the disastrous Greek campaign in Anatolia at the end of World War I. Between the two world wars he spent time studying military tactics in France and lecturing at the military academy in Athens. In 1940 when the Italians invaded Greece Grivas fought in the Greek army and in recognition of his activities on the Albanian front was promoted to lieutenant-colonel. Although the Greek army had inflicted a remarkable defeat upon the Italians (as mentioned above), the Germans then quickly overwhelmed Greece.

During the German occupation of Greece Grivas organised a resistance movement known as χ (the Greek letter *khi*). Besides harassing the Germans his organisation had two other main aims: the return of the king of Greece and the defeat of the Greek communists. To this end he organised assassination and counter-assassination squads. Grivas'

George Grivas, the right-wing guerilla leader

opponents labelled the organisation χ as fascist. During the Greek civil war that followed the defeat of the Axis powers he had to be evacuated from Athens by the British when the communist ELAS (National Popular Liberation Army) tried to seize power in December 1944. After the defeat of the Greek communists he retired on a pension but in 1951 he entered Greek politics, but twice failed to get elected. Disappointed and angry he declared he would give up politics, and it was then he became determined to pursue the cause of *enosis* for Cyprus.

THE FORMATION OF EOKA

In July 1951 Grivas met with Makarios, but apparently the results of this first meeting were somewhat disappointing for the *enotists*. Grivas was determined on a campaign of violence, convinced that only an armed struggle would force the British to relinquish the island. Makarios, however, it appears was not convinced and although he was prepared to condone acts of sabotage, rejected the idea of a guerrilla war. In the following year Makarios and Grivas met in Athens when the former chaired a revolutionary committee. Despite Makarios' scepticism Grivas pushed ahead with his plans for an armed campaign of violence against the British. He returned to Cyprus in October of that year and spent five months surveying the island in preparation for a campaign of violence. He recognised that such a campaign might not necessarily defeat the British militarily, but it would aim to mobilise international opinion on the side of the Cypriots and thereby force the British to cede the island to Greece. After Grivas returned to Athens in February 1953 he started to draw up plans. On 7 March Makarios attended a key meeting of the revolutionary committee which endorsed the campaign and swore an oath of secrecy. The main focus of the campaign would be on sabotage as the geography and scale of the island was unsuited to a guerrilla war. From his experience in the Greek civil war he realised there would be opponents to his tactics and he formed execution squads who would deal with Greek and Turkish Cypriots who opposed or threatened his operations.

By October 1954 he was ready to begin the campaign. However, the British had got wind of the planning in Athens and were refusing visas to visitors from Greece. Grivas therefore decided to sail secretly to

Cyprus and, after being delayed at Rhodes, landed on 10 November in a small craft at Khlorakas, near Ktima. Early the next year he met with Makarios at Larnaca and informed him the Greek government of Papagos now fully supported their aims. It was decided to call their organisation EOKA (*Ethniki Organosis Kyprion Agoniston* = National Organisation of Cypriot Fighters). However, a couple of weeks later there was a setback to their plans when an arms shipment carried in the caique (a light sailing vessel) *Aghios Georghios* was intercepted by a British naval patrol and Socrates Loizides, who had fifteen years previously been banished by the British, and ten others were arrested. Grivas was forced to postpone his sabotage plans as a large quantity of explosives besides boxes of weapons had been seized.

At the magistrate's hearing against Socrates Loizides and the others on 17 March 1955, hundreds of schoolboys delayed the start by mobbing the courthouse, chanting 'Englishmen go home'. The Crown prosecutor was Rauf Denktaş, a London trained barrister, who was later to become the leader of the Turkish Cypriots. At the full trial Loizides was sentenced to twelve years, the others received sentences of between two to five years imprisonment. However, the ease with which the plot to smuggle arms into Cyprus had been discovered, resulted in the British authorities having a false sense of security. Grivas managed to get additional funds from Makarios and a former Greek army officer, Gregoris Afxentiou, found an alternative supply of explosives. On 29 March Grivas met with Makarios and it was agreed that the campaign would start at the end of the month.

EOKA CAMPAIGN

In the early hours 1 April 1955 the EOKA campaign began with a series of explosions across the island aimed at government buildings and installations, including the radio transmitter at Nicosia. At the sites of the explosions leaflets were scattered, proclaiming that with God's aid and with all the forces of Hellenism the Cypriots would overthrow British rule. The leaflets were signed Digenis, recalling the Byzantine legendary hero who had resisted the Arabs, and this became Grivas' code name. Reaction to the campaign was hesitant both in Greece and Cyprus itself. Few it seemed welcomed the idea of a campaign of violence which would disrupt normal life. In reaction Makarios now ordered Grivas to call a ceasefire. Grivas was concerned that any loss of momentum could be damaging and he was particular concerned about the communists, which through the strength of the party AKEL might gain the political initiative.

Grivas, rather than flout Makarios, regrouped and the campaign of violence was not restarted until June. There were essentially four elements to Grivas' plan. The first part involved recruiting youngsters from the schools and using them as messengers, to keep an eye on the British and take part in demonstrations. Grivas calculated that these young rebels would be a pool from which he could recruit the best into his fighting groups. Next he used gunmen against any collaborators with the British authorities or against those Greek Cypriots that opposed his methods or his politics. Thirdly he organised assassinations of British and Turkish Cypriots. Initially, these attacks were aimed against the police and military, but as the revolt continued and the authorities took counter-measures, more and more attacks were aimed against softer targets, civilians. Finally, all Greek Cypriots were encouraged to take part in civil disobedience, passive resistance and an economic boycott of British goods. The main overriding objective was to keep Cyprus in the news, highlight British repression, and thus gain international sympathy and influence world opinion against British rule of the island.

The EOKA fighting groups were trained in sabotage, ambush and execution. The men, and later also women, hid out in the countryside where they could rely on support from the villages and special hiding places were constructed for emergencies. Grivas himself was constantly on the move, making use of disguises and secret boltholes. On several occasion he was almost stumbled on by the British security forces but throughout his campaign he was always able to outwit his pursuers. Grivas demanded fierce discipline from EOKA members and was often critical of the attitude of the Greek Cypriots who were not inured to military action in the way their Greek counterparts had been by the Axis occupation during World War II and the following Greek civil war. The number of core EOKA members was comparatively small and never rose above a few hundred. Despite facing a huge numerical disadvantage on a relatively small island EOKA's guerrilla forces, by keeping to limited objectives, were able to operate with considerable freedom.

THE TRIPARTITE CONFERENCE

In Britain the Conservatives had been returned to power in May 1955. A new Foreign Secretary, Harold Macmillan (who later became Prime Minister) attempted a new initiative, and abandoning the traditional position that Cyprus was a colony and was therefore purely a domestic affair, invited the Greek and Turkish governments' representatives for talks in London. Although the Turkish government immediately accepted, the invitation was an embarrassment for the Greeks. Makarios denounced the conference as a trap and demanded bilateral talks between Britain and Cypriots (or at the very minimum just Greece). The Tripartite conference was doomed to failure as the Greek government argued that only self-determination was appropriate for the Cypriot people. The Turkish representatives, who feared *enosis*, opposed this. The Greek government now focused on appealing to the United Nations to end British rule. However, at this stage there was a refusal to even put Cyprus on the General Assembly's agenda.

JOHN HARDING

The Turkish Cypriot reaction to EOKA was to harden their stance against *enosis*. Later in 1955 leaflets were distributed by *Volkan,* a secret Turkish organisation which criticised the British authorities for their weak security. The British government now seemed to recognise the seriousness of the situation and on 25 September appointed the Chief of the Imperial Staff, Field Marshall John Harding, to be governor with instructions to restore law and order. In response EOKA increased its campaign of violence and by the end of November Harding had proclaimed a state of emergency. On the same day that the proclamation was made a bomb intended for Harding went off in the Ledra Palace Hotel. At the beginning of the next year a Turkish policeman was shot by four EOKA gunman and the incident sparked off riots in Nicosia and elsewhere amongst the Turkish community.

From July 1955 Harding had been in talks with Makarios but when these ended in failure the following year the British authorities decided to deport the archbishop. On 9 March, 1956 just as Makarios was about to board a plane for Athens he was arrested and deported to the Seychelles along with two other clerics and a journalist who was acting as a secretary to the bishop of Kyrenia. The decision had apparently been based on information which showed Makarios to be complicit in the growing incidents of violence that now gripped the island. The next day riots broke out in Greece, but in Turkey the news was greeted with jubilation. However, for Grivas the removal of the archbishop had political advantages and he had now a free hand to conduct his campaign with the intensity he had always wished for. By the time of Makarios exile EOKA had seven guerrilla groups in the mountains, forty-seven in the towns and seventy-five village bands armed with shotguns. Grivas now intensified his campaign and once more attempted to assassinate Harding by having a bomb placed at night in his bed by an agent, Neophytos Sophocleos, who worked in Government House. It failed to go off as it was set at too lower temperature for the cool night and was found by Harding's staff in the morning.

The increase in hostilities resulted in several clashes between the Greek and Turkish Cypriot communities. At the same time the British authorities brought in a series of tough counter-measures, curfews, fines and the closure of restaurants and cinemas. Grivas was concerned that his campaign was being undermined. There were rumours during the spring that several leading Greek Cypriots were now looking for a compromise with the British, but this initiative came to nothing when the Church reasserted its commitment to *enosis*. Harding then increased the pressure on EOKA by ordering extensive operations in the mountains and by mid-August Grivas suspended the campaign on the basis that he wanted to allow renewed negotiations for a political settlement.

The Conservative British government was under pressure at home from the Labour opposition who were convinced the deportation of Makarios was a mistake which served no useful purpose and merely hindered any progress in moving towards a settlement. There was also strong opposition to the death penalty for EOKA members convicted of murder, as this was believed to fuel retaliation killings and create martyrs. Britain, in fact, had moved a long way since the summer of 1954 when Henry Hopkinson, Minister of State for the Colonies, had used the word 'never' in response to a question about independence for Cyprus. By the end of 1955 'never' had become Harold Macmillan's 'sometime', and in the early summer of 1956 there was a proposal for a new plan with a settlement based on self-determination that would eventually mean the surrender of British sovereignty.

At the same time there were also concerns among politicians of all parties that Turkey could well become involved in military action to protect Turkish Cypriots if the government was to concede to a settlement that could lead to *enosis*. Anglo-Turkish relations had been strained since Harding had started negotiations with Makarios and when the government revealed its new plan Turkey immediately rejected the proposal. Fazil Kütchük the leader of the Turkish Cypriots had already made it clear that he was opposed to self-determination and Turkish Foreign Minister, Etem Menderes stated firmly in July that Britian must retain control over Cyprus otherwise the Treaty of Lausanne would be abrogated and chaos would grip the region. The British government was undoubtedly shaken by the Turkish response. In the context of the Cold War and the importance of Turkey as a NATO ally the British government drew back from self-determination for the island. However, self-government was still on the agenda and Lord Radcliffe was despatched to the island to start work on preparing a constitution.

Suez

In July 1956 Colonel Nasser nationalised the Suez Canal and the British Prime Minister, Anthony Eden, began to prepare plans for military intervention. French troops as well as British were to use Cyprus as a base for their operations in Egypt and the concentration on the military build-up resulted in the British counter-offensive against EOKA being severely reduced. This not only gave respite but also was a positive spur for Grivas to resume operations and the truce ended on 29 August when a bomb exploded in Larnaca. During the renewal of violence the

British authorities had discovered large parts of Grivas' diaries which had been abandoned when he was forced to make a quick escape. These were then published much to the embarrassment of the Greek Government as the published extracts revealed the level of their involvement in the revolt against the British. The diaries also implicated Archbishop Makarios in the campaign of violence, which undermined much of the support he had gained from the international community.

By the autumn of 1956 Harding announced a series of stiffer penalties which coincided with the return of troops after the failure of British and French policy over Suez. The respite given to EOKA now ended and there was a dramatic decline in violence towards the end of the year. In December Lord Radcliffe's proposals for a settlement were published and the former attorney general, Criton Tornaritis and Derek Pearson from the colonial office travelled to the Seychelles to discuss the proposals with Makarios.

The Return of Makarios

The Greek government rejected the Radcliffe proposals and in February of the following year put a resolution before the United Nations calling on equal rights and self-determination for the Cypriots. In the end, after a lengthy debate in the General Assembly, a formula proposed by Krishna Menon, India's UN delegate, who called for negotiations towards 'a peaceful, democratic and just solution' won the day. What had emerged was that there was little international support for *enosis*, and the Greek government now worked to persuade Grivas to declare another ceasefire. In March Grivas agreed to a cease-fire on condition that Makarios was returned from exile and negotiations were resumed. The British then freed Makarios who made his way to Athens where he was to meet Grivas. Although the British agreement to free Makarios reduced tension on the island, the consequences were not all entirely helpful. It improved Anglo-Greek relations, but it immediately created a rise in tension between Turkey and Greece. Fazil Kütchük believed that Makarios' release only encouraged EOKA to step up its attacks against Turkish Cypriots and therefore the right solution was to partition the island between the two communities. By the summer all the Turkish Cypriot town councillors had resigned, alleging that the Greek Cypriots had turned the councils into their own political organisations promoting *enosis*. A new underground Turkish movement was formed to counter EOKA. It was to become known as the TMT (Türk Müdafaa Teskilati = Turkish Defence Organisation). The Turkish Cypriots now took the position that they would only drop their demand for partition if the Greek Cypriots gave up their insistence for self-determination, which was interpreted by the Turkish Cypriots as the Greek Cypriot majority demanding *enosis*.

For the British the debacle of Suez appears to have radically changed their thinking. Britain had tried to exert its military power to protect its economic interests and failed. Without the support of the mighty USA, the Western European powers (of yore) could no longer get their way through sheer force as they lacked the necessary military clout. There were those that now argued in the British government that holding Cyprus could serve no useful purpose as Britain's oil supplies must now depend on developing commercial interests with the supplier countries rather than the use of force.

Consequently, Harding had also changed his stance on Cyprus and he now believed it was impossible for Britain to control the whole island against the wishes of the Greek Cypriots and a better position would be to secure a military base against any possible future military requirement. The British government, therefore, moved to the view that a settlement had to be found that would not alienate the Greek and Turkish governments and would protect British interests in the area (the so-called *tri-dominium* solution). The Greek government was also concerned not to stir up Turkey, whose support for partition had become particularly threatening. However, it decided to once more raise the question in the UN and push Britain into granting self-determination.

HUGH FOOT

In December 1957 Hugh Foot was appointed governor to replace Harding. His appointment was a clear symptom of the change in attitude by the Conservative government. Hugh Foot was a liberal with strong socialist connections. He was not new to Cyprus and had served as Colonial Secretary from 1943 to 1945. The Left in Greece and Cyprus welcomed the appointment as a reconciliatory gesture after the military appointee, John Harding. However, the Turkish Cypriots were suspicious and Grivas was positively hostile. He feared that Foot who had influence with the socialists in Cyprus might persuade some Cypriots to settle for a compromise solution that would rule out *enosis*. Grivas immediately resorted to increasing the level of violence to coincide with Foot's arrival. Much of this was aimed at the Turkish Cypriots and as the UN debate got under way street fighting broke out between the two communities. At the UN itself the protagonists took their predictable positions and the debate in the General Assembly which lasted four days made little progress. The Greek motion which sought the principle of equal rights and self-determination, whilst condemning Britain's violation of Human Rights and the atrocities committed against the Cypriot people, failed to gain the necessary two-thirds majority.

At the beginning of 1958 Hugh Foot launched a goodwill mission aimed at winning round the Greek Cypriots. His conciliatory approach culminated in a new plan for a settlement, which consisted of establishing unitary self-government for the island while putting the question of sovereignty to one side. Although Foot's approaches eased tension with the Greek Cypriots the extremist Turkish Cypriots became completely unsettled and the TMT sent a personal warning to Foot, accusing him of favouring the Greek Cypriots. Leaflets were distributed threatening any Turkish Cypriots who co-operated with the British with 'extermination'. At the end of January when Hugh Foot joined the British Foreign Secretary, Selwyn Lloyd, in Ankara for talks with the Turkish government the Turkish Cypriots in Nicosia rioted and seven Turkish Cypriots were killed in two days of fighting with the British security forces. The situation on the island had deteriorated badly for the British who were now facing hostility from both communities.

Grivas had become very concerned about the growing influence of the Turkish government on the British. At the same time he was disillusioned with the 'weakness' of the Greek government. His patience was at an end and he felt that an escalation of violence was the only way to force the British to concede self-determination. He ordered a new boycott of British goods, further passive resistance and greater exposure of British 'atrocities' against the Greek Cypriot community. The campaign of violence was renewed, but the first targets were the Greek Cypriot left wing, especially the communists, members of AKEL and the trade unions. By February after the murder of a couple of trade union members at Lyssi and Komi tou Yialou the PEO (Pancyprian Federation of Labour) was claiming that a civil war had only been averted thanks to the restraint and patriotism of the trade union leaders. The Greek government urged Makarios to intervene. However, the archbishop was only prepared to remind the Greek Cypriots of the need for unity rather than condemn the killings. Recognising, however, the dangers a civil war posed, by April EOKA had essentially switched its focus to attacks on the British.

GUENYELI

Hugh Foot tried to negotiate with Grivas through an intermediary, the lawyer Glafcos Clerides (who later was to become president). It was a risky strategy that was not supported by the British military and threatened to alienate still further the Turkish Cypriot community. The Greek Foreign Minister, Evangelos Averoff, also put pressure on Grivas as Greco-Turkish relations were stretched to breaking point. The surviving Greek population in Istanbul was particularly threatened and the spectre of partition in Cyprus was becoming more real. Rauf Denktaş now joined Kütchük in proclaiming that the British government was going to give into to Greek demands for self-determination and this would mean the 'extinction' of the Turkish Cypriots. On the night of 7 June 1958 a bomb exploded outside the Turkish Press Office in Nicosia sparking off the worst violence between the two communities since the start of the 'Emergency'.

One of the apalling incidents was the massacre of eight Greek Cypriots near the village of Guenyeli. Such were the circumstances of the killings that the British were accused by the Greek Cypriots of colluding with the Turkish Cypriots. A group of Greek Cypriots who were deemed by the British forces as intent on attacking Turkish Cypriots were disarmed and made to walk home past a Turkish Cypriot village where they were ambushed. Despite the findings of a Commission of Inquiry that exonerated the British, there is still a belief amongst some Greek Cypriots that the massacre was 'organised by the British and executed by the Turks'. Although eight Turkish Cypriots were eventually brought to trial for the killings there were no convictions because of lack of evidence.

MACMILLAN PLAN

By the middle of June 1958 the British Prime Minister, Harold Macmillan had constructed a plan, which, it was argued, would break the deadlock between the two communities and the Greek and Turkish governments. The principle of the plan was declared to be that of 'partnership' and its main provision was separate Greek and Turkish Cypriot houses of representatives and a council of ministers presided over by the governor, with the international status of the island to remain unchanged for a further seven years. All sides rejected the plan, and a new wave of inter-communal violence followed. The conflict between the communities reached new heights and there was a steady evacuation of Greek Cypriots from Turkish areas and Turkish Cypriots from Greek areas pushing the island towards *de facto* partition.

By the end of July, fearing outright civil war the British, backed by the Greek and Turkish governments, called for a ceasefire. Makarios, who was still in Athens, was put under pressure by the Cypriots themselves as the conditions on the island worsened, and gave his support to a suspension of the violence. On 4 August 1958 Grivas declared a five day ceasefire. Following the EOKA ceasefire, the Turkish Cypriot TMT also agreed to a cessation of violence. Macmillan went on the diplomatic offensive with both Athens and Ankara in an attempt to win them over to his plan.

With the ceasefire breaking down on the island Makarios revised his position and let the Greek government know that he was now willing to consider independence, and not just self-determination for Cyprus, after a period of self-government under the auspices of the UN, in accordance with the Krishna Menon proposal. On 22 September Makarios authorised Barbara Castle, at the time the vice-chair of the Labour Party, who had been on a visit to Cyprus, to inform the press of his new stance. Barbara Castle was perceived as having taken a pro-Greek Cypriot line, and she had accused the British forces of using unnecessarily violent anti-terrorist methods. While the leader of the Opposition, Hugh Gaitskell had disassociated the Labour Party from her criticisms, he claimed she had been misunderstood. Nevertheless, Makarios hoped that she could influence the Labour Party to take a more partisan position in supporting the Greek Cypriot position as Britain prepared for a general election as the Conservative government's term came to an end.

At the beginning of October the tension in the island increased when the wife of an army sergeant, Mrs Cunliffe was shot dead and her friend seriously wounded. The provoked British security forces reacted with what was later described in the coroner's court as 'entirely unjustified' assaults on innocent civilians. EOKA denied responsibility for the murder of Mrs Cunliffe and the perpetrator was never found, but the killing damaged both the Greek Cypriot cause and the reputation of the British forces. Grivas, however, was becoming steadily isolated as international opinion was moving to favouring independence as a solution for the island's problems.

Paul-Henri Spaak, the Secretary-General of NATO, had been working hard to bring Britain, Greece and Turkey together for a conference to mitigate the threat of Greece leaving NATO over the issue of Cyprus. Initally, the Turkish government had been suspicious of NATO's intentions, but they softened their position with regard to partition and began to show signs of accepting independence as a viable alternative. Although there was a growing acceptance of the compromise solution of independence, all governments needed to buy time before they could convince their publics and Spaak's efforts ended in failure. Attention once more shifted to the UN where a debate was due to start on 25 November. The Greek government pushed for independence for Cyprus in the debate in the political committee of the UN. However, in the end an Iranian motion which called for continued negotiations that went beyond the proposed tripartite conference of Britain, Greece and Turkey by including the Cypriots won the day (31 votes to 22, with 28 abstentions). By the end of the debate the Greek and Turkish foreign ministers, Averoff and Zorlu, were in discussions. These were resumed in Paris at a NATO meeting on 18 December.

Grivas was alarmed by the apparent reconciliation of the Greek and Turkish governments, and recognised that any shared sovreignty of the island would in all likelihood hamper *enosis*. The British on the other hand were tacitly encouraging the rapprochment between Greece and Turkey as ever since Macmillan had come to power, the government's attitude had been that any settlement that was endorsed by Greece and Turkey would serve Britain's purpose. Britain's prime goal was to maintain its military bases in Cyprus and at the same time any Greco-Turkish settlement would only achieve NATO and US support if accorded with this policy. The pressure was such from Greece now that Grivas was forced, against his better judgement, to call another ceasefire on Christmas Eve.

ZURICH AND LONDON AGREEMENTS

Early the next year Greece and Turkey resumed talks on Cyprus once more in Paris. The scene was now set for a summit conference in Zurich. The conference started on 6 February with the two prime ministers, Karamanlis and Menderes and their foreign ministers, Averoff and Zorlu. At one stage it looked as if the talks might collapse when the Turks were insisting on having a base on the island. However, on 11 February 1959 a declaration was signed and Averoff left for London to inform Selwyn Lloyd, the British Foreign Minister, of the agreement. The Zurich agreement was based around twenty-seven articles. It aimed to establish an independent republic based on a Greek Cypriot president and a Turkish Cypriot vice-president; a constitutional court and a high court composed of Greek and Turkish Cypriot judges; the creation of separate Greek and Turkish muncipalities in the five major cities; a Cypriot army of two thousand (60 per cent Greek and 40 per cent Turkish Cypriots) and a mixed police force (with a 70 per cent to 30 per cent ratio). The executive would be a council of ministers, consisting of seven Greek and three Turkish Cypriots, with one key ministry (foreign affairs, defence or finance) always reserved for a Turkish Cypriot. The legislature was to be a house of representatives, elected every five years on the ratio of 70 per cent to the majority community and 30 per cent to the Turkish Cypriots (thirty-five Greek and fifteen Turkish Cypriots). The civil service would also be appointed upon the same ratio. This was distinctly favourable to the Turkish minority, as the demographic ratio was 82:18 in favour of the Greek Cypriots. A crucial element in the constitution would be that both president and vice-president could exercise a veto in relation to security and foreign affairs. The constitution could only be amended or altered if two-thirds of both the Greek and Turkish Cypriots members of the house of representatives were in support. In addition there would be two treaties with the new republic: the first would recognise Britain, Greece and Turkey as guarantors of Cyprus' independence, and the second would give Greece and Turkey the right to station small contingents of troops on the island. The key concessions from Greece and Turkey were the exclusion of any notion of *enosis* or partition.

A conference in London was immediately convened between Britain, Greece and Turkey, and this time with Cypriot delegations from both communities, led by Makarios and Kütchük. The London conference started on 17 February and straight away Selwyn Lloyd, on behalf of the British Government, accepted the Zurich agreement, on condition that two British bases were secured in the final settlement. Makarios was very uncomfortable with several aspects of the agreement, for example, the vice-president's veto and the proportion of power and posts given to the Turkish Cypriots which did not reflect the size of their population. In the end Constantinos Karamanlis, the Greek Prime Minister, told Makarios he must accept the terms of the Zurich agreement, as they were the best he could hope for, given the relations between Greece and Turkey. Makarios had anticipated that he could negotiate away many of the inimical aspects of the agreement but after his discussion with Karamanlis, unless he also wished to challenge Greece, he was faced with a bitter acceptance. Makarios later always made it plain that he was not a willing party to the independence terms, but in the interests of Cyprus he had finally accepted the Zurich and London agreements.

Averoff and Makarios now appealed to Grivas to accept the settlement. Grivas initially refused to endorse the agreement until all EOKA prisoners had been released. He even considered rejecting the settlement entirely, but feared that a civil war might follow and he would be isolated, his arms supply cut off by Greece. When, on 1 March, Makarios returned to Cyprus to be greeted by enthusiastic crowds, Grivas refused to meet with him. However, the British authorities did grant an amnesty to EOKA prisoners on condition that the more dangerous ones would be barred from entering Cyprus before independence. So on 9 March 'relucantly' Grivas agreed to a ceasefire and on 17 March he left the island for Greece. Emaciated and still dressed in battle fatigues he was greeted in Athens as a national hero and promoted to lieutenant-general and granted full pay for life.

THE 1959 CYPRUS SETTLEMENT

Grivas' guerilla campaign had cost the security forces 156 lives and of the 238 civilians killed 203 were Greek Cypriots. Although EOKA claimed they were 'informers', the majority of Greek Cypriots killed were on the political left and opposed to Grivas' right-wing views. Although his ability to avoid capture by the British and to organise terrorist attacks, gave Grivas legendary status and made EOKA into a feared resistance group, ultimately he failed to achieve his political objective. The EOKA campaign, it can be argued (even recognising the importance of the change of policy heralded by Harold Macmillan's decolonisation 'Wind of Change' speech) brought British colonial rule to an end faster than it might have been without the armed resisitance. Grivas, however, also destroyed any chance of a peaceful democratic transition, involving *enosis*. As the notorious commander of the right-wing Greek terrorist group χ and a failed 'fascist' poltician he never fully gained the trust of Makarios or the Cypriot left. In the short term EOKA attacks on the Turkish Cypriot community not only helped the British to pursue their strategy of 'divide and rule', but also undermined Grivas' main political objective as it forced Turkey, as the protector of the Turkish Cypriots, to engage with Cyprus and be a party to any settlement. In the longer term EOKA's activities against the Turkish Cypriots stimulated a much longer-lasting conflict between the two communities, which ultimately led to the actions of 1974.

In April 1959 the Joint Constitutional Commission started work on drafting a constitution within the framework based on the Zurich and

London agreements: experts from Greece and Turkey were joined by Cypriots Rauf Denktaş, Glafcos Clerides and Michael Triantafyllides. Grivas was now advising Cypriots against ratifying the settlement and in the summer Makarios was under widespread attacks from right-wing organisations for accepting an agreement which rejected *enosis*. There was talk of assassination plots against Makarios and the bishop of Kyrenia claimed that *enosis* would be achieved when Grivas became Prime Minister of Greece. Tension was running high in the Greek Cypriot community and it was only when Makarios and Grivas met secretly at Rhodes that the spectre of civil war receded. Then in October a British naval patrol intercepted a boat gunrunning from Turkey, demonstrating that the TMT was still stockpiling weapons. In response Makarios immediately suspended Greek Cypriot participation in the constitutional talks. By November a new political party, the Democratic Union was established and under the leadership of John Clerides, the father of Glafcos; he opposed Makarios at the presidential elections on 13 December.

Despite the extreme tension across the two communities, the elections for president went ahead with little disturbance. Makarios won two-thirds of the Greek Cypriot vote to become president and Kütchük was unopposed, automatically becoming vice-president. The development of the future government's structure proceeded smoothly and British officials started withdrawing, leaving the adminstration of the island in the hands of Cypriot civil servants. A sticking point in determining the actual date of independence for the island proved to be the negotiations over the British sovereign bases, which were only concluded in July. After much wrangling the Treaty of Establishment was agreed and Britain retained two major sites at Episcopi (Akrotiri) and Dhekelia, covering ninety-nine square miles, and agreed to contribute £12 million in aid, earmarking an additional £1.5 million for the poorer Turkish Cypriot community. The sovereignty of the island was protected under the Treaty of Guarantee, which was binding upon Britain, Greece and Turkey. Greece, Turkey and Cyprus were also party to a formal alliance (Treaty of Alliance), which allowed the Greeks to station 950 troops and the Turks 650 troops on the island.

Despite the temporary suspension of participation by the Greek

The signing of the Independence Treaty in 16 August, 1960. Front row l-r shows Archbishop Makarios, Hugh Foot and Fazil Kücük

Cypriot side the constitution for Cyprus had been successfully drafted. It consisted of 199 articles with six annexes and incorporated the body of the Zurich and London agreements. However, in reality the spirit and tone of the constitution was based more upon the strife and suspicion of the two communities than a future model for a democratic Cyprus. With the benefit of hindsight there is inevitably a view, given the history of discord between the Greek and Turkish Cypriots after independence, that the constitution was always unworkable. Undoubtedly even if it had been workable it was complex, or even complicated, as it strove to protect the minority. The disproportionate representation of the Turkish Cypriots in the army, civil service and police, plus the vice-presidential veto was perceived by many Greek Cypriots as a form of 'positive' discrimination which undermined the democratic wish of the majority. From the Turkish Cypriot point of view there was a mistrust of the dominant majority amongst whom some were still committed to *enosis* and even the 'extermination' of the Turkish Cypriot community.

On 1 August a sophisticated electoral system saw thirty-five Greek and fifteen Turkish Cypriots returned to to the house of representatives. On the Greek side there was an easy win for the Patriotic Front:

the Democratic Union boycotted the election on the basis of what they saw as a flawed system and AKEL did a deal with the Patriotic Front which guaranteed them five seats. In the Turkish Cypriot elections Kütchük's Turkish National Party easily won, virtually unopposed. On 16 August 1960 eighty years of British rule of the island came to an end, the independent Republic of Cyprus was declared and Makarios and Kütchük were invested as president and vice-president.

CHAPTER ELEVEN

Independence – Early Years, 1960–1974

By the end of September Cyprus was welcomed into the United Nations as a full member (ninety-ninth) and in the following March the island joined the British Commonwealth. However, although recongised as a fully-fledged nation by the outside world, internally many of its citizens were far from comfortable with Cyprus' new status. Whatever the veracity of the arguments about the Greek and Turkish communities living together in harmony, the withdrawal of the British removed a buffer that had, to an extent, ameloriated confrontation. The tension that existed between Greece and Turkey related to a long history of occupation, oppressive rule and conflict and, despite evidence of past peaceful co-existence in a rural context between the two communities in Cyprus, the reality was that the political and cultural anatagonism between the two 'mother countries' dominated the attitudes and aspirations of Cypriots. At the same time, because of their obligations as guarantor powers and the fact that both had their troops on the island, Greece and Turkey, uncomfortable NATO allies, used Cyprus as a barometer of their relationship.

Britain, thankful to have shed its responsibilities in managing the two communities, and no doubt inhibited by its former colonial role, quietly disengaged so that it would have been difficult to identify how the previous ruling power perceived her true obligations to the fledgling Republic. The British government's concern had been to maintain its sovereign bases, as not only providing her with influence over supplies of oil from the Middle East, but also, under pressure from the USA, as part of NATO's check on the USSR. At the height of the Cold War, Makarios was quick to see advantage for Cyprus in steering a policy of non-alignment. To the Americans Makarios' courting of the Soviet bloc, made him dangerous and ensured Cyprus held a central position on the geopolitical stage which some have thought was not conducive to the development of an independent Cyprus.

The Economy

In 1960 the economic base of the country was dominated by agricultural activity, accounting for 16 per cent of gross domestic product and 45 per cent of the labour market. Manufacturing was mainly limited to processing local agricultural materials. Exports were either primary commodities, such as minerals or agricultural products. A five-year plan was introduced to strengthen the physical and social infrastructure of the island. The road system was improved and nearly all communities were connected to piped water. There was an impressive increase in the number of villages that were supplied with electricity and similarly there was a big expansion of telephone services. Concerns about the uncertain political situation undermined the financial stability of the new Republic and there was an initial flight of capital and considerable emigration, mainly to the UK. There were also problems in collecting direct taxes and the tendency of the government was to rely more upon indirect taxation. Despite some of these difficulties, a steady upgrading of the infrastructure was achieved with an average of about 7 per cent growth in the early years.

The Faltering Constitution

In contradiction to any sense of accepting the new constitution the Greek nationalists had not abandoned their desire for *enosis*. Certainly some of the speeches and statements made by Makarios at the time of independence indicated that he perceived independence as just a stage in achieving the ultimate goal of *enosis*. On the other side the Turkish Cypriot community was now, following EOKA's campaign against British rule, more conscious both of its Turkishness and its dependence upon the policies and attitudes of the Turkish government in Ankara. If Turkey believed that ultimately partition was in its best interests, this was reflected in the stance of the Turkish Cypriots. Many Greek Cypriots were convinced that the Turkish side just wished to demonstrate that the constitution was unworkable and that, therefore, the only way of insuring the security of the Turkish Cypriot community was partition.

In a similar way that the collapse of communism left a vacuum, whereby many former communist countries lacked an experienced political cadre that could run a civil state, the decolonisation of Cyprus failed to devolve executive power to a politically mature group of leaders. Although Cyprus had an experienced civil service (mainly Greek Cypriots) there was a lack of seasoned politicians, who had been schooled in a democratic culture. Such a void is often an opportunity and encouragement to the fanatics and ultra nationalists who manipulate ethnic tensions for their own political and financial gain. Although it would be imprecise to compare the situation in Cyprus to the fall of Yugoslavia, there were those in both the Greek and Turkish Cypriot communities, who had no desire to see an independent Cyprus prosper and who deliberately stoked the fires of ethnic hatred for their own purposes in the same way that some nationalist war lords tore up Yugoslavia. Grivas, now strongly opposed Makarios and worked hard to overthrow the republic.

The constitution itself soon became the battleground between the two communities, as each side deliberately manoeuvred around its provisions to gain advantage. The resentment among the Greek Cypriots at the disporportionate role (30 per cent) of the Turkish Cypriots in the civil service resulted in appointments of Turkish Cypriots being delayed or blocked. The question of the composition of the army became contentious with the Greek Cypriots wanting mixed platoons and the Turkish Cypriots arguing for separate ethnic units. In October in order to avoid integration Kütchük used his personal veto as vice-president and no further attempts were made to build a national army. On 18 December 1961 the Turkish Cypriots, after a series of machinations, vetoed a unified tax bill. The evidence suggests that the Turkish Cypriots were exercising their constitutional right as a lever to put pressure on the Greek Cypriots over another looming crisis relating to the five municipalties. Makarios denounced the 'irresponsibility' of the Turkish Cypriots and threatened to disregard the constitution if it threatened the functioning of the state. With neither side budging no unified tax system could be introduced which, it has been argued, created a substantial impediment to the development of the republic's economy.

Since 1958 there had in reality been separate Greek and Turkish Cypriot municipal governments operating in the five major towns and the Zurich Agreement had made provision for them to become legitimised. Although there is evidence the Greek Cypriots had at first welcomed the separation of local government as this reduced their commitment to support the poorer Turkish Cypriot communities, the Greek Cypriots now saw them as a first step to partition. Even by December 1962 the Municipal Commission had not been able to agree on the appropriate boundaries and so in January of the following year the Greek Cypriots abolished the municipalities and established 'Development Boards' to run the local governments. The Turkish Cypriots countered by establishing their own municipalities. On appeal to the Constitutional Court both sets of actions were ruled illegal. The independent German president of the Constitutional Court, Dr Ernst Forsthoff, and his assistant came under attack with both of them eventually resigning in the in the following year.

From the majority Greek Cypriot point of view it seemed that government had broken down and the constitution had proved unworkable and on 30 November 1963 Makarios put forward thirteen amendments to the constitution. He proposed that the right of veto held by both the president and vice-president should be abolished and that both posts should be elected by the House of Representatives. The latter proposal would have given the Greek Cypriot a majority in the House and a strong voice in the election of the Turkish Cypriot vice-president. He also proposed the abolition of separate majority voting, the separate municipalities and separate justice systems. Many of the other amendments related to the ratio of Greek and Turkish Cypriots in public posts and aimed to bring the proportions in line with the size of the populations. It appears from a later leaked document known as the *Akritas* plan that Makarios aimed to amend the constitution, abrogate the international agreements, advocate the case for self-determination and finally win *enosis* through a plebiscite. Along with the other guarantor powers Turkey was given a copy of the amendments 'for information', but Ankara immediately rejected them, insisting that the constitution was unalterable.

INTER-COMMUNAL VIOLENCE 1963–4

Both sides, as a contingency, had been building up arms supplies and training irregular forces since the Zurich and London Agreements. The impasse posed by Turkey's rejection of the thirteen Amendments was the trigger for violence. On the night of 21 December a series of incidents – who started them is, of course, disputed – led the following day to an all-out assault by the Greek Cypriots on Turkish Cypriots in Nicosia. Hostages were taken and atrocities committed by both sides. It appears that Polycarpos Georghadjis, a former EOKA commander and now Minister for the Interior, co-ordinated previously prepared Greek Cypriot action plans. It was recognised in the *Akritas* document that Makarios' proposed amendments were likely to incite the Turkish Cypriots to stage 'incidents' and that the Greek Cypriots 'counter-attack' should be immediate and decisive. On 23 December, meeting at the Paphos Gate police station, Makarios and Kütchük, came to an agreement and appealed for an end to the fighting. However, more 'incidents' followed and the fighting extended to Larnaca and other areas on the island. Under pressure from the US ambassador and the British deputy high commissioner on 24 December another attempt at a ceasefire was made but soon failed.

On Christmas Day Turkish Supersabre jet planes over-flew Nicosia and the Turkish army contingent, which under the Treaty of Alliance was stationed just north of Nicosia, without consulting with the other guarantor powers, as it was required to do, marched out from barracks and seized control of the Nicosia to Kyrenia road. The Greek force did not move to counter the Turks, but had it done so mostly likely war between Greece and Turkey would have ensued. On 26 December, probably because of the Greek Cypriots fear of a Turkish invasion, the British were able to broker another ceasefire. A British force, under the command of Major-General Peter Young, established a buffer line (the so-called 'Green Line') in Nicosia and Larnaca between the two communities, and took over the main strategic positions held by Greek and Turkish Cypriot forces. At the same time the British Secretary for Commonwealth Relations, Duncan Sandys, flew to the island and managed to negotiate the release of hostages held by each side.

On 1 January 1964 Makarios announced that he had would unilaterally withdraw from the treaties of Alliance and Guarantee. However, Sandys averted another crisis by persuading all sides to attend a conference in London on 15 January. The Greek Cypriots, backed by Greece, demanded a form of 'full independence' that overthrew the 'unworkable' constitution; Turkey and the Turkish Cypriots would agree to nothing less than some form of partition. So the talks stalled. Meanwhile, although the British forces had stopped major violence, both communities accused the British army of bias against them, and used the lull in fighting to re-group and re-arm. For all intents and purposes there were now two separate administrations: the Greek Cypriots controlled most of the island and the Turkish Cypriots had retired to heavily fortified enclaves. Both sides would claim either the constitution was still 'alive' or 'dead' to suit their political purpose of the moment.

UNITED NATIONS FORCE IN CYPRUS (UNFICYP)

In February violence flared up again with an all out attack on the Turkish Cypriot positions in the port area of Limassol. The British government felt they could no longer bear the brunt of the peacekeeping on their own and through the US sought some sort some form of NATO intervention (the so-called Sandys-Ball Plan). This solution was rejected by Makarios, who to preserve his non-aligned position, preferred the UN to be the peacekeepers. In the end the British themselves, exasperated by a situation that was rapidly getting out of hand, took the Cyprus 'problem' to the Security Council of the UN on 15 February. In a unanimous decision by the Security Council the United Nations Force in Cyprus (UNFICYP) was established. The logistical support and largest contingent was to be the British. However, the force would not come into being until the end of March and soon fighting flared up again as each side manoeuvred for advantage. Such was the pressure on the outnumbered Turkish Cypriots that

Turkey threatened to intervene unless hostilities ceased. By the middle of March Greece and the Soviet Union were offering support to the Greek Cypriots and Nikita Krushchev warned the Turkish President, Ismet İnönü, of the dangers of a third world war. With persuasion and financial support from the US and Britain Turkey held back from invading Cyprus, but those Greeks still living in Turkey, in Istanbul, were put under further harassment and expulsion.

On 25 March Sakari Tuomioja, a former Finnish minister, was appointed UN Mediator to Cyprus, but even his arrival on the island was greeted with little enthusiasm. In reality also the stationing of UN troops (with contingents from Canada, Denmark, Finland, Ireland, Sweden and Britain, under an Indian commander) did little to help the situation, as their numbers were small and their powers were limited. Makarios was determined to abrogate the Treaty of Alliance and the Turkish Army still failed to move its contingent back from the Nicosia-Kyrenia road. 'Incidents' continued and in April Georghadjis led attacks on the Turkish Cypriot positions around the castle of St Hilarion. Although U Thant, the Secretary-General, condemned the attack the UN took no action. By the end of May the Turkish government was once more threatening invasion, claiming that the Greek Cypriot side was carrying out a programme of genocide. As Turkish preparations proceeded, the US determined to take action as it could neither afford a conflict between NATO allies nor to see Cyprus become another potential Cuba.

Grivas returns to Cyprus

To head off the crisis President Lyndon Johnson invited İnönü and the Greek Prime Minister, George Papandreou, to Washington for talks, meanwhile he sent Ankara a strongly worded 'secret letter' warning Turkey off any attempt at an invasion of Cyprus. However, Makarios' flirtations with the USSR, his friendship with Colonel Nasser of Egypt, as well as the extreme activities of Georghadjis, the attack on St Hilarion and the disappearence of Major Edward Macey, the British liaison officer to Kütchük, all appear to have helped convince the US that it now needed Greece's support to bring stability to the island.

Grivas was allowed to return to Cyprus (later taking over command of the National Guard) and a large number of Greek reinforcements, both in men and weapons were sent to the island. Nevertheless, Grivas, although he was opposed to Makarios and a useful counter-weight to Georghadjis, was still aiming for *enosis* through the use of violence.

In an attempt to break the impasse Dean Acheson, a former US Secretary of State, through the auspices of the UN mediator proposed that Cyprus should be united with Greece, but Turkey would have a military base, receive the island of Castellorizon from Greece, and two cantons would be set up for the Turkish Cypriots — those that did not want to stay would be compensated. Makarios feared that the *Acheson Plan* would result in *de facto* partition and immediately rejected the proposal. Turkey did not reject the proposal out of hand but wanted to negotiate for a larger Turkish area on the island. Greece in the end decided to support Makarios and also rejected the plan.

At the beginning of August Grivas launched a major offensive in the Mansoura area of the island; the aim was to cut off the arms supply to the Turkish Cypriots being brought into the port of Kokkina from Turkey. When it looked as if the Greek Cypriots would achieve their objectives Turkish jet fighters began straffing and napalming Greek villages. Eventually, following the intervention of the UN security council, a ceasefire was achieved on 10 August. However, prospects for a longer lasting settlement were undermined by the illness and death of Tuomioja who was replaced by Galo Plaza Lasso, an ex-President of Ecuador. He was not trusted by the Turkish Cypriots who were convinced that as a Roman Catholic he would be biased in favour of the Orthodox Greek Cypriots. Although the parties met again to discuss a revised version of the *Acheson Plan*, it was soon rejected and the two communities were once more in a state of stalemate.

NON-ALIGNED CYPRUS

In September Makarios concluded a secret pact with the USSR which was in essence a trade agreement and a means of safeguarding the Greek Cypriot arms supply. This created some division amongst the Greek Cypriots and alarmed Greece, which perceived a change in attitude towards the 'homeland'. Makarios reinforced Cyprus' credentials as an independent state when he spoke forcefully at the Cairo Conference for non-aligned countries, demanding 'unrestricted' and 'unfettered' sovereignty for the Cypriot people to determine their own future without interference from outside. On his way home President Tito of Yugoslavia visited Cyprus and was given a rapturous welcome. This resulted in a flurry of diplomatic activity from Turkey eager to counter Makarios growing prestige among the 'developing nations'.

THE GALO PLAZA REPORT

At the end of 1964 in his report to the security council U Thant was able to refer to a lessening of the violence but in fact the island had become divided. Although the Greek Cypriots had put immense pressure on the Turkish Cypriots, the latter had established enclaves that remained outside Cypriot government jurisdiction. The UN now took the initiative and Galo Plaza Lasso in March 1965 summitted a report based on three rounds of talks with all parties. The Galo Plaza report excluded both *enosis* and partition as a solution. He was opposed to separation of the two communities. His plan rather looked to safeguards for the Turkish Cypriots under the supervision of a UN commissioner based in Cyprus. Ankara reacted angrily to the report and refused to accept Galo Plaza anymore as a mediator. Makarios countered by stating he would not accept anyone else.

The Galo Plaza report was 'noted' – seen by some to equal approval – by the political committee of the general assembly and on 18 December Makarios, through the support of the Greek government, secured a UN resolution that Cyprus should be accorded full sovereignty and independence without any foreign interference or intervention. This was a major success for Makarios' diplomatic efforts among the non-aligned countries. In Turkey the resolution was seen as a serious setback. Only the day before the vote Ankara had confirmed their total rejection of Galo Plaza's report. As a result the pressure on Galo Plaza became unacceptable and on 22 December 1965 he resigned.

The general wish of the UN was now to quickly forge a settlement but Makarios blocked the appointment of another mediator. Although the UN Secretary-General, U Thant, was able to promote talks between Greece and Turkey, no progress was made in bringing the two communities together. Blockades – some permanent, some temporary, but all, denying 'strategic' materials to the Turkish Cypriot enclaves continued. Overall, apart from the odd incident, there was an uneasy peace on the island. Somewhat paradoxically after the success at the UN in the previous year the Greek Cypriots internationally lost ground as more countries came out against any form of *enosis*.

Makarios, concerned about the influence from Athens, determined to build up the police force in opposition to the Greek National Guard. Clerides ordered large numbers of weapons from Czechoslovakia. The threat from Greece receded momentarily as the Greek government of George Papandreou was in disarray and it seemed from the contents of a secret letter that Grivas was implicated in a plot to overthrow Makarios. Early in 1967 the import of the Czech arms increased tension. Although the first shipment of small arms arrived, Turkey was not only able to block the delivery of the heavier weapons, but also threatened to arm the·Turkish Cypriots with a similar quantity of arms. Makarios agreed for the weapons to remain stored in a warehouse, subject to inspection by a UNFICYP officer.

The Greek Colonels

On 27 April Papandreou's government was overthrown by a coup of Greek Colonels, led by George Papadopulos. Because of the large numbers of Greek troops on the island the future of Cyprus was now bound into the political climate of Greece. The Greek Colonels were essentially concerned with two major issues: the first was keeping the political left in check and the second, which was inextricably connected, was Greece's relationship with the USA. Given the pressures now being exerted upon Cyprus, it was perhaps inevitable that Makarios took a softer line on NATO and, therefore, lost some of the influence he previously had with the non-aligned countries. The situation for Makarios was complicated by the outbreak of the Six-Day War on 5 June between Israel and several Arab states. Makarios expressed his support for the Arabs, particularly Egypt, a country that had helped him in the past. At the same time he did not want to alienate Israel.

In August Papdopoulos visited Cyprus and in early September talks were held between Greece and Turkey. The Colonels, on the basis that both governments were unitied in their drive against the communists, hoped to strike some deal with Turkey over Cyprus that would lead to *enosis*. However, the talks ended in failure as the Turks were in no mood to compromise on *enosis*. Meanwhile both communities in Cyprus were reinforcing their positions and incidents involving shootings and bombings continued. In October Rauf Denktaş, who had been 'exiled' for his part in the disturbances of 1963, illegally entered the island but was caught by the Greek Cypriot authorities. After imprisonment, interrogation and much agitation from both communities he was quietly returned to Turkey with his agreement that he would not attempt to return to Cyprus.

THE REMOVAL OF GRIVAS

However, just as that potential flashpoint was defused, Grivas, on 15 November, launched an attack on the Turkish Cypriots in the village of Kophinou in the Larnaca area. An all out assault resulted in twenty-four Turkish and two Greek Cypriot dead. The Turkish government immediately threatened to bomb the Greek Cypriots if the attack did not stop. Under pressure from Greece Grivas agreed to a ceasefire, but against the advice of UNFICYP, he sent armed patrols into the neighbouring village of Aghios Theodoros. The reporting of the attack and the lurid pictures in the press resulted in a strong response from Ankara. On the evening of 17th an ultimatum was delivered to Greece. There were five demands: the removal of Grivas from Cyprus; all Greek troops to leave the island; an indemnity to the Turk Cypriot families who had lost members in the attack; a cessation of the intimidation of the Turkish Cypriot community; and the disarming of the Greek Cypriot paramilitaries. The Turkish army was mobilised on the border with Greece and an invasion force against Cyprus was prepared. The Colonels in Athens knew that Greece was no match for the massive Turkish army and Grivas was immediately flown out of the island to Athens where he resigned his command of the national guard.

The removal of Grivas was not enough to placate the Turkish government and the Turkish president, Sunay, was informing Western countries that Turkey was determined to settle the Cyprus issue 'once and for all'. Apparently bad storms in the Eastern Mediterranean delayed the invasion and this gave the US time to intervene. President Johnson's special envoy Cyrus Vance, supported by the Canadian Prime Minister, Lester Pearson, the NATO Secretary-General, Manlio Brosio and the UN representative Rolz-Bennett, did the rounds of 'shuttle diplomacy'. Their task was not easy as Turkey had before them the example of the Six Day War where Israel had made a pre-emptive strike and was holding on to captured territory despite general world disapproval. The US was able to bring considerable pressure on the colonels which guaranteed that Greece reacted with restraint. The Greek forces on Cyprus were reduced to those allowed by the Treaty of Guarantee and her forces on the border with Turkey were stood down.

At the beginning of December Makarios, recognising that the immediate danger of an invasion had passed, began to threaten the Vance deal by delaying the disbandment of the national guard, on the grounds that the Cyprus government needed a guarantee there would be no Turkish invasion. Vance managed to get the process back on the rails and in the first week of December Makarios visited the departing Greek troops as they were shipped back home. By the beginning of the next year over seven thousand Greek soldiers had departed. Many of the officers stayed on to train the Greek Cypriots, but the Turks did not complain as their own officers were likewise training the Turkish Cypriots.

U THANT

On 13 December King Constantine of Greece tried to overthrow the Colonels, but he received little support and when his attempt failed he and his family fled into exile. However, this unsettled the junta further and this was reflected in their attitutude towards Cyprus. At this point U Thant, in an attempt to establish a longer term solution, proposed that the UN's role on the island be enhanced to include disarming the paramilitaries and taking on additional security responsibilites. However, not only were the Greek Cypriots against an increase in UNFICYP powers, which was perceived as a threat to Cypriot sovereignty, and both the USSR and France, in support of the Greek Cypriots, blocked the proposal in the security council on 22 December. Just a week later a new crisis emerged, when the Turkish Cypriots on the arrival of Zeki Kuneralp, from the Turkish foreign ministry, announced the establishment of a separate provisional Cyprus Turkish administration. U Thant was opposed to this development, expressing his misgivings, and Kuneralp was expelled by the Cypriot authorities.

Makarios, somewhat ironically, through Grivas' attack on Kophinou had been freed from Greek control and on 12 January announced that he intended to hold presidential elections to confirm the electorate's confidence in his government. By over playing their hand those determined on *enosis* had created a reaction in Turkey which demonstrated an 'independent Cyprus' was at that moment the only way forward. Many Greek Cypriots seemed in a state of shock and even the EOKA campaign was criticised as a block to *enosis* – something unheard of since independence in 1960. Makarios' position and his 'independent Cyprus' policy was vindicated when on 25 February 1968 he won 95 per cent of the poll. His opponent Takis Evdokas had espoused *enosis*, in contrast to Makarios' independence policy, but was completely trounced. Ten days earlier Kütchük had been returned unopposed by the Turkish Cypriots as vice-president.

In early March Makarios withdrew most of the restrictions, including the roadblocks, on the Turkish Cypriots. U Thant actively proselytized fraternisation between the two communities and criticised the Turkish Cypriots for still refusing to allow Greek Cypriots into their enclaves. Although there were several incidents and the EOKA day in April, when new Czech weapons were paraded, was not helpful, tension between the two communities was gradually being eased. In June when Clerides and Denktaş, who had been allowed to return to Cyprus, met in Beirut and inter-communal talks were resumed.

ALEXANDROS PANAGHOULLIS

The Cyprus government's relationship with the Greek junta completely deteriorated after Makarios turned away from supporting *enosis*. On 13 August 1968 a failed attempt was made on the life of Papadopoulos, the leader of the Colonels. The assassin Alexandros Panaghoullis was said to have been a Greek army deserter who had been harboured in Cyprus. It was claimed he had links to the Cyprus government and specifically to Georghadjis, the Minister of the Interior and Defence, who subsequently resigned. It seems Georghadjis fell out with Makarios as he was disappointed the archbishop had not stood by him during the crisis. Georghadjis was a significant loss as he had always provided Makarios with vital information about the right wing activities in the island since as a former EOKA commander he had many extremist contacts.

THE NATIONAL FRONT

In March 1969 the extreme right among the Greek Cypriots, no doubt supported by the Greek colonels, formed a new terrorist organisation, the National Front, based at Limassol, which had always been an EOKA stronghold. Their main objectives were destruction of the communists and *enosis*, and their prime targets were left wing trade unionists, the police and Makarios loyalists. According to Glafcos Clerides, writing later, Christakis Tryfonides, an ex-EOKA commander was the leader. The Cypriot government was slow to move against the National Front, leading to the accusation that Makarios found it useful to use this extremist organisation as a counterweight to his more moderate political opposition. This view is born out by Clerides, who states that Makarios had a secret meeting with Tryfonides. It was not until August 1969 that the National Front was finally outlawed as an organisation.

There was growing frustration both in the USA and Greece that the inter-communal talks seemed to be making little progress. Makarios was seen as the main obstacle as he resisted any form of federalism which hinted at separatism. Back in the mid-1960s a Turkish proposal, known as the *Attila Plan*, had prepared a scheme for the division of the island. It is claimed that such a plan was supported by NATO and the colonels and Turkey would now have been amenable to what was labelled 'double *enosis*' – i.e. partition of the island between Greece and Turkey. In January 1970 Makarios visited Athens but clearly in the junta's eyes he remained infuriatingly obstinate and they blamed him for the lack of progress in the inter-communal talks. No doubt to head off any moves towards partition, and appropriately briefed by Makarios,

the Cypriot communist party AKEL contacted the Soviet Union and
through Tass (the official Soviet Agency) accused the West of plotting
against the independence of Cyprus with the purpose of establishing a
NATO base.

POLYCARPOS GEORGHADJIS

On 8 March when Makarios was flying by helicopter to Makheras
monastery for a memorial service for the EOKA leader Afxentiou,
gunmen opened up just as he had taken off. Despite being seriously
wounded the pilot managed to land and Makarios escaped unhurt.
Although Makarios denied it at the time the national guard, presumably
with encouragement from Athens, were involved. It was believed that
Polycarpos Georghadjis was the main conspirator behind the plot and his
arrest was ordered. Georghadjis was stopped from leaving the country as
he boarded a plane for Beirut. However, he was not held in custody and
on Sunday 15 March whilst on his way to a secret meeting Georghadjis
was shot dead, and even to this day no one is certain as to who committed
the murder. In the end four men were convicted for the assassination plot
against Makarios, but it is interesting and perhaps significant that
Georghadjis' widow was not allowed to call witnesses she said would
clear her husband's name. Parts of the media were to claim that
Georghadjis had been killed to silence him because he knew too much
and inevitably Makarios himself was named as being behind his death.

Turkey was rattled by the assassination attempt against Makarios,
suspecting a Greek plot, and sternly warned any attempt to overthrow
the Cyprus government through a coup would be totally resisted by the
Turkish army. Western diplomates went into top gear to reassure
Turkey, fearing a repeat of the 1967 situation. The colonels blamed the
USSR for heightening tension in order to disrupt NATO. On the
island nervousness increased when on 23 May the National Front
seized Limassol Central Police Station, escaping with a huge supply of
arms and ammunition.

1970 PARLIAMENTARY ELECTIONS

Probably as a means of refocussing attention on the constitutional issues
Makarios called parliamentary elections – these were long overdue, and

should have been held five years earlier, but because of the inter-communal problems had been postponed. The real winner of the Greek Cypriot election was the communist AKEL but because of the electoral system the Unified Party, which supported Makarios, ended up with most seats (fifteen). The *enosis* party, DEK, lead by Takis Evdokas did not win a single seat, but the Progressive Party, which was right wing and was led by Nikos Sampson, a former EOKA member, although only winning 17 per cent of the vote, gained seven seats out of the thirty-five.

The relationship between Makarios and Papadopoulos could only now worsen as the junta's aspirations were frustrated and the arch-bishop flirted with the Eastern bloc. The US' and the colonels' concerns over Makarios' anti-NATO policy were aggravated when he made a state visit to the USSR in June 1971. It had probably already been decided to let Grivas return to Cyprus and by the beginning of September, reportedly disguised as a priest, he was back in Limassol. He now formed a new underground movement, EOKA B, with a political wing, ESEA (Co-ordination Committee for the Struggle for *Enosis*) which was launched at the beginning of 1972. Their aim was quite simple and simplistic: the overthrow of Makarios and union with the motherland, Greece. The fact that the political climate had changed considerably since the days when Grivas and EOKA were fighting the British did not appear to have dawned upon him. Even if they were successful in removing Makarios, it was naïve and dangerous in the extreme to think that Turkey would now just stand back and let *enosis* take place.

ARMS FROM CZECHOSLOVAKIA

In January 1972 a Cypriot newspaper revealed that the government had once again been importing arms from Czechoslovakia. It seemed Makarios and his supporters were now intent on forming a militia to help counter-balance the growing firepower of the right wing. It has been stated that the level of weaponry was far in excess of that needed for managing inter-communal violence which perhaps suggests Makarios was preparing for civil insurrection. The Greek junta fretful about Makarios' relationship with the Eastern bloc, feared that the weapons could fall into communist hands. The colonels were also anxious that existing Greco-Turkish relations (where a broad agreement, in relation to 'double *enosis*', on Cyprus' future seemed to have been reached) should not be damaged, demanded that the weapons be handed over to the national guard. Makarios, not unsurprisingly, refused as the national guard was controlled by Greek officers and they were the last people he wished to have possession of the weapons. On 11 February the Greek ambassador, Constantine Panayiotakos, shifted position and wrote a 'stiff note' to the president, calling on Makarios now to place the weapons under UNFICYP supervision, and form a government of national unity. In order to defuse the situation Makarios did agree to place the weapons in a UNFICYP camp, but only after protracted negotiations. Later in the year he also reshuffled his cabinet, giving ministries to those who were less hostile to the Greek junta. The situation remained tense and Makarios was concerned that the colonels would mount a coup. According to Clerides' account, Makarios believed the junta planned something for 15 February. He not only sought help from the USA to put pressure on the Greek regime, but he staged a massive rally in Nicosia in support of himself and his government.

1972 CHURCH SYNOD

Grivas had once more become an embarrassment to the Greek government, as it was clear his provocative activities were undermining their rapprochment with Turkey. Grivas now allied himself with three right wing Greek Cypriot bishops from Kition, Kyrenia and Paphos. They were all staunchly in favour of *enosis* and believed Makarios had betrayed the cause through his 'independence' policy. As members of the holy synod of the autocephalous Orthodox Church of Cyprus they now claimed that under Canon Law it was illegitimate for Makarios to hold both the office of archbishop and president as the political position clashed with his religious duites. The weakness of their argument is clear in that Makarios had already held both offices for twelve years and this was the first time anyone had claimed it was a violation of religious law. On 2 March a Church synod was held where the three bishops demanded Makarios' resignation. He was apparently furious but kept his 'powder dry' and informed them he would respond later. When it was clear the bishops lacked any real support amongst the majority of the clerics, Makarios wrote a letter on 19 March, which in measured terms, spelt out why it was essential for the 'struggle of Cypriot Hellenism' and the 'survival of the Orthodox faith' that he be both president and archbishop.

Sensing there was an opportunity to draw Grivas further away from the Greek Colonels and to neutralise the right wing Makarios sought to find some common ground between himself and Grivas. On 26 March Makarios met with Grivas but the latter was adamantine in his position on *enosis* and the subsequent correspondence between the two reveals that there was no hope of rapprochment. In practical terms it meant that Grivas and his supporters, found themselves in concert with the Greek junta with one objective, the overthrow of Makarios and his government.

Meanwhile the UN was looking to revitalise the inter-communal talks. On the suggestion of the Greek Foreign Minister, Xanthopoulos Palamas, the new Secretary-General, Kurt Waldheim, on 8 June in Nicosia, restarted the talks with a broadened membership. Both Greece and Turkey were invited to send legal representatives to join Clerides and Denktaş. Clerides has subsequently claimed that when the talks ended for the year on 8 December there had been a real chance of agreement but that Makarios had refused to make any concessions on the issue of independent local government for the Turkish Cypriots. In retrospect it seems an opportunity for bringing the two communities together may have been lost.

1973 presidential elections

In January 1973 Makarios called a presidential election as his term of office was due to come to an end. In February he was returned unopposed. At the same time the Turkish Cypriots held a vice-presidential election and Rauf Denktaş was re-elected. After Makarios' election the three bishops who had argued that his holding of the presidential office was incompatible with his role as archbishop renewed their attack. They demanded that Makarios call a synod to consider his position. He refused so they held their own synod in Limassol which when he refused to appear, tried him in his absence, and declared him defrocked. Makarios ignored them and then in July 1973 called his own synod, which was altogether a much larger affair. His synod found the three bishops guilty of attempting to go beyond their powers and declared them defrocked. What might be viewed from afar as a farce in reality created further serious divisions among the Greek Cypriots.

Grivas and EOKA B now increased their campaign of violence with attacks on the police, the seizure of weapons and bomb attacks. In April a socialist politician was murdered and then one of Grivas' own men was killed by Makarios' supporters. In July Grivas kidnapped the Minister of Justice, Christos Vakis, (a plan to abduct George Ioannides, the Minister of the Interior, was also uncovered) demanding the release of all political prisoners in exchange for his freedom. During this period at least two assassination attempts were made on Makarios, but were either foiled in time, or failed.

The Overthrow of Papadopoulos

On 17 November 1973 the students of the Polytechnic in Athens rioted, demanding a return to democracy in Greece. The students were crushed with tanks, but Papadopoulos and his crew did not survive. On 25 November a new government was formed controlled by a another military strongman, Brigidier Demetrios Ioannides, who was even more right wing than the previous regimé. The seizure of power by Ionnides was, it turned out, to have dire consequences for Cyprus.

The Death of Grivas

In January 1974 both Glafcos Clerides, president of the house of representatives and Tassos Papadopoulos, a leading member of the government and future president, publicly criticised Grivas. Clerides was seen as a 'traitor' by Grivas because of his negotiations with Denktaş. Clerides, however, threatened to introduce a motion in the house which would have labelled Grivas as a murderer, but there was a reluctance within the government to initate any procedure which might have made Grivas appear a martyr amongst his supporters. The crisis was defused on 27 January when Grivas at the age of seventy-five died through a heart attack. Makarios immediately seized the opportunity to try to heal wounds by declaring three days of official mourning and a general amnesty for those members of EOKA B who were serving prison sentences. In a gesture of true irony Clerides praised the work of Grivas in a special meeting of the House of Representatives (only those members of AKEL showed any concern about Grivas' real place in Cypriot history by abstaining from an eulogistic resolution). Grivas, despite his widow's wish that he be buried in Athens, was given a state funeral in Limassol with the service being conducted by the three 'defrocked' bishops.

Although there were those in EOKA B who wished to respond to Makarios' call for an amnesty, the movement became split and the extremists refused to be reined in. Only a few days after Grivas' death Kikis Constantinou, the Famagusta area commander of EOKA B organised a raid on the national guard barracks and carried off large quantities of arms and ammunition. Two hardliners, Lefteris Papadopoulos and Nikos Sampson now emerged as the leading figues of EOKA B. They were in close touch with Brigadier Ioannides and made frequent visits to Athens. After two raids on villages in April when the inhabitants were injured and a priest beaten up Makarios revoked the amnesty and on 25 April EOKA B was declared an illegal organisation. At the end of the month Makarios protested to the Greek ambassador about Athens' support for EOKA B and its campaign of violence.

INTER-COMMUNAL TALKS OF 1974

In June the inter-communal talks resumed. This was after a delay during which time a new government in Turkey had been elected, under the leadership of Bülent Ecevit, of the Socialist Party and following a protest from the Greek Cypriots who felt that the introduction by the Turkish Cypriot side of the term 'federal state' undermined the negotiations. The UN Secretary-General, however, was able to broker a compromise over the terms which would be used and once more the two side attempted to pursue a settlement.

On 19 June a massive rally was held in Nicosia and addressed by Makarios who condemned the violence blaming Grivas for his legacy of death and discord. Then on 2 July Makarios sent a letter to Phaedon Gizikis, the president of Greece, complaining about the support for EOKA B and accusing the junta of political murders and plotting against him and his government. He declared that the national guard had become an organisation that conspired against the state. He now requested the replacement of the Greek officers by instructors who could train and reorganise the Cypriot forces. To insure his letter was not ignored he informed local journalists of the nature of the relations with Greece and advised them that his letter to the Greek president would soon be published.

1974 Coup

Ioannides and his closest military officers responded by ordering the Greek commanders in Cyprus to carry out a coup against Makarios. It is interesting that both the USSR and USA gave warnings of a possible coup, but perhaps because the threat had been there for so long Makarios and his government seemed strangely inert, some have said 'complacent', to the danger. Just after 8.am on 15 July 1974 tanks of the national guard led by Greek officers under the command of Michales Georghitsis, surrounded the presidential palace, attacked the archiepiscopal palace and seized the Nicosia broadcasting station. There was heavy fighting but the national guard overcame the presidential guard. Makarios, who had been meeting some Greek schoolchildren from Cairo, was able to escape through the rear of the presidential palace.

The Nicosia radio broadcast immediately that Makarios was dead and that Nikos Sampson was now president. Sampson was an ex-journalist who had been an EOKA member. He was twice sentenced to death by the British in 1957, but had been released from gaol in the UK when a general amnesty came in with the independence negotiations. He then published a couple of newspapers in Cyprus which were fanatically anti-communist and pro *enosis*. He had been a close supporter of Grivas and emerged as a leading member of EOKA B. He soon instituted a purge of Makarios supporters and many left-wing opponents were arrested, tortured and executed. It is believed over five hundred people lost their lives during the short rule of the coup.

Meanwhile, Makarios was able to escape to the village of Palechori. From there he went to Kykko Monastery where it was thought he should travel to Paphos and seek help from the British. He was flown by helicopter to the British base at Akrotiri and put on a plane, which after stopping at Malta arrived in Britain on 17 July. Makarios was taken straight to Downing Street, and Harold Wilson, the Labour Prime Minister, records in his autobiography how he sent out someone to an Orthodox church to get Makarios a clean cassock. Makarios hoped that the British, as a guarantor power under the Treaty of Independence, would take action against Sampson and remove the coup. Wilson and James Callaghan, the Foreign Secretary at the time, assured Makarios that Britain would only recognise him as the lawful president of Cyprus, and advised him to plead his case straightaway at the UN in New York. Makarios flew to the US and on 19 July he addressed the security council, accusing the Greek junta of organising the coup against him.

On news of the coup the Turkish government immediately put their military forces on alert. Sampson had a reputation of violence against Turkish Cypriots, especially at Omorphita in 1963, so not only was there a concern the coup would declare *enosis* but there was also fear for the safety of the Turkish Cypriot community. On 17 July, in the wake of Makarios, the Turkish Prime Minister Bülent Ecevit flew to London to talk to the British government. That evening in Downing Street he met with both Wilson and Callaghan. Ecevit proposed that Britain as a co-guarantor of the 1960 constitution should take joint action with Turkey and intervene to remove Sampson and other members of the coup; or, if Britain was unprepared to take military action to allow the Turkish army use of the British bases on Cyprus. Harold Wilson refused both requests arguing that all the guarantors, including Greece, should try to negotiate a diplomatic solution. However, it was not the intention of the Turkish government at any time to negotiate with the Greeks and at the same time the Greek junta also refused to meet with the Turks.

On 18 July Joseph Sisco, deputy at the US state department, met

Ecevit at the Turkish embassy in London. From the US point of view the greatest danger might have been a conflict between Greece and Turkey, two NATO allies. The US, however, failed to condemn the coup and on the same day that Sisco was talking to the Turkish Prime Minister, the US ambassador in Cyprus, Rodger Davies, actually met with a member of Sampson's regime. There is a view that because of its concerns about Makarios and his flirtations with the Soviet bloc that the US, if it did not encourage, was not adverse to the change to a right-wing, more NATO friendly, government in Cyprus. An even more extreme view actually sees the hand of the US central intelligence agency and the US Secretary of State, Henry Kissinger, not only in collusion with the Greek junta, deliberately encouraging the Sampson coup, but also tacitly allowing the subsequent Turkish response. Either way for the US a solution to Cyprus issue was certain. This time, unlike 1964 and 1967, there was no threat from the US President, Richard Nixon, to deter any Turkish action – although it is true that the US Sixth Fleet did sail towards Cyprus. Had Kissinger given the Turks a green light to partition the island? Kissinger himself was to refer to the uncertainty of American politics at the time, creating hesitancy within the US Government: Nixon was just about to be forced from office because of the Watergate affair. However, was this as some see it a convenient excuse for sitting on hands?

Turkish invasion/intervention

On 19 July Ecevit telephoned his commander-in-chief from London giving him the authorisation for an 'invasion' of Cyprus. There is sensitivity about using the word 'invasion': the official Turkish position was that their forces 'intervened', a legal right under the 1960 Constitution, to remove an illegal regime. However, the subsequent failure of the Turkish army to withdraw from the north of Cyprus after nearly thirty years shows the legalistic position of Turkey to be a sham. Their 'intervention' was in reality an invasion, not linked to the restoration of the 1960 constitution, but a plan to partition the island.

On 20 July, in line with previously prepared plans, the Turkish army moved against the island of Cyprus. Troops came ashore west of

The presidential palace after the July 1974 coup

Kyrenia and paratroopers were dropped in the Mesaoria plain near Guenyeli. The main aim of the Turkish army was to create a wedge, linking Turkish Cypriots holding northern Nicosia with a bridgehead on the coast. Although the invasion had been rehearsed on many previous occasions, the Turkish army underestimated the task. Although there is little evidence to suggest Sampson's regime was in the slightest prepared for the invasion, nevertheless, the national guard put up fierce resistance and there was heavy fighting, especially around Nicosia with the Turkish army taking heavy casualities. There were subsequent claims by both sides of a series of atrocities against their communities and there is still a large number of missing persons, who have never been accounted for, especially from the Greek Cypriot side.

BRITISH REACTION

Britain had reacted to the coup by sending a task force, whose main purpose was to protect British and UN personnel. But why did Britain take no action when as guarantor of the Treaty of Independence it was expected? Later, a British Parliamentary Select Committee found the government did have the legal and the moral right, as well as the military capacity, to intervene. The Labour government did brand the 'Sampson coup' as illegal and the chief of the defence staff at the time, Michael Carver, confirmed that he had been asked about the feasibility of military action to remove Sampson. Apparently, the advice he gave to Harold Wilson was that any use of force by Britain against the coup would not only have risked the animosity of the Greek Cypriot population but would have left British personnel vulnerable. At the time many British families lived outside the Sovereign Bases and could have easily been seized as hostages. Interestingly, at a conference organised by the author twenty years later, Carver argued that, in order to keep the two communities from committing violence against each other, partition was the only long-term solution for Cyprus.

Callaghan, however, was later to write that the government feared another Suez if the British had intervened without the support of the US. Subsequently, in a unguarded remark, Callaghan suggested that Britain nearly came to war with Turkey, but was restrained by the USA. It was also reported by Harold Wilson that when the Turks bombed Nicosia airport British and UN soldiers were put in danger and he warned Ecevit that the Turkish planes would be shot down by British fighters if the attacks continued.

As Turkish troops were landing on the island Makarios was taking part in a Security Council debate. On 20 July as news of the fighting was received a resolution (no. 353) was passed deploring the outbreak of the conflict: all states were called upon to respect the sovereignty of Cyprus; all parties to the fighting were to agree to a ceasefire; there was a demand for foreign military intervention to end; for illegitimate foreign military personnel to leave the island; and the guarantor powers, Greece, Turkey and UK to enter into negotiations to restore peace.

Meanwhile Greece had mobilised its forces and, for a moment, there was a possibility that Greece would declare war on Turkey. However, without far greater air cover than Greece possessed, there was no hope of reinforcing Cyprus, and generally at that time the Greek army was in a fairly parlous state so any direct attack on Turkey through Thrace was ruled out. On 22 July the Greek military junta called for a ceasefire and relinquished power in Greece. It was indeed an ironic twist that the Colonels' Junta should collapse because of the ill-conceived plot to overthrow Makarios. The eminent Greek politician, Constantinos Karamanlis, who was in exile in France, was invited to return to Greece and on his arrival prepared the way for an election and a democratic government. On Cyprus on 23 July, Nikos Sampson stepped aside and was replaced by Glafcos Clerides as president.

GENEVA CONFERENCE

At the same time Ecevit welcomed the return of a democratic government to Greece and accepted the UN ceasefire. However, in breach of the terms of the ceasefire, the Turkish army continued to pour men and arms into the island and extend its control westward. The Turks claimed that their commanders were mopping up snipers and irregulars, but in reality, in line with the *Attila Plan*, the Turkish army was seizing territory in preparation for partition.

On 25 July, following on from the UN resolution, a conference was called, meeting in Geneva, and attended by the three foreign ministers of the guarantors, Britain, Greece and Turkey, James Callaghan, George Mavros and Turan Gunes. Turkey, now with its forces firmly secured on Cyprus, played its hand from a strong position, and refused to consider any settlement which required its troops to withdraw from the island. Finally, on 30 July a declaration was agreed which confirmed the ceasefire and that there should be no extension of the territory now controlled by each side's armed forces, that the Turkish enclaves occupied by Greek or Greek Cypriot forces should be evacuated and military and civilian detainees should be exchanged as quickly as was feasible. The existence of two separate administrations was noted and there was a call for a buffer zone to be set up. The Greek Cypriots felt betrayed by Britain and Greece as there was no demand for the Turks to withdraw their army. It is doubtful if the Turks ever had any intention of keeping to the agreement as their forces continued to expand the territory under their control, nor did the Greek Cypriots evacuate all the Turkish Cypriot enclaves they had seized at the start of the conflict.

On 9 August 1974 the Geneva Conference, chaired by Callaghan, opened. The Greek Cypriots led by Clerides demanded that the Turks withdraw to the ceasefire line of 30 July. Turkey demanded the immediate withdrawal of the national guard from the Turkish Cypriot enclaves. By 11 August the Greeks had conceded, withdrawing troops from the enclaves and releasing Turkish and Turkish Cypriot prisoners. Such was the weakness of the Greek position that they also dropped their demand for the Turkish army to withdraw to the 30 July ceasefire line. Clerides argued for a political settlement that restored the 1960 constitution. Denktaş put forward a plan that created partition and at the same time the Turkish Foreign Minister, Gunes, proposed the establishment of six autonomous Turkish Cypriot cantons. Although Callaghan supported an adjournment for the Turkish proposals to be considered by the Greek and Cypriot governments, the Turks refused and were castigated by Callaghan for their unreasonableness. However, it soon became clear the Turkish presence at Geneva was just diversionary while the Turkish army organised another major assault. On 13 August the Turks broke out of their lines to seize over 37 per cent of the island. Ecevit declared a ceasefire on 16 August having completed the Turkish plan for partition – although, dishonestly, he claimed at the time his intentions were the establishment of a federal state. Over two hundred thousand (a third of the island's population) Greek Cypriots were displaced and fled to the Greek Cypriot controlled south to live in refugee camps.

The Greek Cypriots, understandably, felt completely let down by the West: Britain and the UN had stood by and let the island be divided so that Turkey had seized over a third of the territory, which contained the best agricultural land, for only 18 per cent of the population. The US had not only stood by, but also seemed implicated both in the coup and in the Turkish army's divison of the island. Cyprus had been preserved from communism and the Sovereign Base Areas (SBAs) and the important listening devices that monitored Soviet activities were intact. In reality a price had been paid by both the communities, but inevitably the Greek Cypriots had lost most. It was perhaps, therefore, unsurprising, though nonetheless most regrettable, that a crowd attacked the American embassy and on 19 August the US ambassador, Rodger Davies, and his secretary were assassinated.

Initially, Turkey's action had attracted international sympathy. The Sampson coup had overthrown the legitimate government of Cyprus and the Turkish Cypriot community was undoubtedly threatened. As a Guarantor of the Treaty of Independence Turkey had exercised her

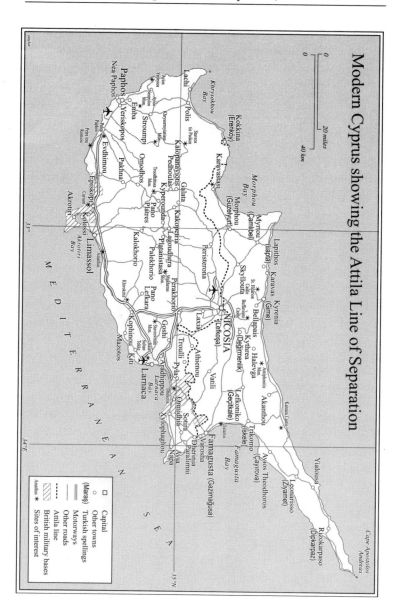

Modern Cyprus showing the Attila Line of Separation

legal right to remove an illegal regime, safeguard the Turkish Cypriots and restore independence to the island. However, international attitudes soon changed after 15 August with the blatant seizure of land and partition of Cyprus by the Turkish army. It soon became clear that the real intention of the invasion was the permanent partition of Cyprus as Turkish Cypriots and Turkish settlers, from the mainland of Turkey, were placed in Greek Cypriots' homes and on Greek Cypriots' land. Britain seemed to comply with this *fait accompli* in a manner that has never been properly explained, when it allowed over 9,000 Turkish Cypriots to be resettled from the SBA of Episkopi in the occupied zone in the north.

UN RESOLUTIONS

Throughout August the UN issued resolutions calling on foreign troops to withdraw from Cyprus and for resumption of talks between the two sides. However, Turkey ignored these resolutions and with hindsight it is possible to see that Turkey's intransigence strained her relationships with both East and West, in such a way that ever since has blighted the country's political and economic development. The US Congress imposed an arms ban on Turkey (was this just window dressing?) but did not extract any concessions on Cyprus. Although the relationship between the USA and Turkey, since the Turkish army's occupation of northern Cyprus, has not been easy, the US has never really pressurised Turkey to sign up to a Cyprus settlement. Firstly, the US supported Turkey because of its strategic position during the Cold War; then, after the fall of the Soviet Union, the US needed Turkey as an ally (along with Saudi Arabia) to help 'police' the Middle East – the airbase at Inçilik in southern Turkey has been crucial in relation to threats from Iran and the conflicts with Iraq. The US is also concerned lest a right-wing government in Turkey might ally with Islamic fundamentalist countries so it needs to ensure the Turkish army, which is the guardian of Ataturk's vision of a modern westernised secular state, remains influential. The Turkish army, for its part, sees control of northern Cyprus as strategically critical to Turkey's security in the Middle East. Even though it is American money that keeps the very fragile economy of Turkey afloat, the Turkish parliament is prepared to flout US wishes, as seen recently in the war against Iraq, when the US was refused access to Iraq across the Turkish border.

ILLEGAL STATUS OF NORTHERN CYPRUS

Ironically, in 1974 opportunities for a fair settlement, which could have healed some of the old wounds, were lost because of the weakness at the time of the Turkish government that depended upon a fragile coalition which had to concede too much to the extremists and the army generals. The consequences of Turkish recalitrance were that only the Greek Cypriot south was recognised by the world as the legitimate government of the Republic of Cyprus and the northern zone was branded as an illegal entity. The Turkish Cypriots in the north, therefore, were isolated both politically and economically. A trade embargo was imposed which has left the economy to stagnate and the Turkish Cypriot community in relative poverty compared to the Greek Cypriots in the south. A buffer zone (the Green Line), patrolled by UNFICYP, divides the north from the south, which was until recently, virtually impassable for all Cypriots, and splitting Nicosia, which is claimed to be 'the last city in Europe to be divided'.

There is no doubt some Turkish Cypriots welcomed the massive displacement of Greek Cypriots in 1974 as an opportunity to gain recompense for the violence and destruction their own community had suffered in 1963 and 1968 – for some 'chickens came home to roost for the Greek Cypriots'. Nevertheless, the indiscipline of the Turkish army in commiting gross acts of violence, looting and destruction against a civilian population and their property had been shocking to the world. Churches, cemeteries and even archaeological sites were desecrated. Anything that had associations with a Hellenic past was wantonly destroyed and, inexplicably, even property which was to be handed over to Turkish Cypriots was also looted and damaged.

In the Greek Cypriot south the pressures on the authorities were enormous with problems of housing, water supply and unemployment. A third of the population now had to adjust to a new way of life with their economic and social patterns dislocated or destroyed. As a consequence of the Turkish actions the Greek Cypriots held the moral high ground and, with the support of the UN, worked consistently to change the political situation. What had been an issue of inter-communal strife had been transformed into one of foreign occupation. For the Greek Cypriots the division of the island was an unjust and illegal act which had to be redressed, so that in the end Greek Cypriots would return to their homes and land in the north. It is fair to observe that some Greek Cypriots found it convenient to forget the violence and death, the injustices and humiliations that had been meted out previously on the Turkish community that had helped create partition.

CHAPTER TWELVE

Post 1974 – The Cyprus Problem

Makarios' Return

On 7 December 1974 Makarios returned to Cyprus to a massive reception from the Greek Cypriot community. Clerides stepped down and Makarios resumed the position of President. He declared a general amnesty for all those who were involved in the coup against him. Although there was an attempt to persuade him to form a government of national unity, Makarios was fearful of alienating the US by including communists in any government. Makarios now realised that he badly needed the US to exert pressure on Turkey to bring about a settlement. He decided in the end to create the National Council, consisting of members from all the political parties, which acted as an advisory body.

Twelve days after Makarios' return to the island inter-communal talks between Clerides and Denktaş were resumed in the presence of the UN special representative, Weckmann–Munoz. Although the Greek Cypriots could claim the stronger moral position they now had to negotiate from a weak political reality. There was talk of an independent federal state, but whereas Greek Cypriots wanted a bicommunal multi-regional federal state, which recognised the disparity in population size between the two commnunities, the Turkish Cypriots wanted a bi-communal, bi-regional federal state, with the two communities treated as equal. In many ways the rhetoric of the two sides was not so far apart, but in terms of their negotiating stance the Greek Cypriots had to be seen to 'win' and Turkish Cypriot side could not be seen to 'lose'. Neither position was compatible or encouraged compromise.

Turkish Federated State of Cyprus

By the middle of February 1975 the talks appeared to have made no progress when on 13 February Denktaş declared the north the Turkish Federated State of Cyprus. On 20 February the UN Security Council met to hear a complaint from the Greek Cypriots about the formation of an illegal state. In March UN Resolution 367 expressed regret at the unilateral action of the north and Secretary-General, Kurt Waldheim, laboured to set up another round of inter-communal talks. These were started in April 1975 and series of rounds were held but, apparently, with little political progress. However, there was an agreement relating to the transfer of refugees and by the end of 1975, over 8,000 Turkish Cypriots had moved from the south to the north. In September the talks were adjourned, but a new round in Vienna was initiated in February 1976. It was agreed each side should present their proposals for a settlement. However, in April Clerides had resigned. He had given Denktaş some proposals but was seen as having acted independently of Makarios and Tassos Papadopoulos was appointed as negotiator in his stead. The talks were then downgraded by Denktaş who sent Umit Suleyman Onan in his place.

MAKARIOS DENKTAŞ MEETING

A new dynamic was brought to the Cyprus problem when Jimmy Carter was elected US President in November 1976. In the run-up to the election he had talked encouragingly about trying to find a solution. So perhaps it was not so surprising that in January 1977 Makarios received a letter from Denktaş proposing a meeting – the first between them for sixteen years. The intial meeting between the two leaders on 27 January was described as a 'breakthrough'. Their talks, apparently, had been friendly and productive. They had agreed to a second meeting that took place on 12 February. At this second meeting they agreed on a series of guidelines: Cyprus would be an independent, non-aligned bi-communal federal republic; the size of the territory for each community would be determined upon the basis of economic viability and property ownership; freedom of movement and freedom of settlement would take into account the practical difficulties which might face the Turkish Cypriots; the powers of the central government would safeguard the unity of the country.

THE DEATH OF MAKARIOS

In March a new series of talks (the sixth round) took place once more in Vienna. Papadopoulos proposed, with the production of a map, that 20 per cent of the island should remain under Turkish Cypriot control within a federal republic. However the Turkish Cypriot side, in contrast to the Greek Cypriots, was concerned that any central government should remain weak. Local talks in Nicosia followed but made no progress and there were threats from the Turkish Cypriot side to settle the abandoned suburb of Famagusta, Varosha. On 3 August Makarios died of a heart attack. He was sixty-four years old and his death marked the end of an era. He was succeeded by Spyros Kyprianou, as president of the House of Representatives, who was returned unopposed after an election the following February.

In April 1978 the Turkish Cypriot side presented its proposal which essentially required dual control at all levels and suggested that a full federal government was somewhere in the future. Although Waldheim saw the proposal as positive, the Greek Cypriot side dismissed the plan, as it believed it was an attempt to legitimise the *status quo* which had been brought about by the Turkish military action of 1974. However, the US now showed determination in trying to find a settlement of the Cyprus problem. In the summer of 1978 Congress lifted the arms ban on Turkey, and by November the US Government, along with the British and the Canadians, had drafted a twelve point plan which was submitted to both sides. In essence the plan proposed a bi-zonal/bi-communal federation and bi-cameral legislature which provided for equal representation of the two communities at the upper level. It was rejected on the Greek Cypriot side as it was seen once more as undermining any central authority. Nevertheless, in May 1979 both sides did agree to reaffirm the guidelines that Makarios and Denktaş had signed up to in 1977. The talks resumed in June, with the issue of Varosha being given priority, but after a week they broke down over the economic boycott of the North and the internationalisation of the problem. Waldheim eventually revived the talks in August 1980 under a UN Special Representative, Hugo Juan Gobbi, but once more there was little progress.

ANDREAS PAPANDREOU

In May and June 1981 both communities held elections. The Greek Cypriots were voting for membership to the House of Representatives, the Turkish Cypriots held presidential elections. There were no surprises and although AKEL (the communists) gained most votes there was no overall majority for any one Greek Cypriot party and Denktaş was returned as the Turkish Cypriot president. By October Gobbi had produced a new initiative which combined all the earlier proposals. Although it too was rejected it became the basis for further negotiations. The relations between the two sides were complicated by the election of Andreas Papandreou's PASOK (Panhellenic Socialist Movement) to government in Greece. Papandreou perceived the inter-communal talks as merely a way of preserving the division of the island and he believed there was a need to put pressure on Turkey to withdraw its troops. In 1982 Papandreou visited Cyprus, pledging his government's support for the territorial integrity and unity of the island and subsequently relations with Turkey rapidly declined.

THE PÉREZ DE CUÉLLAR INITIATIVE

This was the context in which the new UN Secretary-General Pérez de Cuéllar tried to forge yet another initiative. Throughout 1982 de Cuéllar held top-level meetings with both communities and Greece and Turkey. Gobbi had attempted to work behind the scenes and keep the Cyprus problem out of the headlines; the Greek Cypriots had even been persuaded not to raise the issue at the UN General Assembly. However, with the support of the more robust approach of the Greek government under Papandreou, the Greek Cypriots once more took the issue to the UN. On 13 May 1983 a resolution was passed which requested once more the withdrawal of foreign troops, but also called upon all states to help the Republic exercise control over the whole island. This was perceived by the Turks as a major threat and, by the time Pérez de Cuéllar was ready to launch his proposals, Denktaş was preparing to declare total independence.

The Turkish Republic of Northern Cyprus (TRNC)

On 15 November 1983 Denktaş proclaimed the formation of the Turkish Republic of Northern Cyprus (TRNC). The unilateral declaration immediately attracted condemnation, as despite Denktaş' claim that this action would not damage a future federal state, it was in direct contravention of all the UN resolutions. Britain who, under the Conservative government of Mrs Margaret Thatcher, had been reasonably supportive of Turkey, immediately called for a meeting of the Security Council and drafted a resolution condemning the Turkish Cypriot action. On 18 November (Resolution 541) the UDI of the north was roundly deplored as an illegal act of secession. Only Pakistan voted against the resolution. Although Denktaş refused to withdraw the declaration of independence, in January he announced a series of measures designed to show goodwill. There was talk of returning Varosha to the Greek Cypriots, and reopening Nicosia airport under UNIFCYP supervision. Kyprianou dismissed the gesture as propaganda to head off the world criticism of the Turkish Cypriots.

Meanwhile throughout 1984 Pérez de Cuéllar pursued his initiative with a series of 'proximity talks' with the two leaders. On 11 January Kyprianou gave the Secretary-General a document outlining the Greek Cypriot plan for a settlement. In March Pérez de Cuéllar met with Denktaş in New York. In May the Security Council adopted a further resolution once more urging nations to condemn the secession of the north and calling on all countries to deny the TRNC recognition. In September the Proximity Talks began in New York. By November, the US pressure on Turkey was beginning to yield results: the Turkish Cypriot side agreed to a series of concessions. Denktaş was prepared to reduce Turkish Cypriot controlled territory to 29 per cent of the island, and to drop the demand for a rotating presidency. At the same time Pérez de Cuéllar's talks had persuded the Greek Cypriots to accept equal representation of the two communities in the upper house of a bi-cameral legislature.

In January 1985 summit talks between Kyprianou and Denktaş began but, despite initial optimism on both sides, the Greek Cypriots refused to sign a draft agreement and on 20 January the talks ended in failure. The key sticking points for the Greek Cypriots were the withdrawal of Turkish troops, freedom of movement, repatriation of the settlers from the Turkish mainland, and property rights, guarantor powers (to replace those of the 1960 Constitution) and the amount of territory to be returned to Greek Cypriot control. Kyprianou took a good deal of criticism for his rejection of the draft agreement, as the federal solution posed by Pérez de Cuéllar was perceived by many as a serious opportunity to solve the Cyprus problem. In March 1986 the Secretary-General presented a 'draft framework agreement' which was essentially based on the previous formula and was once more rejected.

Turgut Özal

In January 1988 for the first time in ten years, while attending the World Economic Forum at Davos in Switzerland, the Greek and Turkish Prime Ministers, Papandreou and Turgut Özal, met and held talks for a couple of days in an attempt to improve Greco-Turkish relations. Özal was a dedicated European and was determined to lead Turkey into the European Economic Community (EEC). As an existing member Greece had a veto which could block Turkey's application. It was essential to Özal that there was an accord between Greece and Turkey and the Cyprus problem could not be allowed to get in the way of Turkey's membership. This easing of relations between Greece and Turkey resulted in Özal paying a state visit to Greece in June 1988. This was the first visit by a Turkish Prime Minister since 1953.

George Vassiliou

Earlier in February the presidential elections in Cyprus had thrown up an independent candidate, George Vassiliou, who narrowly defeated Clerides. Vassiliou was a successful businessman rather than a career politician and, untarnished by a previous political history, he was able to bring a fresh perception to the search for a settlement. Thus, the thaw in relations between Greece and Turkey and the appearance of a new

Greek Cypriot leader helped create a positive climate for solving the Cyprus problem.

Application to the EEC

On 24 August 1988, meeting in Geneva with Pérez de Cuéllar, Vassiliou and Denktaş agreed to resume inter-communal talks that following September. Both leaders committed themselves to resolving the issues between the two communities through a negotiated settlement by 1 June 1989. By July 1989 both sides had come forward with sets of proposals but these were rejected by the other side. Another attempt was made in the spring of the following year to break the stalemate, but these talks broke down when Denktaş started introducing the concept of self-determination and refering to 'peoples' rather than 'communities'.

In July 1990 the Republic of Cyprus formally applied for EEC membership. The Greek Cypriots in the south of the island had made a remarkable economic recovery after 1974. By 1980s there was full employment; the tourist capacity in the south was greater than it had been for the whole island before 1974 – approximately two million visitors per annum (most of those British holidaymakers); and exports had doubled. It was clear the south would be able mainly to meet the economic criteria of the Common Market. In contrast, the Turkish Cypriots lacked the capacity to develop the resources in the north. The political ostracism and economic embargo of the north left the Turkish Cypriots with an economy and standard of living far behind the Greek Cypriots. In reality the TRNC was not a viable entity but was totally dependent upon the subsidies from Turkey.

'SET OF IDEAS'

Despite the hopes that had attended the Presidency of Vassiliou and Turkish Premier's, Özal's, initiatives with Greece, Pérez de Cuéllar retired as Secretary-General without any progress on the Cyprus problem. In 1992 his successor Boutros Boutros Ghali revived the 'proximity talks' and in August introduced a formula which went under the label, a 'Set of Ideas'. With the break-up of the Soviet Union Ghali was able to command more UN support for his proposals than his precedessors could have achieved, so that the Security Council adopted them unanimously. The crux of his proposals was a federal state with equal communities, a Greek Cypriot president and Turkish Cypriot vice-president, the right of refugees to return home, the three freedoms of movement, settlement and ownership of land. However, he also included in his plan a map, which restored Morphou (one of the most fertile areas on the island) and Varosha (the suburb of Famagusta) to Greek Cypriot control. The Turkish Cypriots found this unacceptable and rejected his 'Set of Ideas', although not in their entirety, so there was still room to negotiate. Denktaş proposed a series of amendments but these were not acceptable to the Greek Cypriot side. There were two major concerns for Denktaş before he could consider moves towards a settlement: the first was recognition of sovereignty for the TRNC and the second was to block the Greek Cypriots joining the European Union (EU). How far his aims were driven by Turkey and how much by his own desire to maintain his own political dominance in the north is a moot point.

'CONFIDENCE-BUILDING MEASURES'

This time it was the Turkish Cypriot side that took the blame for the failure of the Secretary-General's initiative. At the same time, the Greek Cypriot stance changed when, in February 1993, presidential elections took place in the South and Vassiliou was beaten by the narrowest of margins by the seasoned politican Clerides. The Clerides' government, with an eye on the negotiations for entry into the EU, focused its policy towards the settlement on the basis of respecting human rights. In July Boutros Boutros Ghali reverted back to trying to build the trust of each side through the concept of 'confidence-building measures'. This was to involve the opening of Nicosia airport allowing direct flights for tourists (at present all visitors have to fly to the North via Turkey). This would have had an immediate and significant impact on the economy of the North. In reality it would have lifted the damaging trade embargo on the Turkish Cypriots. In compensation Varosha would be returned to the Greek Cypriots. Despite strong US support for the talks in Vienna, the proposal ran into difficulties over the details, with neither side apparently prepared to budge.

Integration with Turkey

The next year the Turkish Cypriots appeared to move away from a federal solution. In July 1994 the European Court of Justice, in response to a referral from a British court, effectively banned the exports of agricultural products from the North to the EU. At the same time a damaging UN report on the treatment of the enclaved Greek Cypriots in the Karpasia peninsular was published. In response to these negative judgements Denktaş threatened to integrate the North with Turkey. Later in the year Clerides tried to shift the situation by offering concessions on constitutional issues if the Turkish Cypriots would support the Republic's application to join the EU. The Turkish Cypriot side, suspicious of the Greek Cypriot offer, preferred to reject the proposal, although there were some Turkish Cypriot politicians who were critical of Denktaş' stance.

Early in 1995 Denktaş issued a fourteen point 'Peace Offensive' in which he rowed back from integration with Turkey and reiterated a bizonal, bi-communal federation. Clerides, in his response, looked to membership of the EU as finding a way forward and called for a timetable to demilitarise the island. In March the French, who held the presidency of the EU, negotiated a deal with the Greek and Turkish ambassadors that altered the whole perspective of the Cyprus problem. Turkey, who had been trying to establish a customs union with the EU as part of the process for eventually gaining membership of the EU, had been blocked by Greece. In return for removing Greek resistance to the customs union with Turkey the EU Council of Ministers agreed that it was not necessary for there to be a settlement between the Greek and Turkish Cypriots before Cyprus could join the EU – in other words the Greek Cypriot part of the island could join without the North. However, this in turn created the potential for a whole series of immensely difficult issues.

The problem of Cyprus' accession to the EU before there was a settlement between the Greek and Turkish Cypriots related to the reactions of both Turkey and the Turkish Cypriots to what would be a dramatically changed political situation. The North had already responded with the threat of union with Turkey if the Greek Cypriots joined the EU. Such an action would rule out for the foreseeable future any chance of Turkey joining the EU. At the same time if the Republic of Cyprus was given membership there would be the prospect of part of the territory of an EU member, not only being in the hands of an illegitimate administration, but also occupied by foreign troops. However, Greece had threatened it would use its veto to block any further expansion of the EU if Cyprus' accession to the EU was held up by a failure to solve the Cyprus problem.

S300 Russian surface-to-air missiles

In May 1996 the British government appointed the experienced diplomat, David Hannay, as the UK Special Representative on Cyprus, but after several shuttle missions he was unable to shift the deadlock. Tensions mounted in the summer, following demonstrations, when there was a series of incidents causing the deaths of some Greek Cypriots on the Green Line (the buffer zone between the North and the South). Then, in January 1997, Clerides announced that he intended to purchase S300 Russian surface-to-air missiles for the protection of a new military airfield near Paphos. This alarmed Ankara, who already felt threatened by the Joint Defence Doctrine agreed between Cyprus and Greece, and Turkey now started warning of a possible pre-emptive strike against the missiles. Relations seemed to be deteriorating badly with the nationalist hardliners on all sides gaining the upper hand.

Richard Holbrooke

The UN, with Kofi Annan as Secretary-General, worked to bring the two sides together once more. The US also increased its effort to bring about a settlement with Clinton appointing Richard Holbrooke, the presidential representative on Cyprus. In July and August talks were held with the two sides first at Troutbeck, near New York, and then later at Lion-sur-Montreux in Switzerland. The UN's aim was to get a broad agreement on a set of principles that would create the framework for a federal state. Legal recognition of the TRNC, however, now became a sticking point for Denktaş. He demanded that there should be equality of treatment between the North and the South: that is that the TRNC be treated as a legitimate state. There was no chance that the Greek Cypriots could agree to recognition of the North, which would be tantamount to relinquishing their claim, which had been endorsed by the UN, that the Republic of Cyprus was the only legal government for the whole island. At the same time the Turkish Cypriot side also argued it could not engage in negotiations as long as the South was going through the process of entry to the EU as this was would lead, according to the 1960 Constitution, to an illegal alliance. So the talks made no progress and broke down.

Denktaş tried to persuade Kofi Annan that the UN would have to recognise that any future talks should be on an equal basis with the recognition of the Turkish Cypriot state. However, in May 1998, the UN Security Council re-affirmed its previous position and in the following month passed another resolution reiterating that any settlement for Cyprus should be on the basis that there would be one state with single citizenship. In July the Secretary-General's special adviser on Cyprus, Diego Cordovez, travelled to the island, primarily to try to persuade Denktaş to rejoin UN brokered talks but without success. Richard Holbrooke and his deputy Thomas Miller also engaged in a fresh round of diplomacy but he declared publicly that the US was not going to try to impose any settlement. Although initially Holbrooke was seen as favouring the North he later blamed Denktaş for a lack of progress and emphatically confirmed that the US would not recognise the TRNC and would not put pressure on the EU to stop accession talks with the Greek Cypriots.

In August Denktaş came forward with a proposal that, in order to achieve a lasting settlement, a Confederation of Cyprus should be established. Not unsurprisingly Denktaş' proposal was rejected by the Greek Cypriots. The UN then repeated its view that a solution should be found in a bi-communal, bi-zonal federation. Alongside this approach Clerides put forward the proposal that the Turkish Cypriots should be able to participate in Cyprus' accession negotiations with the EU without any requirement that they should recognise any legal basis for the application on behalf of the whole island. Denktaş rejected the offer but his action split the Turkish Cypriots as there were those, for example Mehmet Ali Talat, leader of the Republican Turkish Party, who believed the offer could be helpful.

At the end of December 1998 Clerides announced that the deployment of the S300 Russian missiles would not proceed. His government had been under considerable pressure from the UN, the US and Britain to back down on this issue as it was generally perceived as diverting international attention away from finding a settlement. The way now seemed open for the UN to renew its attempt to restart talks.

In March 1999 Thomas Miller, the US special co-ordinator for Cyprus, returned to the island and held talks with both Clerides and Denktaş, but the fact that it was only Miller and not Holbrooke showed that the Clinton administration was shifting its approach. It was not until June that a new impetus for a solution was put on the table when a fresh resolution of the UN called on the two sides to participate in UN sponsored negotiations in the autumn. In August northwestern Turkey was struck by a massive earthquake which killed as many as 40,000 people. The reaction of the Greek and Cypriot governments in immediately sending aid helped thaw the difficult relations that had been building up over the previous few years. In November, Bill Clinton accompanied by his Secretary of State, Madeleine Albright, visited Athens where he promised his own personal involvement in attempting to solve the Cyprus problem. In November the UN was able to sponsor proximity talks, first in New York and then in Geneva.

The issue of the status of the North blocked the progress of the proximity talks and, in an attempt to revive the talks, the UN Secretary-General's special adviser on Cyprus, Alvaro de Soto, visited the island at the end of February 2000. It was agreed a third round of talks would take place and these eventually got under way in July in New York and Geneva. A fourth round then took place in New York in September followed by a fifth round in Geneva, but the recognition of the TRNC still proved to be an insuperable obstacle. Meanwhile the negotiations between Cyprus and the EU continued to move forward, but when the European Commisson suggested that Turkey's application for membership to the EU was linked to the acceptance of a solution to the Cyprus problem, Denktaş hesitated to attend a planned sixth round of talks.

In January 2001 the new Republican administration of George W Bush moved into the White House. The incoming secretary of state Colin Powell confirmed the US' determination to bring a solution to Cyprus which had been 'festering as a sore in that region . . . ' In June the UN, after thirty-six years, renewed its mandate in Cyprus, with some 2,400 peacekeepers patrolling the buffer zone. In July the issue of Britain's Sovereign Bases came to the fore. Although the SBAs as a political issue have been relatively low-key compared with the Cyprus problem there is an understandable irritation and resentment among some of the Greek Cypriots that there are these foreign bases on Cypriot soil. When the British planned to erect some new tele-communications masts, which were thought to be a health hazard, this proved a catalyst for violent demonstrations.

In August the UN Secretary-General, Kofi Annan, met with Denktaş in Salzburg but, by September, the UN Security Council was castigating Denktaş for rejecting the Secretary-General's invitation to new talks. In November Denktaş, in three letters to Clerides, proposed face-to-face talks between the two leaders. These began in December in the presence of the UN Secretary-General's special adviser on Cyprus, Alvaro de Soto.

Kofi Annan Plan

In January 2002 the talks reopened and, although the pace had quickened by the end of March with twenty-two separate sessions completed, there was still no breakthrough. However, as Cyprus entered the last lap of negotiations for entry into the EU the urgency of reaching a settlement was being reinforced by all world governments and agencies. In May the UN Secretary-General, Kofi Annan, visited Nicosia attempting to bring pressure on both sides, stating, 'an historic opportunity exists now to reach a comprehensive settlement'. The talks between the two leaders continued so that by September there had been fifty-six sessions. As the deadline for the acceptance of Cyprus into the EU loomed the UN quickened its activity once more and on 11

Kofi Annan, the UN Secretary-General with President Clerides and the
Turkish-Cypriot leader, Rauf Denktaş

November Kofi Annan tabled his plan for a comprehensive settlement.
The main elements of the 150-page plan, which has been described as a
Swiss-style federation of Greek and Turkish Cypriot constituent states,
were:

- A common state made up of two equal component states in
  indissoluble union
- One single Cypriot citizenship
- A six member presidential council proportionate to the population
  with a ten month rotating presidency
- A transitional government for three years
- A two-chamber parliament – each chamber having forty-eight
  members
- Cyprus would join the EU, but maintain special relationships with
  Greece and Turkey
- Cyprus would be demilitarised and banned from purchasing
  weapons – compliance ensured by UN monitors
- Greece and Turkey would each be allowed to maintain small forces
  on the island

- The constitution would safeguard civil rights
- A reconciliation commission would promote tolerance

A slightly revised version was produced a week later, but any hope of gaining signatures before the December EU summit in Copenhagen were dashed by the Turkish Cypriot side. As Cyprus' accession to the EU was agreed hopes now focused on a settlement being achieved before the new deadline of 28 February 2003.

ELECTION OF TASSOS PAPADOPOULOS

On 16 February Clerides was defeated in the Greek Cypriot presidential elections by Tassos Papadopoulos, who had been very critical in his electoral campaign of the previous regime's handling of the negotiations with the Turkish Cypriots. When it was clear that no settlement could be agreed by the end of February, Kofi Annan extended the deadline to 11 March when he invited the two sides to meet at the Hague in Holland. Despite pressure from the Turkish Prime Minister, Recep Tayyip Erdogan, and a growing frustration among some Turkish Cypriots, who demonstrated in the streets of Nicosia in favour of joining the EU, there was yet again failure in The Hague to reach agreement. Denktaş felt he was unable to accept Kofi Annan's proposal to hold referendums, both in the North and South, on the peace proposal.

Treaty of Accession to the EU

On 16 April in Athens Tassos Papadopoulos signed the Treaty of Accession on behalf of Cyprus joining the EU on 1 May 2004, along with Czech Republic, Estonia, Hungary, Latvia, Lithuania, Malta, Poland, Slovakia and Slovenia, but without the Turkish Cypriots in the North.

In a surprise move on 23 April Denktaş decided to open the crossing points across the Green Line. Extraordinary images showed floods of Cypriots from both North and South crossing over. Many emotional scenes followed and although there have been a few stories of hostility among the two communities the overwhelming impression has been of amiablility and fraternisation offering hope and optimism for the future for the communities of the island.

On 11 June the Security Council renewed the UN mandate for UNFICYP and the Secretary-General, Kofi Annan, along with strong backing from the US and the EU, went into over-drive in an attempt to achieve a Cyprus settlement before the accession date of 1 May 2004. Although Denktaş seemed to pose a severe obstacle to any possiblity of a settlement there was a general feeling among Turkish Cypriots in the North that it was time for change and that they too should have access to the economic benefits of joining the EU. By the beginning of September the three main Turkish Cypriot opposition parties formed an alliance with the principal aim of ousting Denktaş. The alliance pledged that, should they win enough seats in the forthcoming elections in the North, they would form a coalition and appoint a new team of negotiators to bring about a settlement and thereby enable the Turkish Cypriots to join the EU.

THE TURKISH CYPRIOT ELECTIONS ON 14 DECEMBER

The elections to the assembly in the North on 14 December resulted in a tie – with Denktaş' party and the opposition each gaining twenty-five seats. However, significantly, the opposition parties won 50.3 per cent of the vote and on 29 December Denktaş, having little choice, called upon Mehment Ali Talat, the leader of the largest opposition party, the Republican Turkish Party (RTP), to form a government. This provided an opportunity for the UN to reconvene talks, but, although Talat was keen to negotiate a settlement with the Greek Cypriots, the new administration was not in a strong enough position to replace Denktaş as the head of the Turkish Cypriot negotiating team.

FIFTH VERSION OF THE ANNAN PLAN

On 19 February 2004 under the chairmanship of the UN Secretary-General's special adviser on Cyprus, Alvaro de Soto, the intercommunal talks were resumed in Nicosia. The basis of the talks had been agreed, after intensive negotiations, one week earlier at UN headquarters in New York.

In his invitation to the talks the Secretary-General stated, 'I truly believe ... that the plan I put forward ... would permit the reunification of Cyprus through an honourable, balanced and durable settlement that protected and guaranteed the basic interests and aspirations of both sides.'

There were two additional key elements in the process, designed to force a settlement before the accession date of 1 May: if the talks failed to bring about an agreement by 22 March, the Greek and Turkish governments would have one week in which to resolve the differences between the two communities, and if the efforts of Greece and Turkey then failed, Kofi Annan could then use his discretion to produce a settlement plan which would be simultaneously submitted to the Greek and Turkish Cypriots in UN sponsored referendums.

When the Nicosia talks failed to reach an agreement on the settlement plan, Kofi Annan convened a further set of talks including Greece and Turkey, on 24 March, at the Swiss mountain resort of Bürgenstock. However, these talks also failed: the chief stumbling block were the permanent derogations demanded by the Turkish Cypriots which would block the Greek Cypriots' right to return to their homes in the North or to apply to the European Court of Human Rights for the recovery of their pre-1974 property. At the conclusion of the talks on 31 March the Secretary-General tabled a fifth and final version of his plan. It provided for a federal United Cyprus Republic to join the EU on 1 May, subject to its acceptance by both communities in referendums to be held on 24 April.

The main revisions, which attempted to accommodate the key objections of the Turkish Cypriots to the previous versions, to the plan were:

- Turkish Cypriots would relinguish only seven per cent (out of thirty-six per cent held) of land
- The number of Greek Cypriots allowed to return to the North was reduced from twenty-one to eighteen per cent of the Turkish Cypriot population
- Greeks Cypriots would be barred from acquiring property in the North until Turkish Cypriot living standards approached those of the Greek Cypriots

- Greek Cypriots living in the North would be barred from the Senate of the federal state
- Turkish troops would be allowed to remain in Cyprus even after Turkey itself accedes to the EU, but reduced to 650 soldiers by 2018
- After nineteen years full freedom of movement thoughout Cyprus would be allowed

However, even if this new plan was rejected by either side in the referendums the Republic of Cyprus (the South) would join the EU on 1 May and the *acquis communautaire* would not apply to the North.

UN REFERENDUMS ON 24 APRIL 2004

Despite the endorsement of the Annan plan by Greece and Turkey, both Papadopoulos and Denktaş adamantly rejected it. Rauf Denktaş, who had personally stayed away from the talks at Bürgenstock, condemned the plan, stating that it was 'wrenching Cyprus away from Turkey' and if the Turkish Cypriots voted 'yes' he would resign. Papadopoulos on 7 April, in a dramatic television address, urged the Greek Cypriots to reject the plan. He claimed that 'the dangers of a "yes" are non-reversible and far greater than the consequences of a "no" . . . I was given a state to lead, I will not hand over a community'.

On 24 April under auspices of the UN two separate referendums were held in the North and South of Cyprus. The Greek Cypriots rejected the plan for reunification of the island by 75.8 per cent voting 'no' and only 24.2 per cent in favour. On the other hand the Turkish Cypriots voted 64.9 per cent in favour of the Annan Plan and 35.1 per cent against.

There was general disappointment throughout the international community at the Greek Cypriots' negative vote and there was a certain amount of acrimony in the exchanges that followed between the UN, US, EU and the Papadopoulos administration. Athens and the Greek Cypriots, along with the EU, did act to ease the tension among the Turkish Cypriots who had voted 'yes' but appeared to have gained nothing: a package was put together, including financial aid that redirected a sum of 250 million euros from EU coffers to the Turkish Cypriots in the North.

Denktaş rejected a call by Talat to keep his promise to resign if the Turkish Cypriot community voted 'yes' to the plan. Denktaş claimed that the vote had not been a vote of no confidence in himself as President, but that, anyway, he had won as the Greek Cypriot 'no' vote had effectively achieved his aim by killing the plan.

Papadopoulos was anxious to assuage any criticism from the new Greek Prime Minister, Costas Karamanlis, who had supported the proposed settlement. The Greek Cypriot leader visited Athens on 29 April where he stated that 'the Annan plan and all similar UN plans will remain on the table. They don't die and they don't disappear.'

The serious strains between Kofi Annan and Tassos Papadopoulos, exhibited after the Greek Cypriots' rejection of the UN settlement, were heightened when in early June the Secretary-General presented a report to the Security Council on the reasons for the failure of the UN initative which blamed the Greek Cypriots and Papadopoulos in particular. At the same time Annan argued for recognition of the Turkish Cypriots by the international community. There was anger among the Greek Cypriots not only at the proposal to recognise the 'illegal regime' in the North but also at the suggestion Papadopoulos had never really supported the idea of a settlement. The Greek Cypriot President published a strong rebuttal to the UN report and worked hard within the international community on trying to explain why the Greek Cypriots had rejected the settlement.

At the same time the UN Security Council took pragmatic steps to maintain the security of the island by unanimously voting on 11 June for the renewal of the manadate of the UN Peace Keeping Force in Cyprus (UNFICYP).

Life in Cyprus today

When the Republic of Cyprus was established in 1960 the country was still essentially an agricultural society, and this was particularly true of the Turkish Cypriots where over sixty per cent of the population lived in villages. Since then there has been a distinct shift towards urbanisation which was accelerated after the division of the island in 1974 and agricultural products now only account for about twenty-six per cent of exports. Although northern Cyprus still produces citrus fruits for export the mainstays of the island's economy in the South are tourism (nearly two million visitors a year), more recently the shipping industry – with over 1,700 vessels flying the Cypriot flag – and offshore business registrations; the latter explains the growing number of Russians who have an interest in Cyprus. Light manufacturing, in particular textiles, clothing, and leather goods still continues but has suffered some decline in recent years.

For both communities the family has been the most important institution in Cypriot society. At marriage, the parents would give their children a portion of land, if available, Traditionally the groom would provide a house and the bride's family all the household items. Fairly recently this has been formalised into a dowry contract. Since the 1940s the obligation to provide the house has shifted to the bride's parents which may represent a response to the growing shortage of available land. Marriages in the past were arranged, usually through the mediation of a matchmaker. Romantic love was not perceived as a good basis for marriage and, because of the system of dowry, kinship and economic ties, divorce and separation were hardly known. To break up a marriage could have such disastrous social and economic consequences it was almost unimaginable. However, perhaps inevitably, as a consequence of urbanisation and exposure to the Western World, attitudes towards sexual morality are changing. The expansion of the school system has created a greater mixing of the sexes and the increasing number of women in paid work has liberated them from parental control and the old mores. In recent years there has been a dramatic rise in the divorce rate but it is still relatively low when compared with the rest of Europe.

As might be expected the status of women has also changed as they have had greater access to education and increased participation in the work force. Gradually the percentage of women enrolled in education has increased since compulsory primary education was introduced in 1960, so that now across all the levels of education women are equally enrolled. Since the mid-sixties women, mainly Greek Cypriot, have also taken to studying abroad, but after the University of Cyprus was established at Nicosia in the early 1990s the majority of students studying there are female as parents would prefer their daughters to study higher education at home than venture abroad.

Even in the 1990s women are still expected to safeguard the honour of the family. It is the tradition that women have a duty to protect themselves against all criticism of sexual immodesty. Amongst the villagers virginity is still seen as a precondition of marriage, but this attitude is on the wane in the urban areas where a more liberal mode of behaviour is accepted. There is no doubt that the overall nature of Cypriot society is conservative and, for example, Cypriot men are generally reluctant to accept domestic duties – the Cypriot 'new man' is still something of a rarity!

THE FUTURE

The main question now is whether reunification of Cyprus is dead for the foreseeable future or whether some form of settlement – possibly a loose confederation between North and South – can be brought about under the aegis of the EU. There is already some sense of incremental reunification beginning to take place through the general easing of friction in relation to the border controls and the promised financial aid to the North.

Another important significant factor has been the state of the bilateral relations between Greece and Turkey, which have for some time been reflecting a more positive approach by both countries. Turkey's application for membership of the EU was considered by the EU at the end of 2004. The positive response to Turkey's application should have a powerful influence on the Cypriot question. The pressure is now on Turkey to recognise the government of the Republic of Cyprus as it seems very unlikely that Turkey's application for membership of the EU would even be accepted without there being a settlement to the Cyprus problem.

Once more, as in the past, the fate of Cyprus could depend upon the decision of 'others'.

Notes

Notes

Chronology of Major Events

B.C.

Prehistoric

8,800	Mesolithic hunter-gatherers at Akrotiri Aetokremnos
7,000–4,000	Neolithic settlers; for example, at Khirokitia
4,000–2,300	Chalcolithic: Erimi and Philia cultures

Bronze Age

Early (2,300–1950)	Settlers from Anatolia (?); Vounous culture
Middle (1950–1650)	Construction of forts and mass burials
Late (1650–1050)	Increase in trade; immigration from Greece

Iron Age (Geometric)

1050–750	Establishment of the city-kingdoms; Phoenician colony at Kition

Archaic

709	Assyrian (King Sargon II) conquest of Cyprus
c.670	10 Cypriot kings pay homage to Esarhaddon
c.569	Egyptian Pharaoh Amasis controls Cyprus
c.525	Persian domination
499	Most Cypriot cities join Ionian Revolt against Persia
498	Cypriot cities reduced by Persians

Classical

480	Greeks defeat Xerxes at Salamis (150 Cypriot ships in the Persian fleet)
450	Kimon destroys the Phoenician fleet off Salamis
448	Peace of Kallias – Cyprus remains under Persian rule
411	Evagoras recovers throne of Salamis
391	Evagoras rules all of Cyprus

386	Peace of Antalkidas – Persian rule of Cyprus confirmed
374	Evagoras murdered
351	Cypriot kings join Egypt and Phoenicia in a rebellion against Persia, but it is easily crushed
c.335	Birth of Zeno, the founder of Stoicism
338	Battle of Khaironeia – Philip of Macedon dominates Greece
333	Battle of Issos – Cypriot kings support Alexander
323	Death of Alexander

Hellenistic

321	Ptolemy of Egypt allies with four Cypriot kings
311	Ptolemy rules Cyprus with the death of the last king
306	Demetrios Poliorketes captures Cyprus
294	Ptolemy incorporates Cyprus into the kingdom of Egypt
c.264	Death of Zeno
203–197	Strategos of Cyprus, Polykrates, mints his own coins
168	Antiochus IV forced to withdraw from Cyprus by the Romans
130	Physkon flees to Cyprus
106	Lathyros (Ptolemy IX Soter II) is driven out of Egypt and rules in Cyprus
88	Lathyros returns to Egypt
80	Death of Lathyros
58	Cyprus made a Roman province
c.41	Mark Antony gives Cyprus to Kleopatra
30	Death of Kleopatra – Cyprus under Roman rule

Roman

22	Cyprus becomes a separate province
15	Paphos destroyed by earthquake – Augustus rebuilds Temple to Aphrodite
12	Half of Soloi mines leased to Herod the Great of Judaea

A.D.

45	St Paul & St Barnabas visit Cyprus
116	Jewish rebellion on Cyprus suppressed – all Jews expelled
164	Plague devastates island
269	Goths raid Cyprus

324	Licinius collects ships from Cyprus but is defeated by Constantine
325	Council of Nicaea – Cypriot bishops attend

Byzantine Period

330	Constantine inaugurates Constantinople as his Christian capital; Helena (Constantine's mother) visits Cyprus?
334	Calcocaerus' revolt suppressed
343	12 Cypriot bishops signatories at the Council of Sardica
431	Council of Epheseus – confirms Cypriots right to consecrate their own bishops
c.488	Emperor Zeno bestows autocephaly on the Cypriot Church
c.540	Silk industry established on the island
649	The Arab commander, Muawiya, invades Cyprus; Umm Haram buried at Sultan Teke
653–4	Arabs second invasion of Cyprus
c.683	Arabs withdraw from island
688	Treaty between Justinian II and Abd al-Malik demilitarising Cyprus
723	English pilgrim St Willibald visits Cyprus
743	Caliph Walid raids Cyprus
747	Byzantine fleet defeats Arabs off the coast of Cyprus
770	Monks and nuns exiled to Cyprus during Iconoclasm controversy
773	Arab raid – Byzantine governor kidnapped
806	Caliph Harun ar-Rashid raids the island
c.869–76	Cyprus designated a Byzantine *theme*
910	Byzantine admiral Himerius calls in at Cyprus
911	Renegade Greek, Damian, raids the island
c.965	Emperor Nicephorus occupies Cyprus
1042	Failed rebellion of Theophilus Eroticus
1054	Schism between Orthodox and Roman Churches
1071	Byzantium defeated by the Turks at Manzikert
1093	Unsuccessful revolt of the Cypriot governor, Rhapsomates
1097	Cypriot governor Philocates at Laodicea
1099	First Crusade captures Jerusalem; Pisan fleet driven off the island
1102	Cyprus ends ships to helping the siege of Tripoli
1110	The Emir of Beirut flees to Cyprus

1123	Doge of Venice, Domenico Michiel, visits the island
1156	Renaud de Châtillon raids Cyprus
1158	The Emir of Egypt raids Cyprus
1167	St Neophytus founds his monastery
1184	Isaac Comnenus proclaims himself Emperor of Cyprus
1191	Richard I (the Lionheart) of England defeats Isaac and sells Cyprus to the Knights Templar
1192	Templars resell to Richard I

Frankish Period

1192	Cyprus transferred to Guy de Lusignan
1194–1205	Aimery succeeds Guy
1204	Fourth Crusade sacks Constantinople
1205–18	Hugh I
1207	Hugh joins Fifth Crusade
1218–53	Henry I
1220	Orthodox clergy ousted by the Latins
1228	Emperor Frederick II Hohenstaufen arrives in Cyprus
1233	Frederick's adherents on the island are defeated
1248	King Louis reaches Cyprus
1249	Henry I takes part in Seventh Crusade
1253–67	Hugh II
1260	The Pope subordinates the Cypriot Orthodox bishops to the Latin archbishop
1267–84	Hugh III
1271	Sultan Baibars attempts an attack on Cyprus but his fleet is wrecked
1284–85	John I
1285–1324	Henry II
1291	End of Latin rule in Syria with the fall of Acre, Tyre, Sidon, Beirut and Haifa
1299	Mongols invade Syria
1302	Genoese raid Cyprus
1306	Henry II's brother, Amaury, stages a coup
1310	Henry II flees to mainland, but returns after the murder of Amaury
1324–59	Hugh IV
1330	Devastating floods on Cyprus
1345	Fighting between Genoese and Venetians on the island
1348	Black Death kills half the island's population
1359–69	Peter I

1363	Peter I visits England
1365	Peter I sacks Alexandria in Egypt
1369–82	Peter II
1372	Rioting between Genoese and Venetians in Famagusta
1382–98	James I
1385	James I released by Genoese and crowned in Nicosia
1392	James I's son Janus released by Genoese; Henry Percy and Henry Bolinbroke (the future Henry IV of England) visit Cyprus
1398–1432	Janus
1426	Mameluke raid Cyprus – Janus defeated and captured at the Battle of Khirokitia
1427	Janus ransomed but handed over his powers to his brother Hugh
1432–58	John II
1447	Genoese hand over Famagusta to the Office of St George
1453	The Ottoman Sultan Mehmed II captures Constantinople
1458–60	Charlotte, Queen of Cyprus
1460–73	James II
1463	Kyrenia surrenders to James' forces
1472	Peasants' revolt is suppressed
1468	James marries Catherine Cornaro
1473–4	James III
1474–89	Catherine Cornaro
1479	Conspiracy against Catherine suppressed
1489	Catherine cedes Cyprus to Venice

The Venetians

1503	Venetian treaty with the Sultan Beyazit I
1517	Ottomans conquer Egypt and claim rule over Cyprus
1539	Hayrettin Barbarossa raids Limassol
1562	Greeks plot against the Venetians
1565	Ottomans defeated at the siege of Malta
1566	Selim II becomes Sultan
1570	Ottomans invade Cyprus and capture Nicosia
1571	Siege and capture of Famagusta

The Ottoman Period

1572	Expulsion of Latins

1641	Population decline – emigrants offered tax relief if they returned to Cyprus
1673–80	Rebellion of Mehmed Ağa Boyacioğlu
1645	Cyprus became an independent province
1746–48	Pasha Abu Bekir governs Cyprus
1750	Cyprus returned to the control of the Grand Vizier
1764	Çil Osman Ağa killed in a revolt
1765–6	Rebellion of Khalil Ağa
1769	Russians defeat Ottoman fleet at Çesme
1777–83	Haci Baki Ağa governor of Cyprus
1804	Muslim rebellion on the island
1809	Execution of Hajigeoghiakis Kornesios
1821	Greek War of Independence – execution of Archbishop Kyprianos
1833	Series of rebellions on the island
1839	Talat Effendi sent to introduce reforms in Cyprus
1846	Greek Consulate opened in Cyprus
1878	Russians defeat the Ottomans – Treaty of San Stefano; Congress of Berlin – Cyprus Convention leases Cyprus to Britain

The British Period

1907	Winston Churchill visits Cyprus
1912	Lloyd George offers Cyprus to Venizelos
1914	Britain annexes Cyprus
1916	Sykes-Picot Agreement
1919	Lloyd George indicates his intention of transferring Cyprus to Greece
1922	Greece defeated by Turkey in Anatolia – exchange of populations
1924	Treaty of Lausanne – Turkey abandons any claim on Cyprus
1931	Riots against British rule – Government House burnt down
1941	Prohibition on political parties in Cyprus lifted
1944	Sir Cosmo Parkinson gathers opinions about Cyprus' future
1947	Lord Winster's reforms rejected by Greek Cypriots
1950	Church plebiscite (96%) in favour of *enosis*; Makarios III becomes archbishop
1951	Makarios meets with George Grivas
1954	Greece appeals to UN over Cyprus

1955	EOKA begins campaign for *enosis* – tripartite conference held in London
1955–57	John Harding's governorship
1956	Makarios deported to Seychelles; joint Anglo-French operation at Suez
1957	Turkish Cypriots declare for partition – TMT formed
1957–60	Hugh Foot's governorship
1958	Zurich Agreement – Greece and Turkey agree on independence for Cyprus
1959	London Conference – Greek and Turkish Cypriots endorse the Zurich Agreement; Makarios elected president

Independence – Early Years

1960	16 August the Republic of Cyprus is born
1961	Agreement on British Sovereign Bases
1963	Makarios presents 13 amendments to the constitution – outbreak of inter-communal fighting
1964	UN authorises a peace-keeping force (UNFICYP); Grivas commands Cypriot National Guard
1965	UN Mediator Galo Plaza report excludes *enosis* and partition
1967	Greek Cypriots import Czech weapons; Colonels' coup in Greece; Turkish ultimatum after heavy fighting at Kophinou
1968	Georghadjis is implicated in the failed assassination of Papadopoulos, the leader of the Greek Colonels, and is forced to resign
1969	National Front formed to attack communists and overthrow Makarios
1970	Makarios helicopter attacked – Georghadjis murdered; Parliamentary elections
1971	Makarios visits USSR; Grivas returns to Cyprus – EOKA B is formed
1972	Church Synod demands Makarios' resignation
1973	Makarios wins presidential election; overthrow of Papadopoulos by Ioannides
1974	Death of Grivas; Makarios overthrown in a coup – Nikos Sampson becomes president; Turkish invasion/intervention; Greek Colonels step down; Makarios returns to Cyprus

Post 1974 – The Cyprus Problem

1975	Inter-communal talks start; Denktaş declare the north the Turkish Federated State of Cyprus
1976	Clerides forced to resign as Greek Cypriot negotiator at the inter-communal talks
1977	Makarios and Denktaş meet; Makarios dies
1978	Kyprianou returned as president
1981	Greek and Turkish Cypriots hold elections
1982	UN secretary general Pérez de Cuéllar works for a solution of the Cyprus problem; Greek Prime Minister, Andreas Papandreou visits Cyprus
1983	Denktaş proclaims the Turkish Republic of Northern Cyprus (TRNC): UN confirms the TRNC is illegal
1984	Pérez de Cuéllar pursues his initiative with a series of proximity talks between the two sides
1985	Denktaş and Kyprianou hold Summit Talks
1986	Turkish prime minister, Turgut Özal, attempts to ease relations between Greece and Turkey; Vassiliou is elected president; Cyprus applies for membership of EEC
1988	Denktaş and Vassiliou invited to talks in Geneva by UN
1989	Further meeting in New York fails
1991	Parliamentary elections in the south
1992	UN secretary general, Boutros Boutros-Ghali revives proximity talks and introduces 'Set of Ideas'
1993	Clerides elected president
1995	Denktaş issued his 14-point 'Peace Offensive'
1996	David Hannay appointed UK special representative on Cyprus; deaths of Greek Cypriots on the Green Line
1997	Clerides announces the purchase of Russian S300 surface-to-air missiles; Richard Holbrooke appointed US presidential representative for Cyprus; talks between Clerides and Denktaş at Troutbeck, near New York
1998	Clerides elected to a second term as president; Denktaş' 'Cyprus Confederation' proposal rejected; deployment of S300 in the south abandoned
1999	New proximity talks in New York and Geneva
2000	Alavaro de Soto, UN special adviser on Cyprus visits the island

2001	UN mandate, after 36 years, is renewed; riots outside a British Sovereign Base; face to face talks started in December
2002	Kofi Annan, Secretary-General of the UN, tables his plan for solving the Cyprus problem
2003	Papadopoulos elected president in the south; Cyprus signs the Treaty of Accession to the EU
2004	Greek Cypriots reject the Annan Plan; the Republic of Cyprus (the South only) joins the EU

Administration from British Period to Independent Republic

Leased from Ottoman Turkey – High Commissioners

1878   Garnet Wolseley
1879   Robert Biddulp
1892   Walter Sendall
1900   William Haynes Smith
1904   Charles King-Harman
1911   Hamilton Goold-Adams
1915   John Clauson
1920   Malcolm Stevenson

Crown Colony – Governors

1925   Malcolm Stevenson
1926   Ronald Storrs
1932   Reginald Stubbs
1933   Herbert Palmer
1939   William Battershill
1940   Charles Woolley
1946   Reginald Fletcher
        Lord Winster
1949   Andrew Wright
1954   Robert Armitage
1955   John Harding
1957   Hugh Foot

The Republic of Cyprus – Presidents

1960   Archibishop Makarios III Mouskos
1978   Spyros Kyprianou
1988   George Vassiliou
1993   Glafcos Clerides
2001–   Tassos Papadopoulos

Further Reading

ALASTOS, D. *Cyprus in History*, Zeno, London, 1976

ATTALIDES, M. *Nationalism and International Politics*, Q Press, Edinburgh, 1979

COBHAM, C.D. *Excerpta Cypria*, Cambridge University Press, 1895, rep. 1969

CLERIDES, G. *Cyprus – My Deposition*, 4 vols, Alithia , Nicosia, 1989–92

CRAIG, I. & O'MALLEY, B. *The Cyprus Conspiracy*, I.B. Tauris, London, 1999

CRAWSHAW, N. *The Cyprus Revolt*, Allen & Unwin, London, 1978

DENKTASH, R. *The Cyprus Triangle*, Allen & Unwin, London, 1982

DURRELL, L. *Bitter Lemons*, Faber, London, 1957

FOLEY, C. *Legacy of Strife*, Penguin Books, Harmondsworth, 1964

FOOT, H. *A Start in Freedom*, Hodder & Stoughton, London, 1964

HARBOTTLE, M. *The Impartial Soldier*, Oxford University Press, 1970

HILL, G.F. *A History of Cyprus*, 3 vols , Cambridge University Press, 1940–52

HITCHENS, C. *Hostage to History*, Verso, New York, 1997

HOLLAND, R. *Britain and the Revolt in Cyprus*, Clarendon Press, Oxford, 1998

HUNT, D. (ed) *Footprints in Cyprus*, Trigraph, London, 1982

KARAGEORGHIS, N. *Cyprus – From the Stone Age to the Romans*, Thames & Hudson, London, 1982

KYRRIS, C.P. *History of Cyprus*, Nicocles, Nicosia, 1985

LUKE, H. *Cyprus under the Turks 1571–1878*, Humphrey Milford, London, 1921

MIRBAGHERI, F. *Cyprus and International Peacemaking*, Hurst, London, 1998

ORR, C.W.J. *Cyprus under British Rule*, reissue, Zeno, London, 1972

PANTELI, S. *The Making of Modern Cyprus*, Interworld, New Barnet, 1990

POLYVIOU, P. *Cyprus, Conflict and Negotiation*, Duckworth, London, 1980

PURCELL, H.D. *Cyprus*, Benn, London 1969

TATTON-BROWN, V. *Ancient Cyprus*, London, British Museum, 2nd ed. 1997

THUBRON, C. *Journey into Cyprus*, Penguin, London, 1986

VANEZIS, P.N. *Makarios: Faith and Power*, Abelard-Schuman, London, 1971

Historical Gazetteer

Numbers in bold refer to main text

Akrotiri Aetokremnos (Eagles' Cliff):
the first evidence of human occupation of Cyprus, dating from the ninth
millennium BC, comes from a cave. **4**
Amathus: a coastal settlement in the
south, near Limassol, founded before
1000 BC. It remained loyal to the
Persians during the Greek rebellion of
499 BC. In the Roman period it was
capital of one of the four administrative districts but it declined under
the Byzantines. Richard I landed here
before he married Berengaria of
Navarre. Later the Franks used it as a
quarry when developing Larnaca. **16,
18, 24, 25, 38, 40, 51**
***Asinou Church (Panayia Phorviotissa
– Our Lady of the Pastures):*** The
most famous of the painted churches
and often considered the finest
example of a Byzantine church
interior in Cyprus. The church was
built in 1105/6, a narthex added
around 1200 and later paintings in
14th century. Inscriptions inform us
that the original founder of the
church was a certain Nicephoros who
was a high ranking Byzantine official.
The paintings were cleaned and preserved 1965–68. **64**
Ayios Neophytos Monastery: founded
originally by Neophytos in 1159 as a
cave for a retreat, by 1170 a monastery grew up around him. From his
cell he wrote constantly, producing
hymns, ordinances, letters and com-
mentaries. Generally casting a jaun-
diced eye over contemporary events,
he castigated Richard I, Coeur de
Lion, as a wicked wretch. He lived
until the age of 85 years. His cell and
rock-carved chapel are covered in
lavish paintings and inscriptions.
Bellapais Abbey: founded *c.*1200 by
Aimery de Lusignan for the Augustinians. It quickly grew in size and
importance but much of its treasure
was stolen by the Genoese. Sacked
after the Ottoman invasion in 1570 it
became known as a magnificent ruin.
Lawrence Durrell lived in the adjacent village, 1953–55, and the site
became famous to the British through
the publication of his *Bitter Lemons*.
70, 71
Buffavento: the highest of the three
castles of the Kyrenia Mountains.
Initially constructed in the Byzantine
period, it became known as 'the Palace
of the Queen', thought to refer to the
daughter of Isaac Comnenus. It was
later dismantled by the Venetians. **67**

213

Enkomi: an important Bronze Age site, thought by some to be the ancient capital of Cyprus, Alasia. First systematically excavated in 1934 it appears to have been an important copper-processing centre. Eventually abandoned around 1050 BC its inhabitants moved to Salamis. **9, 10, 11, 12, 141**

Episkopï (Akrotiri) and Dhekelia: two British Sovereign Base Areas (SBAs) covering 99 square miles, which were allowed for in the Treaty of Establishment as part of the negotiations for the independence of Cyprus from Britain. **78, 85, 141, 165, 172**

Erimi: a Chalcolithic site near Episcopi, first excavated in 1933, and especially known for its cruciform figurines. **7–8**

Famagusta (previously Ammochostos): the city only became important after the decline of Salamis in seventh century AD. Its name is either thought to be a corruption of its earlier title, Ammochostos, or a corruption of the *Latin Fami Augusti.* By the 13th century it had become one of the most important ports of the east Mediterranean. After the fall of Acre it became home to many Christian refugees and was the chief port for the Levant. Famous for its wealth it became a prize for the Genoese who took control in 1372. By the time James II drove them out in 1468 the city had declined and much of its land was uninhabited. After 1489 the Venetians rebuilt the walls. From September 1570 until August the following year the city was besieged by the Turks. During the Ottoman period the city went into serious decline until 1906 when the British revived the fortunes of the city and it became the main port for the island. A railway was built and ran from Morphou through Nicosia to Famagusta, but was abandoned in 1951. After independence a thriving tourist industry developed but this came to a halt when the city was captured by the Turkish army in 1974. With the subsequent division of the island much of the city, including the suburb of Varosha, has been abandoned. **28, 67, 78, 79, 80, 82, 83, 84, 86, 88, 95–7, 122, 177, 179, 182**

Golgoi: an archaeological site said to have been originally settled by Greeks from Gorgos near Corinth. **40**

Guenyeli: a Turkish village to the north-west of Nicosia where in 1958 eight Greek Cypriots were killed. Such was the nature of the killings that the British were accused of colluding with the Turkish Cypriots in their deaths. **135–6, 167**

Hala Sultan Tekké: originally a Bronze Age town which appears to have been destroyed *c.*1175 BC. Now the site of a octagonal mosque built in 1816 which houses the tomb of Umm Haram, who was the maternal aunt of the Prophet Mohammed and reportedly was killed by a fall from her mule *c.*AD 649 during an Arab raid on the island. **9, 53**

Idalion (Dhali): founded in the Bronze Age it was virtually abandoned by the fourth century BC. **16, 21, 28**

Kantara: the name is thought to derive from the Arabic for 'bridge'. The castle was built in ninth century AD and is the most eastern of the castles on the Kyrenia range. Isaac Comnenus took shelter here but eventually surrendered to Richard I. It was linked by a system of signal fires to Buffavento, St Hilarion and Nicosia. **67, 74**

Khirokitia, Cyprus' largest and best-preserved neolithic site, discovered in 1934, dating from the sixth millennium BC on the south coast half way between the cities of Limassol and Larnaca. **4, 84**

Kokkina: a Turkish enclave which resisted Grivas' attack in 1964. It is now outside Turkish control and is supplied by sea and land convoys under UNFICYP protection. **151**

Kolossi: the camp of Isaac Comnenus which Richard I captured in 1191. In 1210 Hugh I gave the land in the area to the Knights Hospitaliers. After the loss of Acre in 1291 it became their headquarters until it was briefly in the hands of the Templars. It later became a Commandery when the Hospitallers transferred their headquarters to Rhodes in 1310. The castle was damaged by the 15th century Mameluke raids and was rebuilt by the Grand Commander Louis de Magnac. The estate produced madder and sugar and is still famous for its Commanderia wine. After the Ottoman conquest the castle fell into disrepair and was only restored in 1933. Today it is a delightful tourist site with fine views of the surrounding countryside from the top of the four-square keep. The remains of the sugar factory are of interest with its five large vaults. **85**

Kophinou: a clash here in November 1967 between Greek and Turkish Cypriot forces led to an ultimatum from Ankara to the Greek Colonels. As a consequence Grivas was banished from Cyprus and over 7,000 Greek troops were withdrawn. **154**

Kourion (Curium): an ancient city site; dating from the Neolithic era it was probably settled by Dorians from mainland Greece at the end of 16th century BC. The city joined the rebellion against the Persians in 499 BC and then later lent support to Alexander at the siege of Tyre. It became very prosperous under the Romans and in Late Antiquity converted to Christianity. After Arab raids in 7th century its bishop transferred to Episkopi and the city faded into insignificance. **12, 16, 24, 39, 49**

Kykko Monastery: (corruption of *kokkous* meaning acorn, referring to a giant oak tree which stood in the area). Founded at the end of 11th century it is said by a hermit monk Esaias, who cured the Emperor Alexios' daughter of sciatica. In return the monastery received an icon of the Virgin said to have been painted by the Evangelist Luke. It has been destroyed by fire five times. The first time in 1365 when it was rebuilt by Eleanor of Aragón, Queen of Peter I. It was burnt down again in 1541 and 1751. In the 18th century Kykko developed a close association with Russia, which lasted up 1917, and received many gifts becoming the wealthiest and most powerful monastery on the island. In 1821 the Abbot Joseph was a victim of the Turkish massacres and the monastery was ransacked. Archbishop Makarios was a novice at Kykko and is buried nearby. **106, 124, 165**

Kyrenia (Kerynia): by 10th century BC it was a Greek settlement and it had an important role as the main port in the north during the Roman and Byzantine periods. The Lusignans built a castle on an earlier Byzantine fort which was attacked by the Genoese in 1374. In 1570 the castle was surrendered to the Turks without resistance. After centuries of decline it was revived by the British and until the division of the island in 1974 had a well-known 'colony' of retired British officials. **16, 25, 61, 67, 74, 83, 85, 88, 102–3, 167**

Kythrea: a village in the north which was the site of a Neolithic settlement dating to fourth millennium BC. Fed by a natural spring it was colonised later by the Greeks. It became an early Orthodox See, but was destroyed by the Arabs at the beginning of the ninth century. In 1928 a larger than life bronze statue of the Roman Emperor Septimius Severus (193–211 AD) was found nearby. **41**

Lapithos: a Bronze Age settlement which after the revolt against the Persians in 499 BC was ruled by a Phoenician dynasty. Under the Romans it became the administrative capital of the north. After a raid in seventh century it surrendered to the Arab commander Muawiya. **12, 16, 21, 25, 27, 31, 38, 53**

Larnaca (Kition): a coastal trading site, dating from 13th century BC. The settlement appears to have been destroyed by an earthquake *c.*1050 BC. After which it appears to have been resettled by the Phoencians and

remained in their hands until 312 BC. It was the birthplace of Zeno who left for Athens in 313 BC. In the seventh century AD it was frequently raided by the Arabs. Under the Lusignans it was known as Salina or Salines, taking its name from the nearby salt lake. After the Genoese took Famagusta many merchants moved here and it became known as Larnaca. Under the Ottomans its importance grew. In 1878 when the British took over Cyprus Sir Garnet Wolseley landed here. **101, 103, 112, 114, 118, 127, 132**

Limassol: the origins of the city are obscure and it was not until the decline of its neighbour to the east, Amathus. In 1191 Richard I, *Coeur de Lion,* married Berengaria of Navarre here. Under the Lusignans the city was developed and the Knights of St John cultivated the surrounding vineyards. From the fifteenth century the city was damaged by earthquakes and raided by the Turks. During the Ottoman period it was described by travellers as being in a ruinous state. Under the British it began to prosper as wine and carob exports grew. After independence the port and shipyard was further expanded. George Grivas died and was buried here in 1974. **67, 74, 76, 79, 92, 105, 106, 118, 120, 122, 149, 157, 158, 159, 162, 163**

Makheras (Monastery of the Knife): founded around 1148 by two hermits from Syria who were said to have found an icon of the Virgin in a cave nearby. The Byzantine Emperor, Manuel Comnenos granted land and an annual stipend to the monastery. The monastery was completed in 1190 by the abbot Nilos, who went on to be the Bishop of Tamassos. One story claims that in 1337 the wife of Hugh IV, Alix d'Ibelin, insisted on entering the sanctuary of the church, which in the Orthodox faith is forbidden to women, and was instantly struck dumb. (She apparently only recovered her speech three years later when she witnessed the miracle of a relic of the true cross surviving a test by fire at Tokhni). In 1393 during an outbreak of plague James I and his court took shelter here. In 1530 and 1892 the monastery was destroyed by fire. The present buildings mainly belong to the reconstruction that was completed in 1902. In 1957 the EOKA commander, George Afxentiou, died in a hide-out near to the monastery after a prolonged engagement with British troops. **158**

Marion: to the south-east of Polis, said to have been founded by the Athenians in 7th century BC. An important centre for the copper industry the city was destroyed by Ptolemy I in 312 BC. A few decades later the city of Arsinoë was founded nearby and called Polis during the Lusignan period. **12, 16, 21, 25, 28, 40**

Maroni: a Bronze Age trading site in the south. **9**

Nicosia (Leucosia): thought to be near the ancient site of Ledra, there is some evidence of Roman buildings and mention of a Byzantine fort. It was developed under the Lusignans with a castle, palace and monastery. By the Venetian period the population had grown to 16,000. However, the fortifications were incomplete when the Ottomans invaded Cyprus

and after a six-week siege in 1570 the city was completely sacked. During the British period it was the seat of the High Commissioner and in 1931 Government House was burnt down in riots against British rule. After 1974 the city was divided by the so-called 'Green Line' between the Greek Cypriot south and the Turkish Cypriot north. Although it contains few outstanding buildings it is a charming city with its centre close to the old Venetian fortifications. The Cyprus Museum houses the national collection of antiquities. Next to the Archiepiscopal Palace is the Byzantine Museum, which has a fine collection of icons. **65, 67, 69, 71, 74, 79, 82, 84, 93–5, 98, 100, 114, 120, 127, 129, 134, 135, 148–50, 167, 173, 179, 182, 187, 189–91**

Panayia Khrysorroyiatissa (Monastery of Our Lady of the Golden Pomegranate): founded in 1152 by a hermit Ignatios after the discovery of an icon of the Virgin. Little is known about the monastery until it was rebuilt by Panaretos, Bishop of Paphos, in 1770. After a bad fire in 1967 Archbishop Makarios helped rebuild the monastery and the appropriately named Abbot Dionysios revied its winery.

Paphos: developed as the most westerly port of Cyprus under the Ptolemies it replaced Salamis as the capital. Under the Romans the city was known as Augusta Claudia and legend had it that St Paul received a whipping here. In the fourth century AD Paphos was devastated by earthquakes and with the capital being transferred back to Salamis the city went into decline. After a series of Arab raids the port was abandoned. Although reused as a port during the Crusades, according to various accounts, it was a miserable place. The Turks rebuilt the old Lusignan fort which had been destroyed by the Venetians. During the Napoleonic Wars the British established an agent here and later under British rule the port was dredged. It is now an important tourist centre with an excellent museum of antiquities. In Kato (Lower) Paphos there are surviving Roman remains with remarkable mosaics on display in the House of Dionysos , the Villa of Theseus and the House of Orpheus. **12, 16, 19, 25, 27, 30, 35, 38, 39, 42, 43, 47, 49, 54, 65, 76, 82, 184**

Petra tou Romiou: a group of rocks on the coast to the south of Paphos. The small pebble beach here is celebrated as the legendary site where Aphrodite (Venus) – the goddess of love – came ashore. The rather prosaic Homeric tradition of her birth was replaced in classical times by a much more racy myth: when urged by his mother Gaia, Chronus castrated his father Uranus and cast the severed genitals into the sea. The white foam that arose gave birth to Aphrodite who was carried by Zephyrus (the West Wind) to the shores of Cyprus. In Western poetry and art there have been many descriptions and depictions of this scene. The most famous painting of Aphrodite's birth is perhaps that by the Italian Renaissance artist Botticelli, which shows the naked goddess being gently carried on the sea in a seashell. Nearby is the Sanctuary of Aphrodite at Palea Paphos where up to the Christian period her cult was worshipped. Even now the concept of Aphrodite, the epitome of love and beauty, has its hold on the island – mainly as a commercial for the tourists!

Prophitis Elias Monastery: of post-Byzantine construction the buildings were restored in 1899. Now used by the Forestry Department.

Salamis: said to have been founded by Teucer, the son of Telamon, the legendary king of Salamis in 11th century BC. It replaced Enkomi after its destruction by an earthquake *c.*1050 BC and was the first Cypriot city to issue its own coinage. Under its famous king, Evagoras, it became the capital city and symbolised Greek resistance to the Phoenicians. However, in 306 BC Demetrios Poliorketes destroyed its walls. Under the Ptolemies Paphos became the capital and Salamis slipped into decline until it was rebuilt by the Roman Emperor Constantinus II in 350 AD and renamed Constantia. St Barnabas came from here and was said to have been martyred at the hands of the Jewish population. Sacked by Muawiya in the seventh century it was abandoned in favour of nearby Famagusta. The first serious archaeological excavation took place in 1880. **12, 16, 18, 20, 21, 22, 23, 24, 25–6, 27, 38, 39, 42, 43, 47, 52, 54**

St Hilarion: Once the abode of an anchorite called Hilarion a monastery was established on this site in the Kyrenia range after 10th–11th century. Used by Isaac Comnenus as

The gymnasium at Salamis

fortified eyrie. At the beginning of 13th century the Lusignans strengthened the fortifications and paid a key role in the conflict against the forces of the Emperor Frederick II. The castle was further developed in the 14th century and the Lusignan Court used it as a summer residence. In the 15th century the Venetians dismantled some of the fortifications. **47, 67, 74, 150**

Soloi: founded as one of the 10 Hittite kingdoms founded in Cyprus around 700 BC, It was said that its original name of Sillu was changed in honour of the Athenian statesman Solon after he visited the city. In 498 BC the city held out for four months against the Persians. During the Roman period it became important as a centre for the copper industry and its beautiful theatre was built during second century AD. **12, 16, 19, 24, 25, 39, 40, 49**

Sotira: an archaeological site, excavated 1947–54 in the south near Limassol, which has given its name to a late Neolithic culture 4,500 and 4,000 BC. **6, 7**

Stavrovouni: the mountain site of a monastery. Originally the mountain was called Olympos and had a temple to Aphrodite built on its summit. Helena, the mother of the Roman Emperor Constantine, was said to have brought part of the True Cross here from Jerusalem and founded a monastery in 327 AD. The first monastery was destroyed in 15th century and was only resettled by monks in 17th century. The present building dates to 19th century. **47, 61**

Tamassos: famous for its copper mines it became a Phoenician colony *c.* 800 BC. The mines were given by Alexander the Great to the king of Salamis and were later leased by Herod the Great. The mines were largely abandoned by the second century. By fourth century AD it became a centre of Christianity. **16, 21, 40, 43**

Troodhitissa Panayia Monastery: founded in 1250, it is said to house a sacred icon of the Virgin that had been brought over, in the 8th century, from the Anatolian mainland during the time of Iconoclasm. The icon is associated with a belt with silver buckles which is said to cure barrenness in a woman if she wears it. The present church dates from 1731 and although further buildings were added these were destroyed in a forest fire at the end of the 18th century.

Troödos: the range of mountains dominating the centre of the island.

The British built a summer camp near the summit, Mount Olympos (1952m; 6404ft) – now a radar/communications station . It was here that the French poet Arthur Rimbaud in 1880 helped build the summer residence for the High Commissioner. It is now both a winter and summer resort with several nature trails for walkers. **1, 3, 5, 40**

Vounous: site of Early Bronze Age tombs where metalwork and representations of bulls were found suggesting connections with Anatolia. **8–9**

Index